Praise for
Growing Together without Growing Apart

'This book by Lt Gen Rajeev Kanitkar offers a lucid, vivid, and honest account of Lt Gen Madhuri Kanitkar's life and career. It captures the trials, challenges, and long stretches of separation that come with two people navigating successful military careers together. Having worked alongside Madhuri at HQ IDS, I could clearly see her grit, drive to succeed, pursuit of excellence, and forward-thinking mindset reflected throughout the narrative. As more women step into roles in the armed forces, this book stands out as a source of inspiration, motivation, and practical insight into the unique personal and professional demands of a life in uniform. A compelling and highly readable account.'

—**Admiral R. Hari Kumar**, PVSM, AVSM, VSM (Retd)
Former Chief of Naval Staff, Indian Navy

'This remarkable book offers an inspiring and deeply motivational account for young couples. At its heart is a strong message about the power of commitment—the foundation for building a successful marriage while navigating life's many challenges. It also serves as a powerful source of encouragement for those aspiring to careers in both medicine and the armed forces.

Lt Gen Rajeev and Lt Gen Madhuri Kanitkar stand out as true role models for their academic excellence, professionalism, and unwavering integrity. Their story shows what it means to grow together without losing oneself, and how to support each other while excelling in demanding careers.

Growing Together without Growing Apart offers valuable insights on balancing relationships, ambition, and responsibilities. It is a book that will no doubt inspire many young readers to walk a similar path—with purpose, partnership, and perseverance.'

—**Air Marshal Bhushan Gokhale**, PVSM, AVSM, VSM (Retd)
Former Vice Chief of Air Staff, Indian Air Force

'This book is a captivating account of an extraordinary couple who began their journey in the Indian Armed Forces almost side by side. What follows is an inspiring story that evolves into an exceptional narrative, culminating in both of them achieving the rare honour of retiring as the first lieutenant general couple from the prestigious Indian Armed Forces. Together, the couple exemplified what it means to strike a fine balance between demanding professional responsibilities and a nurturing personal life, raising grounded children and leaving a lasting impact in their respective fields.

Growing Together without Growing Apart is not just a story; it is a profound source of inspiration, chronicling a journey that has left an indelible mark on the armed forces and society at large. Congratulations to Lt Gen Rajeev Kanitkar for bringing this remarkable story to life.'

— **Lt Gen B. K. Chopra**, PVSM, AVSM (Retd)
Former Director General, Armed Forces Medical Services

'"He was not around, yet he was always there"—this one powerful line captures the essence of the remarkable journey of the Indian Armed Forces' first-ever three-star couple, Madhuri and Rajeev. This must-read book shows how a marriage between two luminous stars can thrive, not through constant proximity, but on shared purpose, unwavering commitment, and a love that bridges every distance.

Growing Together without Growing Apart is more than just a memoir. It is an inspiring guide for couples striving to balance ambition with affection, and to celebrate each other's success with mutual respect, pride, and grace.'

—**Raghunath Mashelkar**, FRS; Padma Vibhushan,
Padma Bhushan, and Padma Shri awardee
Former Director General, CSIR; Former President, INSA;
and Former President, Global Research Alliance

'I am very pleased to share my thoughts on the book *Growing Together without Growing Apart*, which vividly captures the extraordinary journey of my friend Madhuri and her husband Rajeev. Having known this three-star general couple closely over the decades, I have had the privilege of witnessing their exemplary careers.

I wholeheartedly endorse this well-written book and recommend it to young professionals, doctors in particular, as a source of inspiration on how to balance demanding careers with family life and do so with courage and aplomb.'

— **Dr R. N. Srivastava**, Consultant, Paediatric Nephrology
Former Professor, Paediatric Nephrology, AIIMS;
and Former President, Indian Academy of Paediatrics

'Lt Gen Madhuri Kanitkar is truly an inspiring figure, admired not just for her professional achievements, but for the grace and strength with which she has lived her personal life too. She stands as a shining example of integrity, compassion, discipline, and unwavering dedication.

This book offers a rare, authentic ringside view of her extraordinary journey, capturing her steadfast commitment to her family, her profession, and her nation.'

—**Lt Gen P. M. Hariz**, PVSM, AVSM, VSM (Retd)
Former Army Commander, Indian Army

'Reading *Growing Together without Growing Apart*, penned by Rajeev, has been a thoroughly engaging experience. The challenges faced by two professionals trying to balance career and home are portrayed with warmth and honesty, all set against the unique backdrop of the armed forces. Madhuri's journey—as a soldier, doctor, and teacher—is brought to life in Rajeev's distinctly personal and heartfelt style. The anecdotes from service life and Madhuri's no-nonsense way of dealing with tough situations make the book hard to put down.

contd...

I strongly recommend it, especially to young couples striving to balance work, life, and shared dreams.'

—Dr Soumya Swaminathan
Chairperson, M. S. Swaminathan Research Foundation;
Former Chief Scientist, WHO

GROWING TOGETHER *without* GROWING APART

An Inspiring Journey of Service, Sacrifice, and Shared Dreams

LT GENERAL RAJEEV KANITKAR
LT GENERAL DR MADHURI KANITKAR

HAY HOUSE INDIA
New Delhi • London • Sydney
Carlsbad, California • New York City

Hay House Publishers (India) Pvt Ltd
Muskaan Complex, Plot No. 3, B-2, Vasant Kunj, New Delhi – 110070, India

Hay House LLC, P.O. Box 5100, Carlsbad, CA 92018-5100, USA
Hay House UK Ltd, 1st Floor, Crawford Corner, 91-93 Baker Street, London W1U 6QQ, UK
Hay House Australia Publishing Pty Ltd, 18/36 Ralph St., Alexandria NSW 2015, Australia

Email: contact@hayhouse.co.in
Website: www.hayhouse.co.in

First published by Hay House India, 2025
10 9 8 7 6 5 4 3 2 1

ISBN 978-93-6611-536-8 (Hardback)
ISBN 978-93-6611-207-7 (Ebook)

Printed at Thomson Press

FSC www.fsc.org MIX Paper | Supporting responsible forestry FSC® C010615

Hay House is committed to a sustainable future for our business, our readers and our planet. This book is made from Forest Stewardship Council® certified paper.

We dedicate this book to strong and steady mothers. One of them, Saroj, was instrumental in nurturing three sons, and the other, Hemalata, guided and mentored three daughters while raising them. Though their circumstances were different, they were united by a shared set of values rooted in the SHIP principle: Simplicity, Humility, Integrity, and Perseverance. These values helped both of us face life head-on with practicality and determination and serve Mother India with pride.

Contents

PART V
ADVISORY ROLE AND ADMINISTRATION

PART VI
HIGHER LEADERSHIP AND MANAGEMENT

Foreword

I read *Growing Together without Growing Apart* with great admiration and deep interest. It would not be out of place to express a certain sense of satisfaction in having played a part—however small—in bringing this project to fruition.

My first interaction with the couple was on *Baatcheet*, a YouTube programme hosted by my daughter, Saina, the CEO of Demonstrative Learning. I particularly enjoyed engaging with Madhuri. She came across as a determined woman, brimming with novel ideas, deeply rooted in sound cultural values, and strongly supported by her husband, Rajeev. He was initially hesitant to join the conversation, but Saina wouldn't take no for an answer. Before long, we were immersed in an engaging discussion about life in the armed forces which included their triumphs, challenges, and shared accomplishments. The conversation naturally veered towards leadership values and the art of converting adversity into opportunity. At its core was the emphasis on caring, sharing, and navigating life's highs and lows together.

In June 2022, I had the opportunity to meet Madhuri again at the vibrant campus of the Maharashtra University of Health Sciences (MUHS), where she had taken over as vice chancellor following her retirement in October 2021. In a remarkably short span, she had initiated transformative changes in the institution. During that visit, I also met Rajeev, still steadfast in his support. Within two years, Madhuri had turned the MUHS campus into a living example of Mission LiFE, based on the principles of reduce, reuse, and recycle. By optimising available resources and transforming *karmacharis* into *karmayogis*, the #MUHSparivaar had become an inspiring role model for students and faculty alike. Today, the green, plastic-free campus is among the most impressive I have seen across the country.

Recognising the richness of their journey, I suggested that Madhuri consider writing about her time in uniform for the benefit of a wider audience. However, her demanding schedule left little room for such an endeavour. She felt Rajeev was better suited to the task. Tragically, towards the end of that year, Rajeev suffered a sudden brain stroke and was left with dense hemiplegia. Yet, with a soldier's resolve, he faced the early challenges head-on and, by late 2023, had made significant strides in recovery. To keep his mind engaged and help rewire his brain, Rajeev began writing about their shared journey in the military.

During my visit, I witnessed how Madhuri had channelled the same spirit and dynamism from her defence forces days into her new role as vice chancellor. She began by overhauling infrastructure and introducing automation, which brought transparency and improved administrative efficiency. More importantly, she breathed new life into the human dimension of the organisation, transforming every stakeholder into a co-owner of her vision to make MUHS a centre of excellence. Her energy, optimism, and drive have permeated the institution and resonated at the highest levels of the state government. Her vision of positioning Maharashtra as the fountainhead of quality, affordable medical education, and cutting-edge research is steadily becoming a reality.

In *GTGWA*, Rajeev skilfully presents their journey in a compelling and accessible manner. The initial chapters provide context, tracing how the couple seemed destined to meet and grow together. As the narrative unfolds, it becomes evident that every challenge they encountered was met with open dialogue, mutual support, and a determination to transform obstacles into opportunities. Their story is deeply rooted in the values of camaraderie, community, and resilience, hallmarks of the armed forces, and timeless lessons for any organisation.

A career in the armed forces demands consistent excellence at every level. Madhuri's visionary thinking and forthright approach often invited scrutiny, but her brilliance and commitment to organisational success always saw her through. The latter part of the book underscores her significant contributions to policy and leadership, making it essential reading for anyone interested in these domains. Her creative, open-minded perspective, paired with clinical precision in translating policy into action, remains her hallmark.

It is important to note that this book is Rajeev's independent account, with Madhuri's role focused on reviewing the manuscript for factual accuracy and offering her reflections on each phase of their journey through concise postscripts that follow every chapter, lending authenticity and clarity. In that sense, it is neither a conventional biography nor a straight forward autobiography; it is, as one might say, a biography in auto mode. This distinctive format breathes life into the narrative, making it both engaging and deeply resonant for anyone navigating a similar path.

Growing Together without Growing Apart is a powerful and uplifting read as well as a tribute to partnership, purpose, and perseverance.

With love,
—**Kiran Bedi**

Prologue

We often wonder ourselves how we achieved this distinction, each of us having served nearly thirty-nine years in the prestigious Indian Armed Forces. I am frequently asked questions and invited to share our life experiences. While our colleagues and family have always been extremely supportive, the journey has certainly been challenging.

In today's world, where youngsters seek mentors and role models, and couples look for #CoupleGoals, I felt that our story might hold some relevance. With me neck-deep in my new role, Rajeev—now with time on his hands and the inclination to write—took up the task of authorship. This time, it served the purpose of growing together while being together post-retirement.

We have had an amazing life together while being apart, with me doing most of the talking and Rajeev doing most of the listening! I have always been the eternal optimist; Rajeev, the calm and practical one. I am constantly in a mad rush; he is the patient, composed counterpart. And the list goes on.

They say opposites attract. They say marriages are made in heaven. But what is often left unsaid is this: marriages must be held together here on earth by mere mortals, weathering every storm and learning to grow together without growing apart!

We spent nearly twenty-four years apart while progressing professionally in our respective careers. It wasn't easy. Sometimes, we were both rising at the same pace. At other times, one of us had to take a step back to let the other surge ahead.

With that in mind, Rajeev—who has always been better with words—decided to pen down my life story from his point of view, deeply intertwined with his own. It is, in a sense, an auto-biography—a biography written in auto mode. However, the aspect of *uski kahaani, usi ki zubaani* (her story as told by her) was equally important. And so, after each chapter, I have taken the liberty of adding a postscript.

Before I sign off, I must also declare a small conflict of interest: Rajeev has written this book, and being the doting husband that he is, I am sure it is biased in my favour. You are most welcome to read between the lines to sense his perspective and appreciate his magnanimity. What impressed me the most was how much he registered along the way while remaining incognito in faraway places. He wasn't always around, and yet, he was always there. Chivalry of the armed forces at its best.

With that, I wish you a joyful reading experience!

—Lt General Dr Madhuri Kanitkar

Part I

Where It All Began

Chapter 1

A Date with Destiny (Que Sera Sera)

The Never-Ending Train Journey

10 June 1978 was an eventful day. I was commissioned into The Poona Horse on this day as a second lieutenant (a single star adorned our proud and tough shoulders) after graduating from the Indian Military Academy (IMA). I was awarded the silver medal for being second in the order of merit. It was a joyful moment. Approximately a year earlier, I had been the recipient of the President's Gold Medal (PGM) for topping my batch at the National Defence Academy, Khadakwasla.

My parents had forgone the occasion of witnessing the passing out parade (POP) at Dehradun due to an impending wedding in the family. However, my father's elder brother, Madhav Kanitkar, and his wife, Sumati Kanitkar (fondly addressed as Madhu Kaka and Sumati Kaku), attended the parade in their absence along with my younger brother, Umesh Kanitkar who was 12 years old at the time. All of them were very dear to me. They were thrilled to see the march-past proceedings that day. My Kaka and Kaku were scheduled to move on to the pretty hill station of Mussoorie after the POP, while Umesh was to return with me to Pune.

When passing out of IMA, newly commissioned officers are issued a fairly large component of uniforms and field exercise equipment. All of it gets packed into a big steel trunk, a large holdall, and an equally spacious kitbag, all of which can be identified from a mile away (literally). With all this baggage in tow, Umesh and I managed to board a bus at Dehradun's crowded bus stand. We reached New Delhi Railway Station in time to board the Jhelum Express on the evening of 10 June 1978.

The wedding for which my parents had stayed back was that of my cousin sister, Madhuri Bhat, daughter of my mother's younger sister. The marriage was slated for 12 June 1978, and I was expected to reach for the reception that evening. Consequently, for the long journey from Delhi to Pune, seats had been reserved for the two of us by an acquaintance. The tickets were to be delivered to me at the Delhi railway station. However, this rendezvous did not take place due to some miscommunication.

I suddenly realised that the train would be arriving at the platform in the next 15 minutes, and we still did not have our tickets. Without them, we could not board the train. Instinctively, I decided to buy ordinary tickets for the non-reserved compartment. I asked Umesh to guard our luggage and ran down to the ticket counter. By a stroke of luck, I managed to obtain them. All the while, I kept hoping that a miracle might still 'deliver' the reserved tickets. But that was not to be.

Soon, the Jhelum Express chugged in, and all hell broke loose. The train was already overflowing with passengers. My request to open the entry door initially fell on deaf ears. Fortunately, someone who wanted to get down from the compartment opened the door a wee bit. As soon as he did, the supreme physical fitness achieved through our yearlong training at IMA kicked in. I pushed Umesh inside the vestibule and asked him to help me with the luggage as much as he could. The only place that offered us some space was the WC vestibule right next to the entry door. Into that space, I pushed all our luggage, stacking it one on top of the other and 'topping' it off with Umesh at the pinnacle. I found myself a place to stand next to the entry door and, with a big heave, closed and locked it.

Hurrah! There we were for the next 36 hours and more—hours that seemed never-ending. I was unhappy about our discomfort, especially for Umesh, who was still a child, but relieved that we were aboard the train and would arrive in time for the wedding reception on 12 June.

And so it was that we reached Pune in a ragtag fashion, completely exhausted, in the afternoon of 12 June 1978. I do not recollect how I managed to take care of Umesh during the train journey. It is to his credit that he did not complain and took this unique experience in his stride. We reached home a bit dishevelled and got down to unpacking our luggage after some much-needed rest.

With the excitement of being a newly minted officer of the Indian Army still bubbling within me, I soon got ready to attend the evening reception of my cousin's wedding. Coincidentally, she was marrying a smart army officer from the corps of EME, Capt Vishwas Bhat, who later retired as Lt Gen Vishwas Bhat, DGQA.

Date with Destiny

Having met most of the people I knew at the reception venue, there came a lull in the proceedings, and I decided to take a breather. I do not recall if I deliberately walked past a couple of very pretty girls sitting nearby. Nor do I recall going up to them and asking if they were the Khot sisters (though I am told that I did!). My memory suggests that I was surprised to be suddenly addressed by one of those lovely damsels, asking if I was Rajeev, who had just been commissioned into the Indian Army.

Whatever the truth, I soon found myself conversing with Madhuri and her sister Nilima. Their family was well known to my mother's elder sister (*maasi*). My maasi's husband and the sisters' father were close colleagues in the railways. Due to this common network of friends and family, Madhuri and Nilima were also attending the wedding. And here I was, with no inkling of this unexpected turn, first bumping into my proverbial destiny.

Soon enough, it was time for the two sisters to return home. Not being late was the norm in those days. Under strict instructions from their grandparents, with whom they were residing, they rose to leave. And out of nowhere, the young second lieutenant sprang to life with chivalry, volunteering to walk them home, which was not too far away. Happily, we continued our interaction for some more time.

Having left them at their residence, I returned to the reception venue. I did wonder if I would ever meet them again. As I neared the venue, I merged back into the proceedings. After some time, the reception wound down, and the newlyweds disappeared into their magical future.

It was not until later that events took a pleasant turn, heralding the best times of our lives. As we look back, 'The Day We Met' became 'Our Date with Destiny'. 12 June 1978 was a red-letter day in our journey together.

Looking Back

As I savour those magical moments in life, I often wonder about the uncanny coincidences and occurrences that sometimes offer no explanation. My cousin's wedding date was fixed for the 12th of June, and my graduation ceremony was on the 10th of June—just enough time to reach the reception venue if I was smart enough. I was keen to greet my cousin and her husband on their wedding day, which propelled me to reach Delhi as early as possible to board the Pune-bound train.

Bad luck struck in the form of missing out on the reserved tickets. But just in the nick of time, I made a quick decision to travel unreserved, even though my younger brother would have been very uncomfortable. Despite the long queue for train tickets and the overflowing compartment, Umesh and I managed to board the train for a journey that initially seemed impossible and subsequently felt never-ending. This laid the ground for my impending rendezvous with Madhuri and Nilima Khot later that evening. It was a coincidence that they and I attended only the reception part of the wedding due to time constraints. A coincidence that they noticed me, and I noticed them, without really knowing each other. We had heard of each other within the circle of family and friends but had never had the occasion to meet. A coincidence, perhaps, that we bumped into each other because none of us knew too many people at the event, and we were looking around for some company. And, coincidentally, we appeared to have a desire to meet each other, which led to a brief conversation. A coincidence that I met Madhuri at Madhuri's wedding! And to top it all, Madhuri was named Madhuri because my cousin, born two years earlier, was a very pretty girl.

In the context of such coincidences and occurrences, nothing could be truer than the famous adage, 'Marriages are made in heaven.' It was in the aftermath of that singular meeting that subsequent events gave rise to our enduring story.

Postscript by Madhuri

Destiny was in play even before the 12 June 1978! While at Fergusson College, I was drawn to the uniform and had already made up my mind to don it after being impressed by the smart cadets from NDA strolling around Deccan Gymkhana on any given Sunday. Meeting a freshly minted, chivalrous young officer had a lasting impact on me and influenced my decision to join the Armed Forces Medical College. This set the stage for our paths to cross again without too long a wait.

Chapter 2

Growing Up the Sanskaaram Way

The Early Years

Madhuri was born in the small town of Dharwar in Karnataka on 15 October 1960. She is the eldest of three sisters. Her father, Dr Chandrakant Khot, was a brilliant man who completed his graduate studies in engineering at the young age of nineteen! Too young to be employed, he pursued doctoral studies in microwave telecommunication in the early 1950s and completed them in record time. He then joined the Indian Railways in their signals and telecommunication department.

A strict disciplinarian and a meticulous person, he instilled in his children a mindset of 'can do and must do' for anything and everything. To him, being a girl carried no negative connotation and thus, his daughters were expected to handle life's daily challenges independently. He always exhorted them, 'Learn to fish in order to feed,' and 'Fight if you are right.' He encouraged them to take on responsibilities traditionally reserved for boys. His guidance was clinical and to the point, with an unwavering eye for detail. For him, righteousness and rightful conduct were inseparable. Hard work, integrity, diligence, competence, courage, and conviction were his guiding principles, and he embodied them in his own life—principles that his daughters absorbed deeply.

Madhuri's mother, Hemalata Khot (née Dhakappa), was a gem of a person. Lovely and lively in her own special way, she epitomised kindness, affection, generosity, and a large-hearted nature. A deeply spiritual person, she instilled in her children the values of truth, prayer, simplicity, gratitude, empathy, forthrightness, creativity, consideration, and compassion in a meaningful way. Together, both parents provided their children with a positive environment for growth throughout their childhood. Their guidance and encouragement ultimately shaped them into responsible citizens as they stepped into adulthood.

Threads of Belonging

To truly understand Madhuri, one must look closely at the people who shaped her early years—her parents, grandparents, siblings, teachers, and extended family. They were her first teachers, her earliest audience, and her enduring compass through life.

- **Mother's Parents**

Madhuri's mother hailed from Sirsi, a small town in northern Karnataka. Her parents were conservative yet held a progressive outlook. A joint family environment prevailed in their large house in Sirsi, where the family had small business interests in textiles and spices. There was a constant flow of people in and out of the house, all of whom were treated with respect and generosity. At the same time, there was a strong emphasis on good education for all children, regardless of gender.

Madhuri and her sisters often spent part of their annual school vacation in Sirsi, immersing themselves in the semi-rural environment with great joy. It was here that they observed and absorbed the simplicity and generosity of village life—values that Madhuri and her siblings internalised deeply.

- **Father's Parents**

Madhuri's paternal grandparents were in a different league altogether. They had married under unusual circumstances. Her grandmother had become a child widow at the tender age of eight. However, her maternal uncle ensured that she received a good education at the Maharshi Karve Stree Shikshan Sanstha in Pune—an institute that has been focused on educating girls, especially orphans and child widows, since the turn of the previous century.

Extremely intelligent and sharp, this twinkle-eyed lady met her match while studying medicine at B. J. Medical College (BJMC) in Pune in the late 1920s. Her future husband, deeply influenced by Gandhian philosophy—particularly the 'practice what you preach' principle—was also a student there. During one of his philosophical discourses, he spoke about the importance of being mindful and supportive of child widows, extolling the virtues of choosing them as life partners to help integrate them into normal society. After his address, Madhuri's grandmother stood up and forthrightly asked him if he would practice what he preached if such an occasion arose. Without hesitation, he replied in the affirmative. She then revealed that she was, in fact, a child widow and asked if he had the courage to marry her. And that was that.

Both of Madhuri's grandparents were strong-willed personalities. At the end of their studies, they married in a simple ceremony. Soon thereafter, they went to inform their parents of their marriage. However, they were not accepted at home, having defied all prevailing societal norms and protocols. As a consequence, when an opportunity arose to serve as medical professionals for the British government in the jungles of Africa, they volunteered and shipped themselves off to an unfamiliar and challenging terrain.

It is worth mentioning that all three of their children—two sons and a daughter—were born in the vicinity of dense African jungles. And Madhuri's father, in particular, had an extraordinary birth. In the absence of a gynaecologist, the grandmother conducted her own delivery with only a paramedic's assistance while the grandfather was away on a medical call. Such were the incredible circumstances that shaped this family.

The grandmother instilled in her children the fundamentals of resilience, determination, and hope. Their early education in Africa took place entirely at home under her sharp-eyed supervision. So effective was her teaching that when the family returned to India after several years, Madhuri's brilliant father cleared the entrance exams for a class higher than his age would have normally permitted.

During their growing-up years, Madhuri and Nilima (her nearest sibling, two years younger) often stayed with their grandparents, who had by then settled in Pune. They served as the girls' local guardians throughout their schooling and continued in this role during Madhuri's studies at Fergusson College and later at the Armed Forces Medical College.

Madhuri's grandfather was philosophical and indulgent with his grandchildren most of the time. The grandmother, however, was a tough cookie. Keenly aware of the limitations imposed by societal norms—especially concerning the girl-child—she was a no-nonsense person. She insisted that her granddaughters be given the freedom to develop themselves fully. She encouraged them to be independent and fearless and cultivate a do-or-die attitude in their pursuits. Her overarching knowledge of the scriptures and their practical application to daily life was deeply instilled in her grandchildren. Though diminutive in stature, she possessed the personality of a fearless tigress. As a role model, she played a significant role in shaping a strong value system in her grandchildren, leaving an indelible mark on their lives.

- **Teachers and Mentors**

Madhuri studied in numerous schools during her pre-college years due to her father's rotational job requirements, each with its own uniqueness. Her early schooling began at St. Anne's Convent, a Jesuit school in the heart of South Mumbai. While the school upheld a strict disciplinary code, compassion was always a strong element of its teaching curriculum.

During her childhood, she also got the opportunity to study at an international American school when her father was posted as the scientific attaché at the Indian embassy in Tokyo. While refining her English skills, she was greatly drawn to the remarkable aspects of Japanese culture. Cleanliness, courtesy, politeness, punctuality, self-discipline, and civic consciousness left a deep impression on the entire family. However, given the high cost of schooling in Japan, Madhuri and Nilima were sent back to India for their further education. They were admitted to Dastur High School for Girls, a boarding school in Pune, where strict daily regimens were emphasised. Cleanliness, honesty, and integrity were instilled as core moral values. As the elder sister, Madhuri was given the responsibility of looking after Nilima in their new environment. Much to Nilima's dismay, she took this role rather seriously! Their sibling bond flourished in this setting.

After a couple of years in the hostel, their parents decided to transfer them to St. Joseph's Convent, another reputed school in Pune. During this time, they lived with their paternal grandparents. This arrangement gave them the dual advantage of growing up under the disciplined oversight of their razor-sharp grandmother and the tolerant nature of their grandfather. At school, their teachers nurtured values of care, empathy, and understanding.

When their parents returned from Japan, the family relocated to Lucknow, where her father was stationed at the R&D complex of the railways. It was here that Madhuri completed her high school education under the watchful guidance of her senior teachers. Her biology teacher, Dr Gon, took a particular interest in her academic journey. Though she was equally proficient in mathematics—her father was a wizard at the subject—he foresaw in Madhuri the potential to become a compassionate and skilled doctor. Under the combined influence of her father and teacher, she chose biology as her primary focus for high school.

Madhuri had a stellar academic record, and she proved her mettle by securing a top rank in the class 11 CBSE exams. She also qualified, not once but twice, in the National Talent Scholarship exams, making everyone proud.

For her 12th-grade studies, Madhuri returned to Pune and joined Fergusson College, staying in the college hostel. Her classmate and close hostel buddy, Suchitra Purohit, the daughter of an Air Force officer, became a lifelong friend. Over forty years later, their bond remains strong. The year at Fergusson College marked her first true experience of independence. It was also a crucial period, as her 12th board exam results would determine her eligibility for professional courses. She aimed to compete for a seat at Pune's only government medical institution, B. J. Medical College (BJMC), which also happened to be the alma mater of her beloved grandparents.

However, another possibility arose when Suchitra encouraged her to consider the Armed Forces Medical College (AFMC) in Wanowari, located within Pune's Military Complex. A familiarisation visit to AFMC proved to be an eye-opener. The well-organised infrastructure, clean and green surroundings, and the disciplined atmosphere appealed to her deeply. Right then, she decided, along with her friend, to make a sincere effort to gain admission to AFMC. The sight of the uniform left a lasting impression, subtly influencing her eventual decision. Incidentally, it was during this time that destiny brought us together for a brief meeting—an episode that may have further reinforced her choice of a military career.

Madhuri's 12th-grade results were no surprise; she once again topped in multiple subjects and led the merit list for BJMC. However, she had also applied for admission to AFMC with the support of her grandparents, who were her local guardians. When she secured admission to AFMC, she excitedly informed her father in Lucknow of her new achievement. And then, all hell broke loose!

Her father questioned her decision to commit to a military career without thorough consideration and was upset that he had not been consulted. Under his insistence, she withdrew from AFMC and joined B. J. Medical College. When he later asked his own parents why they had allowed Madhuri to apply to AFMC, her grandmother cryptically replied, 'Your daughter should fly on her own wings.'

Madhuri, however, was deeply unhappy about leaving AFMC and pleaded with her father to reconsider. Seeing her unwavering determination to embrace the military way of life, he eventually relented. As a final condition, he warned her that if she ever changed her mind, he would not be able to help her leave the military service or pay her way out of the bond. Madhuri accepted these terms without hesitation. She then reached out to AFMC, which was kind enough to reinstate her admission. She was destined for a career in uniform, and she ensured she kept her date with destiny!

- **Siblings**

Madhuri is the eldest of three sisters. With an age difference of two years from Nilima and nine years from the youngest, Rashmi, she naturally felt a strong sense of responsibility. Hailed as 'Tai' by them, she quite enjoyed her stature! Perhaps the first shoots of natural leadership sprouted in this fertile environment.

As they grew up, it became evident that all three were gifted with sharp intelligence and photographic memories. The youngest, Rashmi, perhaps took the cake in this regard. Nilima turned out to be extremely quick-witted and spiritually inclined. Madhuri, always in a mad hurry, did everything quickly and meticulously—perfection was her motto. They also possessed a convivial appearance and carried themselves with grace. Each one influenced the others positively, and they all grew into brilliant professionals in their respective fields. As the eldest, Madhuri internalised a nurturing role and became the go-to person when needed. She continues to be a role model in terms of maturity, understanding, compassion, and empathy.

- **The Friends Circle**

Madhuri exhibits a cheerful disposition and natural vivacity, much like her mother. Her helpful, sincere, and friendly nature drew a large circle of friends at different stages of her life. The first real set of close friendships took shape in Lucknow during her senior school years. Being bright and quick on the uptake, she often helped others with their studies. Engaging in both indoor and outdoor activities with her friends created strong bonds. A similar trend continued through her college days in Pune and later at AFMC. Her robust and happy attitude ensured that she retained a close-knit circle of trusted friends, whose unwavering support has been a source of strength throughout her military career.

- **The Joint Family System**

Another significant influence in Madhuri's life was growing up within a larger family circle, where her parents were well-regarded. Her father's academic brilliance and her mother's warm personality were admired by all. The extended family had migrated to different regions for education and livelihood, but they remained connected. As the children grew up, they visited each other during annual school vacations and lived together without regard for status or stature. This fostered a strong social network that thrived on community functions and togetherness. This simple and unassuming way of life became an integral part of Madhuri's nature and has served her well throughout her life.

Pigtails to Cocktails: A Vibrant Upbringing and a Lively Personality

Within this milieu of simple *sanskaars* (values), Madhuri grew into a vibrant and lively personality. From the very beginning, there was an element of novelty, simplicity, and humility in the environment around her. The social backdrop was conservative yet progressive. Her paternal grandmother exhibited exceptional resilience in the face of adversity, while her mother embodied a cheerful yet spiritual disposition. Her father was strict and stern but had a modern outlook. Best of all, there was always a feeling of trust and confidence within the family. As the eldest of the three siblings, Madhuri assumed a leadership role early in life, one she has continued to refine throughout her professional career.

The emphasis on meticulousness with sincerity of purpose, compassion for those less fortunate, and the importance of spiritual grounding to maintain calm during crises were critical influences in her formative years. Over time, a sense of quiet contentment seeped into Madhuri's being as she navigated life on her own terms. Close and reliable friends provided a solid support system along the way. Gender differentiation was never an issue while growing up, and an independent perspective was always encouraged. This upbringing made all three sisters bold and uncompromising. Righteous conduct was a hallmark that was deeply respected within the family.

Thus, in the summer of 1978, as Madhuri transitioned from minor to independent adult (she was about to turn eighteen that October), she made the life-altering decision to join the armed forces for a professional career in the army. Her father respected her choice, and the rest is history. And so, in July 1978, she finally joined her alma mater for medical studies—the Armed Forces Medical College (AFMC), the launchpad for her illustrious career. Her time at AFMC holds a special place in her life and will receive separate attention in this narrative. At this juncture, it suffices to say that the sanskaars she absorbed during her upbringing laid the foundation for the principled conduct she would uphold in her chosen field over the next forty-five years.

When she joined AFMC, she was a petite, pigtailed girl, full of life and good cheer, looking ahead to an exciting future. By the time she graduated with flying colours, she had transformed into a strong personality, ready for new challenges and a new life in the armed forces. In a lighter vein, she had successfully completed her journey from 'pigtails to cocktails.'

Postscript by Madhuri

I never realised how the impressions made on the soft clay of my mind would shape my later life. Each impression described is etched in memory, and every person has contributed in their own way. Rajeev forgot to mention his own role! He was the solid rock, the pillar of support, the anchor that ensured I remained on track while I learnt to fly—the wind beneath my wings then and now.

Chapter 3

AFMC: The Amrutam Sarovar

Backdrop

Armed Forces Medical College (AFMC) is a one-of-a-kind institution. Boys and girls enter its portals at the young age of seventeen or eighteen, all rough and raw. It is a co-educational institute where students graduate as basic doctors after four years and six months of rigorous study. Given the specific requirements of the armed forces, the entry ratio of boys to girls at AFMC was historically one girl for every five boys—a ratio that has only improved slightly over the years.

Madhuri encountered a small hurdle during the admission process when her petite frame was found to have a low haemoglobin count, which could have made her unfit for entry. However, she convinced the medical examination officer of her fitness, citing her sporty and sprightly appearance. That cleared her way to joining her new alma mater.

Upon graduation, newly minted doctors are commissioned into the Armed Forces Medical Corps as officers, holding a rank equivalent to a lieutenant in the army. As a norm, fifty per cent of the hundred male graduates are granted permanent commission (PC), while the rest receive short service commission (SSC). SS officers are expected to serve in the armed forces for an initial period of five years, though those who choose not to serve at all have the option to leave by paying the amount specified in the service bond. SS officers who later seek a permanent commission must undergo a selection process and are accepted based on the organisation's requirements.

Among the female graduates, only one in twenty is granted a permanent commission. This is awarded to the top-ranked female candidate in the selection process, which considers factors beyond academic merit. This peculiar limitation would later impact Madhuri's career.

First MBBS

The first two months of settling in at the new establishment were indeed exciting. Besides getting to know their batchmates, the new entrants also became familiar with their seniors. Friendly ribbing by the senior girls in the hostel was an accepted phenomenon, testing both physical and mental endurance. Most girls took it in their stride, while some took longer to adjust to their new life.

During the initiation phase, boys were required to wear white shirts and black pants, while the girls presented themselves in an all-white or mismatched salwar-kameez combination, with heavily oiled braids secured by bright red ribbons. This made them noticeable from a mile away, earning them the colloquial nickname 'The Penguins.' At the end of the two-month initiation, the bedding-in process culminated in a splendid bash-up party. Madhuri, with her cheerful nature, ever-present smile, and quick wit, stood out from the very beginning. She was selected as 'Miss Social' by the batch.

Soon, it was time for the AFMC sports festival. With her abundant energy and athletic abilities, she was crowned the fastest sprinter among all the girls. She proved that the doctors who had cleared her during the entrance medical test had been right to place their trust in her. It was during this time that she was christened 'Speedy' by her batchmates—a name that stuck with her throughout her career in the Armed Forces.

Beyond athletics, Madhuri participated in numerous co-curricular activities, including the dramatics society, adventure camps, the students' scientific society, basketball, and more. These activities fostered a sense of accomplishment, camaraderie, and confidence. However, they also encroached on study time. While thoroughly enjoying her new lifestyle, Madhuri found herself struggling academically during her first pre-semester exams. She was shocked when she actually flunked one of the internal exams—a lesson that stayed with her, not only at AFMC but throughout her career. She quickly realised the necessity of time management and prioritisation. Refocusing her energies, she never looked back, no matter the distractions.

As the first semester exams approached, Madhuri relied on her natural inclination as an early riser. She found that her best concentration came in the quiet hours before dawn, when even the Sun God had yet to appear. Around 5 a.m. soon became her favourite time to study. Up and about in a jiffy, she would dedicate the next two to three hours to her studies, revising the previous day's topics and preparing for the day ahead. She took brief notes in her bold yet neat handwriting and was ready to hit the road post-breakfast.

Madhuri had a quick-reading ability and a razor-sharp memory. The visual images in her medical books became invaluable aids to her recall. She could focus on the essentials of any subject and summarise them concisely. Her creative ability to sketch neatly and quickly also enhanced her presentation style. These skills allowed her to answer queries and exams in a precise yet holistic manner, making her answer sheets both succinct and comprehensive. This mastery over her mind and thought process enabled her to tackle complex medical concepts methodically and efficiently.

With this inbuilt capability, she appeared for her first semester exams and, to her delight, passed with flying colours.

She realised that her morning study routine, combined with sincere (if not perfect) class attendance and an emphasis on the practical aspects of medicine, helped her absorb the intricacies of medical studies with relative ease. This became her unbeatable formula for success at AFMC and beyond.

The end of the first term was followed by a highly anticipated term break. Having fared well in her exams, Madhuri enjoyed her first holiday at home in Lucknow with relish. Refreshed and recharged, she returned to campus ready for the challenges and events the new term would bring.

During the new term, the inter-medical collegiate sports tournament was scheduled for February 1979. Madhuri could not count herself among the taller girls. However, it appeared that she had a knack for dribbling and assisting in effective plays. Before long, she found herself being groomed for the girls' basketball team. And now, another coincidence took place. While Madhuri rejoined AFMC for her second term, I had arrived in Ahmednagar (120 km from Pune) for the young officer's course (YO's course) at the Armoured Corps Centre and School (ACCS). As a student officer, I shared a room with a dear friend, Daljit Singh. Sometime in early February, he mentioned that he was thinking of scootering down to Pune to meet a friend at AFMC. Pune being my hometown, I thought it would be a good idea to join him and spend the weekend there. It also struck me that the pretty girl I had met six months ago was now a student at AFMC and perhaps this unforeseen opportunity could be used to meet her again. Hopefully, she would recollect our interaction from that occasion. Daljit was happy to hear that I also knew someone there and encouraged me to come along. So, I decided to give it a go and mentally started preparing for the rendezvous. Of course, Madhuri had no inkling of this play of destiny. She was likely continuing with her date with basketball, excited to be representing her college in the tournament.

The much-awaited day was here. Daljit and I set out on the rickety but faithful Lambretta scooter and reached AFMC on a pleasant February morning. After meeting Daljit's friend, we made our way to the girls' hostel, located adjacent to the basketball court. With some apprehension, I requested someone to send a message to Madhuri. She was obviously not expecting any visitors, but a little later, she breezed into the room.

I was hoping she would recognise me. But with one look, she said, 'I think you must have come to meet someone else,' and started to walk out of the room. Everything seemed to be going exactly as I had feared. With some hesitation, I reminded her of our earlier meeting, hoping to jog her memory. She looked at me with a little more interest, and suddenly, a flicker of recognition appeared. Though I felt relieved, I wasn't entirely sure she remembered the occasion until she pointed out that I looked very different from my IMA graduation days.

Following this encounter, we all sat down in the visitor's room and had a laugh over the incident. Even then, she appeared completely at ease, confident as ever. I debated whether it would be polite to ask her out for a meal the next day if she was free. Looking back, I find it hard to believe that inside the quiet me, there lurked someone bolder! And so, at the end of our first meeting, I asked her out for lunch the next day. I was thrilled to receive a positive reply.

The Place, a sought-after eatery in those days, was the venue for our meal. Madhuri and I often look back at that first luncheon and agree that we had 'found' each other then. After lunch, emboldened by our conversation, I asked if we could stay in touch. Her emphatic 'Yes,' accompanied by her imperfectly perfect smile (I always say she possesses a set of imperfectly perfect teeth), made my day.

In retrospect, we often marvel at the number of coincidences that ensured we met again. Destiny had brought us together briefly months ago. Now, it had orchestrated a second meeting, one that set in motion the beginnings of our eternal and wonderful togetherness.

Post that first meeting, both of us stayed in regular contact through small notes, and I looked forward to meeting Madhuri on the weekends. In the early stages, whenever I went down to Pune, a friend would accompany me. The presence of a good friend helped in overcoming conversation voids! And I thought I was handling the situation maturely until one day she said, 'Next time, could you please leave behind your friend?' Well, the directions from higher HQ were clear. I was a little taken aback, but it signified that she trusted me fully and that no one else was necessary when we were together.

The days seemed to roll by both fast and slow—fast when we met and slow in between. She organised her studies in a way that allowed her to be free whenever I could visit on a weekend. I too was busy with my own course studies and was doing fairly well. I would use my travel time to read my study notes whenever I took the bus (which was more often than not) and stay prepared for exams. I think we managed this study-and-enjoy routine rather well and also got to know each other better.

As her second term was coming to an end, so was my YO's course. That meant I would soon return to my unit in Jammu, and she would be on her way to Lucknow for her holidays again. Our periodic weekend meetings were likely to come to an end, and a lurking sense of losing out set in.

When it was time for her to travel by train from Pune to Lucknow, I promised to meet her at the railway station during its scheduled ten-minute halt at Nagar. However, due to some mischief, all the young officers were suddenly sent out on a cross-country run with packs on our backs at the exact time my 'date' at the railway station was supposed to take place. I was apprehensive that I might not make it in time, but I took off at blistering speed and managed to complete the course in record time, much to my own surprise. Still in my dusty battle fatigues, I rushed into the station just as the train rolled in. That rendezvous remains one of my strongest memories. I think it was then that the first inklings of a commitment to each other appeared on the horizon.

Soon thereafter, I returned to my unit, and both Madhuri and I fared well in our end-term exams and assignments, which made us happy. We realised that we could overcome distractions and continue to excel in our professional aspirations. Instead of being a hindrance, our support for each other became an inspiration.

Madhuri returned from her sojourn and immersed herself in her studies with full fervour in the second half of 1979. This term was important as her first MBBS exams were scheduled at the end of the semester. She remained consistent in her academic routine, and her theoretical thoroughness and proficiency in practical aspects had been noticed by her faculty. She also continued participating in co-curricular activities, albeit on a lower scale.

On my end, after completing my YO's course, I returned to my unit and soon absorbed myself in my professional endeavours as a young officer. As tankmen, we were expected to know our equipment and men like the back of our hand. It meant serious soldiering, and in my continuing exchange of notes with Madhuri, I would often describe to her how the tank was my first love!

Soon, it was time for her first MBBS exams. She exuded an air of confidence, without any sign of fear or nervousness. It was a battle she seemed to relish, and soon she emerged victorious, achieving the top rank in the university! The winning streak had just begun, and it would soon become a habit.

With her first MBBS done and dusted, it was once again time for her to head home and let her hair down. Meanwhile, in Jammu, I learnt that I had been assigned another professional course at Ahmednagar, commencing in January 1980. This meant I could once again catch up with Madhuri in Pune on the weekends. The course duration was almost five months, coinciding with Madhuri's fourth semester. Destiny seemed to be reinforcing the theory of coincidences with gathering vigour.

Second MBBS

By topping the first MBBS exams, Madhuri's academic excellence became evident. She was a keen learner, always on the lookout to gain knowledge outside of class time, with a special emphasis on the practical aspects. Over the next five months, she continued to focus on her studies at AFMC. At Nagar, I pursued my professional studies with equal seriousness.

I would visit Pune on most weekends and, at times, sit in the college library while she completed her assignments. Time seemed to pass quickly on such occasions, but the pauses in between allowed our relationship to progress gradually. We realised that our personal natures were different; I was the quiet type, while she was an extrovert, full of life, with a spring in her step. Perhaps we balanced each other out.

Those months passed all too quickly, and soon it was time for her term break and for my return to my unit. She continued to excel in everything she took on. Her success followed the same path she had already established in her academic career before joining AFMC. I, too, worked hard and managed to top my professional course. These small achievements encouraged us to believe that we brought out the best in each other. Without explicitly stating it, we would each put in extra effort to perform well in our respective fields.

Once again, it was time to part in the summer of 1980. We had been good friends for the past year and a half, and our families knew we had struck up a close bond. I had been thinking that we needed to give our relationship a sense of permanence, and it felt right to ask Madhuri if she felt the same way. So, as is my usual wont, when I went down to Pune to say goodbye, I gingerly asked her if we could commit to each other on a permanent basis. She turned around and simply said that it was already understood! It was a happy culmination of our time together.

Soon, we departed for our respective locations, deciding to inform our parents about our commitment and hoping they would be as happy as we were. In a way, we were already getting accustomed to the routine of meeting, greeting, and departing—a pattern that would define our lives for years to come. In the following months, Madhuri and I remained at our respective stations. We began writing to each other more often. I think my lack of talkativeness was compensated by my frequent letters. In those days, telephone calls were expensive and not easily accessible!

Sometime in the second half of 1980, I had the opportunity to represent the Services Cricket Team. The initial practice camp was in Pune, which gave me a brief opportunity to meet Madhuri. Meanwhile, her fifth-term semester exams were fast approaching, and she tackled them with her usual discipline and determination. Exams for her were like temporary challenges which she relished. They always encouraged her to strike with hope and anticipation. And so, as always, she cracked them in her characteristic style before heading off for her term break.

As 1980 drew to a close and Madhuri was still on her break, I received word that I would be attending another professional course at our alma mater in Nagar. Looking back, it seems as though someone up there was ensuring that our relationship moved forward with certainty and strength. Seeing this opportunity, my parents proposed to Madhuri's parents that our commitment be formalised. After reflecting on our bond, they gave their consent. And so, on the solemn occasion of Republic Day, 26 January 1981, Madhuri and I were engaged in the presence of our close relatives and friends, marking the beginning of our eternal journey together.

Following the engagement ceremony, I returned to my course studies, and Madhuri to hers. Her Second MBBS exams were due at the end of the sixth semester. During this period, I had the misfortune of losing my identity document during one of my visits to Pune, which led to a formal inquiry into my misdemeanour. The repercussions in such cases are generally severe, but I was certain that I must state the truth during the investigation. I was blamed for not being adequately careful, and upon completing my course (in which I excelled once again), I reported back to my unit, which was out on training manoeuvres. Immersed in training, I soon became oblivious to the loss of my identity card.

The training exercise went well, and my conduct was appreciated. My course results also arrived from Ahmednagar, and my good performance was duly noted by everyone. While we were still in the field, the inquiry proceedings landed on my commander's desk. Though he was taken aback by my carelessness, he appreciated my honesty and initiated action that did not negatively impact my career. I felt indebted, but the experience also strengthened my resolve to follow the righteous path throughout my service.

While all this was happening at my location, Madhuri completed her exams with confidence and flair. Her iron discipline—early morning study sessions, attentiveness in class, and emphasis on practical aspects—helped her excel with ease. She was happy with her performance and, once again, received top honours in the university.

Third MBBS

The seventh semester heralded the final lap of the MBBS curriculum. The burden of studies grew heavier, but Madhuri did not get bogged down. Instead, it only made her more resolute, and she doubled down on her study routine with greater focus. Madhuri and I continued our long-distance relationship and eagerly looked forward to each other's letters.

Madhuri's term break came and went. The eighth term was the penultimate semester, and the momentum towards the final term picked up pace. Towards the end of April 1982, as I was settling down at my unit after a hectic training event, I was asked to report to my unit HQ. I was pleasantly surprised to learn that I had been posted to ACCS as an instructor in the YOs' wing based on my qualifications. I had no inkling that this was going to happen. I had just completed four years of service, and it was not standard policy to move out of the unit so early. But destiny has its peculiar ways of turning matters around.

A year had passed without us being able to meet, which, in a way, worked in Madhuri's favour, allowing her to focus entirely on her studies. The news of my posting was completely unexpected, and both of us were thrilled. It meant I would be in Nagar for the next two years—just 120 km away—making it possible for us to meet frequently. Destiny and coincidence continued to be close friends.

I reported to my new assignment in May 1982 and began settling into my role as an instructor. Meanwhile, in Pune, Madhuri returned from her semester break and resumed her studies. Short case and long case became a routine reference in our conversations. She spent most of her time in the library, where she found quiet and peace. At Nagar, I busied myself with preparing my teaching notes, which meant my trips to Pune were spaced out at longer intervals.

While all this was happening, our parents began discussing our marriage. Both families felt it should take place as soon as possible, and we agreed. By then, we had been together for nearly four years, and it was only fitting that we take our relationship to the next level. We knew there would be many challenges ahead—our postings, setting up a home, and frequent travel between locations. Frankly, we had no answers to these questions. The only certainty was that we had chosen each other of our own volition, we liked and cared for each other, and we were committed to doing whatever was necessary to support one another and make our life together work.

With that, the process of finalising the wedding date began. Soon, Madhuri's exam schedule was published, and her exams were set to conclude on 12 November 1982. Conveniently, 16 November 1982 happened to be Padwa, an auspicious day. There was, however, a small hitch: as a student at AFMC, Madhuri was not expected to marry before completing her academic course. After a brief discussion, we decided to go ahead with the wedding in the hope that she would sail through her exams, given her track record!

We settled on a simple one-day ceremony. Both our families, being down-to-earth middle-class households, agreed to share all expenses equally. The wedding and reception would be held at the same location on the same day. To simplify logistics, we chose the open assembly hall of a school in Mumbai as the venue. A simple solution for a complex event! And with that, the wedding planning was complete.

The final exams were now close. Madhuri appeared a little concerned, but I knew she was well-prepared and ready to give her best shot. One by one, every paper was attempted with due diligence, and the final practical on 12 November 1982 was an event of significance. It marked the beginning of the home stretch for both of us. Four days later, we would be tying the knot for our onward journey together.

Finally, D-Day arrived. Early in the morning on 16 November 1982, my parents and I proceeded to the marriage mandapam. Soon, the *vidhis* (pre-wedding ceremonies) began. Madhuri looked lovely and dapper in her wedding attire. Fresh out of her exam routine and with no worries, she seemed as elated as I did. However, in the middle of the solemn proceedings, there was a sudden flutter—the postman had just delivered a telegram to Madhuri's father. Everyone waited with bated breath. It was a congratulatory message from one of her teachers and mentors. Internal evaluations indicated that Madhuri had performed extremely well and was likely to be the university topper once again. A wave of joy swept over the gathering. The vidhis resumed, and finally, the moment of betrothal arrived. Four and a half years in the making, this was 'THE' moment for us. Finally, we were together—always to be together. That was the thought that passed through my mind.

At the end of the day, after a small send-off ceremony, Madhuri travelled back with me to our home. Now Madhuri Kanitkar, she was welcomed into the Kanitkar household as the Lakshmi-Saraswati combination, bringing happiness to all. In short, Rajeev Kanitkar and Madhuri Kanitkar had arrived on the scene. It had been a long but happy journey, and we looked forward to an enduring partnership in the days to come.

Niranjan Ranasinghe, my friend and colleague from the Sri Lankan Army, had invited me to his beautiful country for our post-marriage vacation. We flew to Colombo via Chennai and spent a wonderful holiday in that lovely locale. Meanwhile, Army HQ had kindly agreed to post Madhuri for her internship at a hospital in Pune, adding to our joy.

Her batch was to be the first to graduate and be commissioned as officers in a military parade. As pioneers, they underwent rigorous marching practice to set the standard for future batches. Over time, the Q batch refined their drill, and the parade was a resounding success on 27 December 1982. Following this, the main awards ceremony took place. Madhuri was awarded the Kalinga trophy for her outstanding academic achievements and the President's Gold Medal for her commendable all-round performance. Her achievements have since been recorded on the history boards at AFMC.

The Amrutam Sarowar (The Lake of Immortality)

AFMC, as an institution, played a crucial role in shaping the raw and rough students of the 1978 Q batch into resilient and responsible officers of the Indian Armed Forces. Hard work, sincerity, loyalty, and camaraderie became part of their DNA. Respect for teachers and elders became second nature, while discipline and civic consciousness were deeply instilled. As they progressed in their studies, they realised they would graduate as soldier-doctors, responsible for life-and-death situations in challenging operational environments. Consequently, these young men and women developed a maturity rarely seen at such an early stage of life.

The environment at their Amrutam Sarowar had instilled a spirit of nation-first without them even realising it. For all those who pass through the portals of AFMC, the nectar from this Sarowar will continue to provide sustenance when needed. As they spent their last day at AFMC, nostalgia gripped them. Everyone was eager to take on their next assignment at designated military hospitals. Upon completing their internships, they would be posted as full-fledged doctors—an exciting prospect. With enthusiasm (and perhaps a hint of sorrow), they bid farewell to their alma mater. 1983 beckoned, and it was time to say 'Happy New Year' with zest and gusto.

Postscript by Madhuri

Four and a half years seemed unending while waiting to be married. I remember my mother's concern when I mentioned a friend whom I was seeing regularly when I was not yet eighteen! She seriously asked if I had the courage to complete a rigorous four-and-a-half-year course to become a doctor or if I would rather get married and become a housewife. I quietly replied that Rajeev was just twenty-one, and since the army did not encourage marriage before twenty-five, I could surely complete MBBS while waiting. From that moment on, we both knew we had made a commitment—to each other and to our respective careers. Life's destination was clear, but at the time, we did not know that the journey would be far from a fairy tale.

Part II

Laying the Foundation

Chapter 4

Internship: The Forging Furnace

Our First Home: United Even When Apart

1983 BEGAN WITH AN ETERNAL LESSON THAT BECAME AN integral part of us over time—together yet apart. Madhuri reported to M. H. Kirkee for her internship, and I resumed my duties at ACCS. We had a family home in Pune where my elder brother, Sanjeev, and his wife, Padmaja, lived. My parents were scheduled to shift into the same abode after my father's retirement a little later. However, Madhuri felt that she needed to stay in a different place and be independent. As an intern, she would have odd working hours, which could cause disturbances whenever she went in and out of the house. Secondly, it would allow us to spend time together during my short weekend visits. Both of us were keen to get used to living separately yet together whenever feasible.

Madhuri's grandparents owned a house in Pune that was vacant, so we decided to move in there. Though no specific mention was made, my parents were probably unhappy about this arrangement. We, too, did not bring up the issue, as there was no clear solution to a matter that involved sentiments. Nevertheless, since the two houses were within walking distance, frequent visits to each other naturally resolved the issue over time.

Setting Up, Settling In

Making a house a home is easier said than done. Firstly, the process was largely left to Madhuri in my absence. Secondly, Madhuri's knowledge of cooking was fairly limited, and mine was almost non-existent. Her mother was an excellent cook, and Madhuri had picked up a few things from her—more by observation than practical experience. But super-efficient Madhuri took on the challenge with verve. The kitchen essentials were soon acquired, the existing furniture was rearranged, and the house was made functional for daily life. It would be fair to say that this house became our first home, where we felt comfortable and eagerly looked forward to our short but memorable weekends together.

Fortunately, we were blessed with wonderful neighbours: Madhuri's paternal aunt and uncle, along with their three lovely children (Veena Atya, Bipin Kaka, Rupa, Reshma, and Rohit). Atya and Kaka became our unstated godparents. Anytime something was unavailable in our house (especially kitchen supplies), it would magically be replenished from theirs. I still remember the wonderful cups of tea that Atya would so often prepare for us. Madhuri also hired a maid to help with household chores, and, over time, the essentials of running a home slowly fell into place.

The hospital where Madhuri reported for work was about five km away. In those days, she had an old scooter, which she used for commuting to and from the hospital, as well as for other errands. It was under these circumstances that she began to take on life independently, with spirit and aplomb.

The Hospital Routine

One universal truth is that internship is tough business. The intern is expected to be the first person on duty in the morning and the last to leave in the evening. He or she is required to know the résumé and clinical findings of every patient in the ward. Suitable annotations have to be made in the case sheet daily. In addition, interns are expected to be familiar with various aspects of patient administration, including diet requirements, the state of hospital linen, and even details of caretakers, if any. Resolving constraints also fell within their domain of training. In brief, the intern is literally the workhorse of the hospital.

Madhuri, with her bright outlook on life and intense dedication to training, took all this in her stride. She acknowledged that the 'internship furnace' was the foundation on which she would refine her clinical skills. Hence, she worked with full gusto and unwavering determination. Despite her sincerity, her supervisory specialists often found something wanting in her efforts. At times, she was admonished for inadequate knowledge despite being a bright officer. It was also noted that she had received preferential permission to stay at home due to her married status. These incidents may have been intended to push her to work harder, but to her, they appeared to be deliberate attempts to downplay her academic achievements and 'put her in her place.' There was no solution to this ingrained issue except to soldier on and prove that she was better than the best at every juncture. Consequently, she prepared herself to deal with such encounters on an ongoing basis.

Though a tough cookie by any measure, Madhuri, at that young age, was vulnerable and not yet mentally attuned to the negative undercurrents she experienced. During my periodic visits to Pune, I sensed her concerns about this issue. But the brave girl that she was—and is—she would not cry over spilt milk. Around the halfway mark of her internship, she decided to move out of our fondly built home to the Officers' Mess. This allowed her to remain within the hospital premises 24/7, reducing the administrative burdens at home that took up much of her after-work time.

Slowly, her seniors' attitudes began to change as she excelled in her clinical work. As the days passed, she was sought out for her input on complicated cases, which gave her immense satisfaction. In a strange way, learning by fire proved to be a blessing in disguise. By the time she completed her training at M. H. Kirkee, she had earned a reputation for being rock solid in her clinical abilities. She appeared to have a gift for quickly analysing complex cases and the courage to voice her opinions. She also developed the confidence to act decisively and without fear. During a crisis, she would neither flinch nor crumble under pressure. She knew what to do and how to do it. In the process, Madhuri came into her own and was now ready to apply her newly honed skills as a budding doctor in the field.

The Absent Husband

For me, this was a new experience as well. Together for the first time, it was also my responsibility to try and make our home functional. My instructional responsibilities spanned multiple fields of work. However, by now, I had been at ACCS for more than six months, and most of the preparatory work for my job requirements had been completed. Hence, whenever feasible, I would inform my superiors and proceed to Pune over the weekends. These were great times, full of anticipation on the way out and full of longing on the way back.

Sometimes, I would use my motorcycle (a Yezdi, the replacement for the old Jawa bike at the time) to travel to Pune but soon realised that taking the bus was a better option. It saved me the fatigue of driving and allowed me time to read my notes. It was also safer than riding a bike alone. However, the downside was the inflexibility of the bus schedule. I would leave Nagar after working hours on Saturday and return on Monday mornings. My return journey would start at 4 a.m., with Madhuri dropping me off at the bus station on her two-wheeler. Strangely, even at that hour, the bus would be almost full, and Madhuri's presence often helped me find some space for myself. These intermittent weekend rendezvous became a hallmark of our early years—together, yet apart.

An incident with a tinge of melancholy marked our first wedding anniversary in November 1983. Both of us had been eagerly looking forward to it. But then came an unexpected spoiler. In the forces, we have a system called Bara Khana (a colloquial term for having a meal with troops), where officers and troops partake in a meal together to celebrate an event of significance. I do not recall the specific occasion, but I suddenly realised, just before our anniversary, that I was expected to attend the dinner as it was an official event. This meant I would not be able to travel to Pune for our celebration. Madhuri was understandably upset with this turn of events. On my part, I felt I could not ask for leave when an official event was scheduled.

To compensate, Madhuri decided to visit Nagar for the day. While I attended the Bara Khana, she had a Chota Khana in the mess room by herself. It was a poor substitute for our first anniversary, and both of us felt disheartened. Over time, however, we learnt to take such occurrences in our stride as part of humour in uniform. Events like these, I suppose, helped us develop resilience beyond our years and taught us to accept destiny with humility.

The Soldier's Doctor

Madhuri's internship at M. H. Kirkee had been a rewarding experience, despite a few challenging moments. One of the highlights was that we got to spend many weekends together. Her internship was scheduled to conclude in December 1983, around the same time I was to return to my unit on posting. She requested a posting to Jodhpur, where my unit had moved from Jammu. Having acquired the necessary skills to be a soldier's doctor, she was determined not to look back. Army

HQ was most helpful and issued her posting orders to a Field Ambulance located on the outskirts of Jodhpur Cantonment. She was required to report there in March 1984.

This was a fortunate turn of events, and it struck us that perhaps we could start thinking of expanding our family. In early 1984, my posting orders arrived as well. I was to head back to my unit in June, and we looked forward to finally being together in a real sense. The process of packing and hiring a truck to transport our luggage was a new experience, one that would continue periodically for the next forty years.

Basic Military Training (BMT)

Madhuri's batch was the first to be commissioned as officers in a military parade at AFMC. In fact, the lady officers of her batch were pioneers, being the first to be posted to field units upon completing their internship. Before proceeding to their new units, all interns were required to attend Officer's Training School (OTS) in Lucknow for basic military training, a program designed to transform young doctors into soldier-doctors.

It was an exciting time for the batchmates to reunite after a year of rigorous internship, and they looked forward to enjoying their time in Lucknow. However, the reality of tough training painted a different picture. Their routine included demanding drill practice, battle physical efficiency tests (BPET), and weapons training in the mornings, leaving them exhausted by the time they had to report for classroom lessons. These sessions covered various aspects of military tactics and administration in both field and peace establishments, equipping them to perform their military duties more efficiently.

At the time, there were no specific regulations for testing the physical fitness of lady officers. They were expected to meet the same standards set for their male counterparts, which proved challenging. The instructors provided some leeway while assessing them, but Madhuri decided to test herself against the prescribed standards and performed quite well. However, she was convinced that this discrepancy needed to be addressed, considering the physiological differences between men and women. Determined to rectify this, she took up the issue and ensured that a separate set of standards was eventually introduced to assess the physical fitness of women officers. Conviction-driven action remained her trademark throughout her service.

This period of training was, in many ways, great fun. During their free time, the batchmates would share countless stories of their internship days. Outings to favourite dining spots in the city were common. However, this combination of military training and good-hearted banter was about to end, after which they would all proceed to their new units to begin life as soldier-doctors. And though Madhuri obtained a delta grade for her performance, she did not top the course. Apparently, there was some jubilation that she was beatable! Such are the humorous angles of an intensely competitive environment in the armed forces.

In March 1984, upon completing the course, Madhuri was promoted to the rank of captain. From Lucknow, she proceeded to her new unit near Jodhpur. There was excitement and curiosity within the troop fraternity upon hearing that a lady officer was being posted to their unit for the first time in its history. They likely wondered how this new presence would fit into their daily routines. Where would she reside? Would she attend PT parades early in the morning with the troops? Would she join them on the games field in the evenings? What kind of duties would she undertake in the unit? And if military operations became imminent, would she move to the border areas with the others? This speculation was not limited to the troops; similar questions lingered in the minds of the senior command hierarchy as well.

When Madhuri reached Jodhpur by train in March 1984, a suitable reception party was sent to receive her at the railway station. They assumed she might be apprehensive and unsure of herself in a new place and role. However, as the train came to a halt at Jodhpur Railway Station, the newly minted 'soldier-doctor,' cheerful as ever, jumped sprightly onto the platform. She looked around confidently to see if help was at hand. Spotting a group of AMC personnel nearby, she waved to them with poise, probably taking them by surprise. Soon, she was assisted with her luggage and escorted to the field hospital with dignity and decorum.

After spending a couple of months in Jodhpur, she applied for leave to assist me with packing up in Nagar. That same month marked her parents' 25th wedding anniversary. So, in mid-May, we all spent a wonderful family vacation at Mahabaleshwar, a hill station near Pune. We took long walks around the local lake and indulged extensively in the famous strawberry ice cream, so much so that by the end, we realised we had more than our fair share.

As we were preparing to return to Pune, Madhuri experienced the first inklings of a likely addition to our two-person family. Medical tests in Pune confirmed the happy news—our first baby was on the way, and our joy knew no bounds.

Postscript by Madhuri

Everything had been on fast forward since completing my MBBS course—going from student to wife just three days after my exams, to intern within fifteen days, and an officer the next month! There was too much on my plate, and I was glad Rajeev was there to help me find my feet. He supported my decision to live by myself after marriage. The tightrope I walked in those days taught me to balance work and home and to develop the strength to handle most things alone, as destiny would demand in the future. The binging on strawberry ice cream—and the sudden aversion to it—had another reason: early pregnancy! However, neither of us knew it then.

On the career front, our basic military training had been great fun, but by the end of it, I realised that our responsibility as doctor-soldiers was now truly at hand, as I departed for my new unit. From this point on, I would be independently responsible for the health of our troops and their families. It would be my first battlefield—providing practical medical care—and I looked forward to my new role with a little apprehension, but also with great eagerness.

Chapter 5
The Jodhpur Interlude

Forerunners at the Field Hospital

Madhuri reported to her new assignment in Jodhpur with great anticipation. The CO of the medical unit was an experienced and mature officer. In his first interaction with Madhuri after her arrival, he assured her that she would have an interesting tenure in her new setup. He appreciated her strong credentials and the reputation she had gained at AFMC and M. H. Kirkee. After the initial formalities, he indicated that arrangements were being made for her to stay in the divisional HQ Officers' Mess, as there was limited scope for the privacy she might expect.

The soldier that she was, Madhuri immediately told him that she would prefer to stay in the unit lines with everyone else and would manage to put in place the necessary arrangements for her stay with the assistance of her colleagues. She expressed appreciation for his concern but insisted on first trying the option of staying within the unit premises. After giving it some more thought, the CO agreed to her suggestion. And so began an interesting first field tenure for Madhuri.

The unit lines were located away from the main built-up areas of the cantonment and were fairly secluded. The living quarters for troops and officers were in temporary reconstructed huts (colloquially called TRHs). As the name suggested, these were simple, rudimentary structures providing temporary shelter in the absence of permanent accommodation. The beds were made of steel pipes and nylon straps, laid out against the walls of the barracks with walking space in between. Water shortages were common, and drums of water were available from which one could help oneself if the overhead tank ran dry. A section of the barrack towards the end, partitioned by a thin wall, was allotted to her. A few curtains were added to provide enhanced privacy. The barracks for the men in the unit were also in close proximity, and their bathing point (as it is called in army language) was just outside the officers' barracks. So, every morning and evening, Madhuri found herself within earshot of their friendly banter. It was in these surroundings that Madhuri began her role as a soldier's doctor.

Another interesting incident took place during Madhuri's first couple of months in Jodhpur—her interaction with the general officer commanding (GOC). This was the first time lady officers had been posted to field formations, which necessitated careful planning for their employment. Would they stay back at the rear base and manage administration, or would they be deployed in active field hospitals? Would they be able to withstand tough field conditions? Would they require more privacy than others, and how would that impact the overall administration? The safety of lady officers in the field also required consideration. These questions had gained significance.

It was in this context that one day, Madhuri received a summons from the divisional HQ. The GOC was keen to meet the new officer at the field hospital and hear her views on the matter. After some small talk, he asked the important question: What would she do if the division moved out for war? Would she prefer to remain in the rear? Without batting an eyelid, Madhuri replied that she would prefer to be in the field with her men, doing her best to provide medical care at the battlefront.

What about privacy? She explained that even in the unit, she had refused to shift to the relative safety of the divisional

Officers' Mess and had chosen to stay in the unit lines. She joined the soldiers in every activity, whether PT or sports. If she could integrate with her troops in peacetime, she reasoned, it would be even easier in the field, where everyone was more attuned to each other's needs. Privacy would be managed just as she had handled it in the peace-time location. As for operational dangers, they were the same for everyone. Not for a moment did she see herself as part of the rear party just because she was a woman.

With a small chuckle from the GOC, the matter was settled. He liked Madhuri's spirit and, after this conversation, probably felt more at ease about the issue. Such were the initial uncertainties surrounding the employment of lady officers in wartime.

The Daily Routine

Life in the field hospital was a new experience. A field hospital in peacetime is not heavily committed. It is expected to keep its equipment and stores in a state of readiness so that it can mobilise for operations at short notice. The doctors and technical personnel, in particular, set up a small outpatient department (OPD) to care for a portion of the military clientele in the station and/or integrate into the local military hospital to enhance its functional capacity. In the overall context, there is a tendency towards underutilisation of equipment and personnel.

Soon after settling down, Madhuri felt that the limited use of personnel and equipment needed a review. Accordingly, she suggested to the CO that they could open up a part of their stores and increase the scope of their peacetime utilisation. This would enhance manpower skills and improve their readiness to deploy at short notice. The CO liked the idea and decided to implement the suggestion.

Consequently, Madhuri got down to plenty of work in her new unit. She believed that all medical officers must be capable of handling basic cases of all kinds and that referrals to specialists should be made only in deserving cases. This approach had a positive effect, and the unit became known for its professional stance. Madhuri integrated smoothly into the professional routine. Her medical knowledge and strong clinical acumen earned special praise from the CO of the military hospital. She found great satisfaction in being the soldier's doctor.

At the field hospital, she also joined the troops for PT parades and on the sports field. Her happy-go-lucky attitude was well received, and she soon started enjoying her daily routine. There was professional work to do, along with time for physical fitness, exercise, and sports—a perfect combination in the early part of her career. This practice eventually shaped her philosophy of a fit mind in a fit body.

Together for the First Time

Madhuri and I travelled back together to Jodhpur in early June. We stayed for a few days in my regiment's Officers' Mess until we could arrange for a house. Due to a shortage of military accommodation, we hired a private house for the interim. It was a few kilometres away from our workplace, and both of us travelled on our two-wheelers to and from work. While Madhuri continued her routine of tending to patients in her unit OPD, I got busy with regimental activities. As the adjutant of the unit, I was responsible for coordinating all administrative and operational matters. Consequently, I found myself spending long hours at the office. Often, I would miss lunch, which upset Madhuri. Looking back, I regret not handling my office pressures in a more balanced manner.

As the days passed, Madhuri's pregnancy started weighing on her more. On days when she remained at the military hospital as the duty medical officer (DMO), I would meet her only the next day. Though we were posted together, our respective routines frequently kept us apart. At home, Madhuri took on the responsibility of running the household. Going to the market added to her burdens. Though I tried to pitch in, it was not enough, and we wondered whether we would be able to handle the precious life on its way. Madhuri needed companionship, something I was not sensitive enough to recognise. I expected her to be a tough soldier, which was unfair, and she pointed this out when I was unable to accompany her for important medical check-ups. All the same, we battled on!

Alongside, there were many enjoyable moments as well. On one occasion, we invited unit officers and their wives to our place for high tea. It was Madhuri's first attempt at cooking for a large group. To keep it simple, the menu focused on *pav bhaji*, a well-known Maharashtrian dish. After a hearty round of refreshments, the main dish was served. We were happy that everyone appeared to be enjoying themselves until we noticed most of them reaching for a glass of water! That is when we realised the bhaji had received a double dose of spices. The mouth-watering dish had taken a turn; it was now making our eyes water instead. But everyone declared it was the best meal they had ever had. Fortunately, the dessert helped overcome this homely disaster.

A few months later, we were allocated official quarters. We were happy, as it meant better security and having friends nearby. By then, Madhuri was late into her pregnancy and needed to take greater care. However, she was suddenly earmarked for temporary duty (TD) at another location four hours away. Roads in those days were in poor condition, making for a bumpy journey that would not be good for her. A request was made to divert the duty, but it was not accepted, so Madhuri prepared to move the next morning.

However, her CO was determined not to let this pass. That evening, we had gone to the army open-air theatre in Jodhpur for a movie. As luck would have it, the GOC also dropped in to watch. During the break, Madhuri was suddenly summoned to interact with him. We wondered what it was about and soon found out. Her CO had approached the GOC to inform him of the issue affecting her. The GOC called for her, enquired about her health, and quickly realised that sending her on duty in her present condition would be inappropriate. He immediately directed his HQ to make the necessary adjustments.

Madhuri's predicament was resolved thanks to her CO's perseverance and a GOC who was mature and discreet. Keeping her health in view, her CO suggested it would be more appropriate to shift her to the military hospital for the remainder of her tenure in Jodhpur. This would provide greater stability and facilitate regular medical check-ups. Army HQ responded positively and side-stepped her to the military hospital. The CO, a kind and considerate person, gave her a fond farewell as she departed for the hospital.

At the Military Hospital

Madhuri's shift to the new surroundings was smooth. She had gained a reputation for exemplary professionalism and was warmly welcomed into the hospital fraternity. Madhuri loved clinical work and immersed herself in the hospital routine with gusto. Meanwhile, she had entered the penultimate month of pregnancy, and working long hours was becoming increasingly difficult. She had to decide when to avail leave in anticipation of the big day.

At the time, the leave facility for a mother was not very generous. Besides two months of maternity leave, she could avail two months of annual leave and another two months of half-pay leave which was subject to the commanding officer's approval. The tendency was to take leave as late as possible to ensure the mother could tend to the baby for at least three to four months before rejoining duty. Keeping in mind the expected delivery date, Madhuri commenced her leave in early January 1985.

I was trying to be as helpful as possible to ensure she was not overburdened. My unit was due to move out for training into the deserts of Rajasthan, but my CO was kind enough to permit me to stay behind until the baby arrived. The due date passed, yet there was no sign of our little one. It seemed the little one was quite comfortable in the womb. Only when the doctor started preparing for an operation, citing safety concerns—which Madhuri was reluctant about—did the baby finally decide to make his presence felt. And so, a little past 7:30 p.m. on 22 January 1985, we were blessed with a bonny son, hale and hearty.

Thrilled, we conveyed the good news to all, including my CO in the training area. The next day, Madhuri and the baby were shifted into a special room, both doing well. My parents had decided to join us in Jodhpur to help in my absence. Their arrival was a godsend and put us at ease.

Early that afternoon, we suddenly heard a commotion outside the hospital room. Through the window, we saw a cavalcade of military vehicles approaching. Soon, a bevy of officers from my unit burst into the room, singing a congratulatory song. On hearing of the new arrival, my CO and other officers had driven down a good 200 kilometres from the training area to felicitate the baby's birth. They brought along a huge cake, which was cut with great enthusiasm to celebrate the occasion.

We had not yet decided on a name for our son, but the unit officers had. They nicknamed him 'Ranveer'—a name symbolising a hero on the battlefield. Our regiment is known for its battlefield bravery, and our unit motto is '*Ranveer Jai Sada*,' which translates to 'The brave are always victorious.' A toast was raised to the baby and the mother, followed by a few lively songs. We were deeply moved by this kind gesture, and the memory remains imprinted in our minds to this day.

A few days later, Madhuri and the baby returned home. We wanted to have his naming ceremony before I departed for the desert. After some deliberation, we settled on Nikhil. In Sanskrit, *Nikhil* translates to 'complete in itself,' embodying strength, bravery, and boldness. It is also considered another name for Lord Vishnu. Everyone liked the feel of the name, and so it was decided that Ranveer would be formally addressed as Nikhil, while Ranveer remained his regimental identity.

For the next six weeks, Madhuri cared for little Nikhil with assistance from my parents. Though she was a doctor, she would often worry about his health. He had a fair complexion, and the intense cold of Jodhpur, combined with the dust in the air, seemed to affect him adversely. She would frequently bundle him up against the cold and rush to the paediatrician for consultations. Each time, the doctor would simply remove his excess layers to make him more comfortable. And in return, Nikhil would thank him with a big spray of pee, while Madhuri would burst into laughter.

On my return from the training area a few weeks later, my parents went back to Pune. Now, we were on our own once again. Half of Madhuri's leave had already passed, and in the days ahead, I knew Nikhil would be in my care. I was a little apprehensive, but I knew I would do my best.

Madhuri's father was posted in Gorakhpur at the time, and we decided to visit him. Sometime in March 1985, we ventured out with Nikhil to Gorakhpur. It was a joint air and rail journey to make the trip as short and comfortable as possible for him, as he was no more than eight weeks old. After a few days, I returned to Jodhpur while Madhuri stayed back a little longer for her first real break from a hectic schedule. She resumed her duties at the end of April 1985, and I took on the responsibility of looking after Nikhil.

I had watched Madhuri bathe Nikhil, but when I tried to replicate it, I found the technique quite complicated. In my attempt to find a simpler solution, I came up with the 'Three Bucket Drill.' I would gently lower Nikhil, holding him under both armpits, into the first bucket to wet him. This was followed by applying soap and scrubbing. Once done, I would shift him into the second bucket to rinse him. Finally, he would go into the third bucket for a final wash, and the bathing session would be complete! I suspect Nikhil liked my simple system. It was relatively safe, as it ensured I wouldn't drop him while bathing him, and it was assembly-line efficient!

The next task was drying him up. For this, too, I devised a method—the 'Three Towel Drill.' I would lay out three towels in a row on the bed before starting this drill. Once the bath was done, I would commence the 'Rolling-Up Drill' to dry him off. Instead of trying to hold up the little baby to dry him, I found it more convenient to roll him on the soft towels. Three to four turns one way and back again ensured he was all nice and dry. Simple solutions to complex issues became my chosen method for navigating fatherhood.

Nikhil had very light skin, and the heat of the Jodhpur summers troubled him greatly. My solution was to pick him up in my arms and rest him against the grill of the water cooler. The strong, cool breeze would calm him down. However, the water cooler often wouldn't work due to power outages. The answer to this problem was to pour a bucket of water all over the room floor. The natural evaporation would provide some relief, though not always satisfactory. Madhuri found my methods quite amusing, but they worked, and I could manage them independently. Those were the days of our early parenthood.

SS to PC Dilemma

At this stage, Madhuri was a short service officer. SS officers are considered for permanent commission upon completing two years of service. At that time, she was pregnant, and in the army, that meant she was deemed 'unfit,' making her ineligible to apply for PC. She waited another year before it was time to decide whether to apply.

It was a million-dollar question! We deliberated over the issue carefully. Given her experience, she wasn't sure if she wanted to continue. Nikhil was still very small, and balancing his care with her duties would be no easy task. Would she be able to do justice to both? Moreover, at present, we were together, but what about the future? Madhuri's father was still in service, and he had the responsibility of caring for his aged mother and disabled sister. My parents, though retired, couldn't always be available for long-term support. They lived in Pune with my elder brother, who had also been blessed with a son. My parents were already helping with his care, making it impractical for either set of parents to be available to us consistently.

As far as I was concerned, I felt that it would be unfair to Madhuri if she could not pursue her medical profession. She was academically brilliant and a superb clinician. By any measure, this combination deserved to flower and grow. Of course, saying it was one thing; doing it was a whole different story. So, we did consider the option of Madhuri settling down on the civil side, where she could pursue her medical profession while looking after Nikhil. At least she would have more stability while I moved around, and local assistance in our hometown would be more readily available. It was an attractive option but also had its drawbacks. Both of us liked a disciplined and orderly life. In some ways, Madhuri had decided to sign up at AFMC after meeting me and had looked forward to a military life. We liked the organisational strengths of the army. The camaraderie within military units is unique and not available elsewhere. Also, we could hope for postings together periodically, as there was a central government policy that aimed to post married couples to the same station whenever possible.

Such was the dilemma that confounded us. While I was keen for her to stay on in the army, it was she who would bear the brunt of responsibilities—managing military duties, running the home, and raising our child. Hence, it would be unfair of me to press too hard on this issue, so I left the final call to her. After more thought, we realised there were no sure-fire answers to all our queries. Settling down in the civil setup would be easier for Madhuri, but that would mean we would always be apart as long as I stayed in the army. If she stayed on, there was a better chance of being together on occasions, but handling all the responsibilities would be much more demanding. Finally, we decided that she should apply for PC, and if, at a later stage, life became too difficult to manage, she could request release from the army.

Based on this broad logic, Madhuri applied for PC in mid-1985. PC vacancies for women were limited. However, Madhuri's performance during her internship and the military orientation course at Lucknow had been excellent. Subsequently, her sterling service in the field hospital and the military hospital was also well appreciated. All this ensured that she was granted PC on her first attempt.

From the time I returned from my field training in March 1985 to early 1986, we had a fairly long stay together as a family. We enjoyed watching Nikhil grow. His appetite was so voracious that Madhuri and I often had to sit on either side of him, feeding him together just to keep up. As soon as one spoonful disappeared into his mouth, the next had to be ready for quick ingestion. If not, his bawl of annoyance could awaken the entire neighbourhood. His intake proportions were quite generous, and by the time he was eight months old, he was veering towards the obese side. Nikhil had to be put on a diet at that tender age, as his doctor mother knew the ill effects of early obesity!

In January 1986, we had a wonderful first birthday party for him in our unit mess. Nikhil started walking at just nine months old, and by his birthday, he was already racing around.

He sported golden locks, and with his winsome looks, he could win over everyone's heart.

In the first half of 1986, I had to leave for a field training event followed by a course at one of our training institutions. I was away for six months. Madhuri endured that interregnum on her own and had a tough time, especially when Nikhil was unwell. In the second half of the year, I focused on preparing for the Defence Services Staff College (DSSC) exam, scheduled for September 1986. The preparation required intense study, which meant Madhuri's responsibilities continued without respite.

The exams were just around the corner when a war-like situation arose, and the regiment was mobilised for operations. All of us looked forward to some real action, and studies had to be put aside for the time being. As the year-end approached, diplomatic efforts managed to stave off military action, and alert levels were eventually downgraded.

Sometime in January or February 1987, I returned to prepare for my DSSC exams, scheduled for April 1987. I was confident of doing reasonably well, but I floundered in one of the papers. I was disappointed, but Madhuri simply said that if I had found it difficult, others would have too. She predicted that everything would turn out fine, and she was right. When the results were declared in June, I had qualified with flying colours. Congratulations poured in from many quarters. This meant that in June 1988, I would have to proceed to Wellington, near Coimbatore, to attend the prestigious course at the Defence Services Staff College, nestled in the Nilgiris.

In the meanwhile, orders had been received for our unit to move to Suratgarh in November 1987. This shifted our focus back to Madhuri and Nikhil. It was evident that they would not accompany me to Wellington. Either she would continue in Jodhpur, or if selected for PG training, she might shift to AFMC in Pune, where home support would be available.

Towards the end of our stay in Jodhpur, I remember an evening when we were visiting the new CO of the military hospital. By then, Nikhil had become quite a chatterbox. Fizzy drinks were his favourite. Upon reaching the CO's house, Nikhil was politely asked for his preference. Prompt came the reply: 'Soft drink.' Very soon, he was offered one with an orange hue. Without batting an eyelid, he announced that he preferred a dark one. Quickly, someone brought him a glass of Coca-Cola. He turned up his innocent face and quipped that he liked his drinks only in a bottle. By now, we were downright embarrassed to see our young man elaborating on his specific preferences. There was a scramble to fetch him his choice. The CO, a thorough gentleman, soon put us at ease by praising Nikhil's wit. This amusing tale continues to be one of our abiding memories.

Application for Postgraduate (PG) Training

Madhuri applied for PC and PG training concurrently. As per the extant rules, only PC officers could be selected for PG training. The SSC interviews were scheduled well before the PG course, and Madhuri was confident she would be granted her PC before the PG selection was undertaken. However, since the PC results were not declared in time, her PG training application was turned down! She had to wait another year before she could be considered for the specialist course.

When she applied the next year, she once again did not find herself on the selection list. Selection for PG training was largely based on performance in the Medical Officer's Junior Command Course (MOJC) and the Annual Confidential Reports earned by officers during service. In addition, officers with high MBBS merit were selected after three years of service. Madhuri had performed extremely well in her MBBS exams, and her professional performance was highly appreciated. Hence, there was no reason for her not to be selected for PG training.

Madhuri was very upset, and rightly so, and she decided to catch the bull by the horns. She was convinced that she deserved fair consideration, and her fight-for-what-is-right principle came into focus. She sought an interview with the concerned authorities to understand why she had been passed over. When she presented herself in Delhi, she was told that she did not possess adequate merit. She was aghast and requested them to recheck their facts. When she pointed out some anomalies, she was told that those aspects should not be her concern.

In view of the foregoing, she requested a meeting with the overall head of the Armed Forces Medical Services (AFMS). The gentleman was gracious enough to hear her out and called for all the inputs on the issue. Seeing her impeccable record, he accepted her request. However, all the PG vacancies at AFMC had already been allocated, and hence, Madhuri was permitted to undertake her training at the Indian Naval Ship Hospital Asvini (INHS Asvini) in Mumbai.

The entire episode took place in mid-December 1987. The vacancy allotted to Madhuri had to be filled by 1 January 1988. This meant that Madhuri would have to rush back to Jodhpur from Delhi, pack up all her belongings, and travel to Mumbai with our three-year-old son. Thereafter, she would have to register for the PG training within the stipulated time.

Magical Madhuri took all this in her stride. Within a week of her return from Delhi, she packed up the entire household on her own. Friends chipped in to help. At the last hour, train reservations were unavailable. One of our dear friends, who was travelling on the same train, offered his reserved seat to her and roughed out the overnight journey in the corridor outside. Madhuri continues to remain grateful for his thoughtful gesture.

Three days before the cut-off date, Madhuri reached Mumbai and submitted the documents for registration with a big sigh of relief. The battle for PG training had been won. It was now time to master her technical skills a notch further, and she was ready for that. Where there is a will, there is a way became the mantra for the long journey ahead.

Postscript by Madhuri

Jodhpur remains a memory bank of sentiments and emotions. In our first military station together, our very own maharaja of Jodhpur, Nikhil, was born, and the first two big decisions in life were made despite all odds—one, the decision to take a permanent commission, and two, the decision to pursue post-graduation in paediatrics. Looking back, I realise how important it is to make quick decisions and then work towards making them successful, instead of procrastinating and being a non-starter.

My first success in swimming against the tide and standing up for my rights in a firm but polite way taught me great life lessons. The young girl with dreams in her eyes was waking up to reality. For the two of us, Jodhpur will always remain special.

Chapter 6

PG Storm in the Mumbai Cup

Our interlude at Jodhpur had been a mix of joy and tough times. But being together had helped us navigate real-life situations reasonably well. Now that we were separated once again, my mind was filled with apprehensions, centred on the uncertainties that would surround her daily routine in Mumbai while she underwent specialist training.

Settling Down in the Mumbai Environs

Madhuri's courage and conviction enabled her to take up the issue of PG training with her superiors and resolve it appropriately. Her spirit was slightly dampened by the fact that she was not able to undergo training at AFMC, a world-class institution with a strong teaching structure. She missed the feel-good factor of training in familiar surroundings. However, Madhuri is made of sterner stuff. Not one to sit back and mope, she decided to put the memories of the PG battle behind her and get down to her training in Mumbai with full enthusiasm. Her motto has always been that challenges need to be turned into opportunities, and this she did with a bang and flourish.

She quickly settled down with her parents in Mumbai. The naval hospital where she was to carry out her training was also located in close proximity. Nikhil hit it off with his grandmother and soon became attached to her. With Nikhil off Madhuri's immediate concerns, she was relatively free to utilise her time in the best possible manner. Along with Madhuri, another naval officer, Sheila Mathai, had also been nominated to undergo PG training at the same hospital. Both of them being good friends proved to be a great advantage during their three-year training period.

Mumbai has some of the best teaching hospitals in the country, and the spectrum of patient clientele at any time is humongous. From a clinical point of view, there is no better place to train in any given speciality. To avail this advantage, it was essential to travel long distances in crowded Mumbai to visit specific hospitals. Together, they devised a master method of quick movement based on two-wheelers and the famous local trains of Mumbai. This combination provided the most practical method to beat the traffic blues of the city.

After attending to all their responsibilities at INHS Asvini, they would proceed to the civil hospitals in Mumbai to see additional patients, attend clinics, or read in the library. It meant herculean efforts but also resulted in great learning. This was a big opportunity under severe challenges. I was located at Suratgarh at that time, and as usual, we underwent a long annual training season that lasted till March-April 1988. It had been six months since I had parted company with Madhuri. When I had originally appeared for my DSSC exams, the broad plan in my mind was that after the Jodhpur tenure, if I cleared my exams, I would do the one-year DSSC course at Wellington and then proceed on a staff appointment for two years. During the same period, Madhuri would complete her PG training in Mumbai while staying with her parents. By then, we would have stayed separately for three years, and perhaps our HR departments might consider posting us together. It was in our minds that we should try and be together every alternate posting. Both of us had different job specifications, and we realised that postings in the same station may be difficult on a continuous basis.

When my training schedule terminated in Suratgarh and our unit had settled down to the normal peacetime routine, I requested my CO to grant me long leave, after which I planned to join the DSSC at Wellington in the first week of July 1988. Without hesitation, he gave me the permission, and I was quite overjoyed. Over the next few days, I packed my bags and said goodbye to the unit to join Madhuri and Nikhil.

At Mumbai, I was happy to see that Madhuri had settled into her daily schedule, thanks to the comfortable support system in place. The grandmother-grandson duo had become inseparable, and the grandfather too had made alterations to his office routine to spend time with Nikhil. While I was there, Madhuri and I made tentative plans for her and Nikhil to join me for short durations at Wellington. At the end of June, I proceeded on a happy note to the Staff College, looking forward to our rendezvous in the Blue Mountains of Coonoor.

The Mumbai-Coonoor Interregnum

For all practical purposes, Madhuri and I were mentally prepared to be apart for a period of three years, interspersed with brief get-togethers. It was going to be a long haul and our first real test of separation post-marriage. I reached Coonoor towards the end of June 1988 for my DSSC chapter, while Madhuri continued with renewed vigour in Mumbai. The intense schedule of assignments kept me quite busy, as was Madhuri with her training.

A few months down the line, Madhuri and Nikhil joined me at the college during our mid-term break. We stayed within the Officers' Mess complex where I resided. In those days, I did not possess a car, and my means of transportation was a brand-new scooter, which came in greatly handy during the break. All three of us, along with our backpacks, drove down the steep mountain roads of Coonoor to the Mudumalai Sanctuary, a few hours away. We greatly enjoyed our stay in the natural environs of the sanctuary. At one point, we even made a dash to save ourselves from a marauding elephant. Those were great times, which we still remember vividly.

When Madhuri's vacation ended, we took leave of each other as per our SOP (standing operating procedure).

PG Training: To Continue or Not

Around November or December of 1988, we found ourselves facing a decision-making crisis. Madhuri's father was nominated as the head of their training institute at Hyderabad, and he was to report there in mid-1989. This implied that Madhuri's support structure would fold up, making it impossible to continue her PG training while caring for Nikhil. Madhuri's first reaction was to consider giving up her specialist training, which I felt was not fair. The only other option was for me to be posted to Mumbai upon completion of my course in order to assist her.

In the normal course of events, an officer on completion of the staff course is posted to an operational appointment in the field. Not obtaining that experience can negatively impact an officer's career. However, I felt that I should step back a little to contribute to her professional advancement. It involved accepting a non-operational appointment in Mumbai. The risk of a blemish on my service record due to a compassionate posting was real, and she felt that I should reconsider. I was sure in my mind that I should initiate this move to tackle our present challenge and too much debate on pros and cons leads to indecision.

My application on this account was acknowledged promptly by Army HQ, and subsequently, I found myself posted to Mumbai in a low-key administrative appointment. Someone remarked that 'I was axing my own feet,' but at that point in time, I had to reset my priorities, and I had no hesitation in doing that. Personally, I was happy to be of assistance to Madhuri and contribute to our son's care.

In Mumbai, Madhuri packed up her belongings and applied for married accommodation in the naval pool. As luck would have it, a couple of new buildings were in their final stages of completion and were expected to be available for allocation in June 1989. When Madhuri's parents moved out of Mumbai in May 1989, she availed some leave and joined me in Wellington for a short period after dropping off our son with my parents in Pune.

While Madhuri was at the college with me, we received the news of accommodation allotment. She moved back to Mumbai and shifted into the new accommodation, which was on the ninth floor of a building overlooking the Arabian Sea. What else could one wish for in Maximum City? We decided to look forward and move ahead with hope and gratitude.

Mumbai Meri Jaan

For the next two years, Mumbai became the lifeline for us. For army officers, being posted to Mumbai is like manna from heaven. The facilities in terms of education, entertainment, and ease of living are outstanding. Though I had come to Mumbai at some risk to my career, that thought never bothered me. I had made up my mind that whatever responsibility came my way would be discharged to the best of my ability. Being extremely sincere, I knew I would always go beyond the call of duty to fulfil my responsibilities, even if they were not high profile.

We began our life in Mumbai in naval accommodation. As mentioned earlier, it was a new building, and hence its systems were not functioning efficiently. The most glaring issue was the elevator system. Electrical failures were rather frequent, and we often had to walk up nine floors to reach our house. Madhuri faced a bigger problem because she had to go to the hospital often, and a non-functional elevator meant walking up and down those nine floors repeatedly. On one such occasion, while proceeding for an emergency call at 4 a.m., the elevator stopped midway due to an electricity failure. There was no one around to help her at that early hour and no way to exit from the vestibule. But like a good clinician, she reasoned that there was no use panicking, as the earliest assistance would arrive when one of the early risers tried to use the elevator. Subsequently, the elevator doors were opened mechanically, and she was pulled out from the vestibule stuck between two floors. It was a unique experience, tackled with a cool head in her inimitable style.

We were fortunate to admit Nikhil to a good school. In the vicinity, there were facilities for horse riding and other sports, and I had the time to introduce these activities to him. Even as he was enjoying his school days, he gave us a real fright on one occasion when he did not return home in the school bus. Nikhil was just about five years old at that time. We rushed to the school to check if he had been mistakenly left behind but there was no sign of him anywhere. We wondered if we should report the incident to the police. As a matter of caution, we decided to go home to see if someone else had dropped him there. There we found a non-flustered Nikhil leaning against the door, looking very accomplished. Due to some misunderstanding, the school bus had departed from the school without him. Not finding anybody around, he had walked up to a taxi driver in the vicinity and asked if he could be dropped off at his house. Probably the address displayed on his identity card helped the kind gentleman bring him home. That wonderful person did not even take the taxi fare, nor did he leave his contact number. We were distraught that we could not contact him to convey our gratitude.

It was also in Mumbai that we bought our first family car—the Maruti 800. To put together the necessary funds, we used all our savings, amounting to all of INR 50,000! Another INR 30,000 was raised as a loan from the bank, and the last INR 30,000 (to make a grand total of INR 1,10,000) was obtained as a returnable loan from Madhuri's father. It was a significant amount in those days. We were proud of our new acquisition, and it helped us move around with ease for the next ten years all over the country. Soon Madhuri began her driving classes in the new car, and within a couple of months, she acquired due proficiency and became Mumbai-ready.

Another interesting incident that occurred during our Mumbai stay concerned our respective identity cards. Both of us had ventured out for some work that required us to carry our identity cards. It was a one-time requirement, and since we were in civil clothes, the cards were kept in Madhuri's purse instead of being secured to our apparel as per the SOP.

On our way back, we stopped for a short while along the coastal road to catch the sea breeze. On returning home, we realised that Madhuri had mistakenly left her purse on the sea wall parapet. My mind went back to an incident a decade earlier when I had misplaced my identity card. On this occasion, both of us were in the same boat. It was a critical situation, but we addressed it with a cool mind.

First, we went back to the location where the purse had been left and looked around on both sides of the sea wall. However, we had no luck. Slowly, we drove back, thinking of the repercussions and the next line of action. It was incumbent upon us to report the loss within twenty-four hours of the incident, and we also needed to keep our superiors informed.

Since there was no telephone at home, we went to the duty medical officer's (DMO) room. We were just about to reach for the telephone when it suddenly started ringing. Thinking the call was for the DMO, he answered it. Suddenly, we heard him say that Mrs Kanitkar was very much a part of the naval hospital, and by coincidence, she was actually present in the same room. The caller wanted to speak to her urgently.

Not knowing what the matter could be, she took the call. The speaker on the other end asked Madhuri if she had lost anything recently. Madhuri could not believe her ears but told him about the evening's incident. It turned out that the gentleman speaking to her had been sitting next to us on the sea wall and had observed us leaving. He had noticed that Madhuri had left her purse behind, but before he could react, we had already departed. He then perused the purse's contents and found our identity cards in it. By sheer coincidence, he had served in the Military Engineering Services for a while and understood the importance of identity cards. Seeing from the card that Madhuri was a doctor, he took a hunch and made the effort to call the DMO at the naval hospital to check if she served there.

Though it was late, he agreed to wait for us to reach his house, which was an hour's drive away. At midnight, we recovered the important documents with a great sigh of relief. For a long time, we marvelled at the miracle of Mumbai. The loss had occurred in a city of ten million people, but by a stroke of luck, a conscientious person had come to our rescue. Our feeling of gratitude was beyond measure.

Life, however, moved on quickly, and I turned my focus to the primary reason I had come to Mumbai: Madhuri's specialist training. It was going to be her firm base from which her clinical career in the forces would emanate. I had completed my staff course, which, for me, was the anchor on which I could hope to proceed with reasonable success. Madhuri spared no effort to obtain the requisite experience to become an excellent clinician. In this quest, Sheila was a mirror image of Madhuri. In their endeavours, both of them criss-crossed the length and breadth of Mumbai. They worked so hard that they appeared to be all over the city at the same time. Their energy levels were unsurpassed, and they became famous as the 'Paediatric Twins of Mumbai.' Both of them were—and are—very strong personalities. They would not tolerate interference with their training programme and consequently garnered yet another nickname for themselves: the No-Nonsense-Females (NNF).

Sheila went on to become a vice admiral in the Navy, and the two remain good friends.

The three years of PG training were coming to an end. Due to Madhuri's intense academic activity, Nikhil and I spent most of the time with each other for company. It was difficult to replace Madhuri in taking care of Nikhil, but this challenge was also an opportunity, and I quite enjoyed those times, watching him grow over the two years. After Madhuri's final exams in January 1991, she would be due to move to a hospital as a specialist for the first time. Newly qualified specialists are normally posted to a hospital where another senior specialist acts as a mentor. I was scheduled to return to my unit in Babina, a small military station in central India. Accordingly, Madhuri applied for a co-locational posting. Army HQ did not agree to post Madhuri to Babina due to various constraints but consented to place her at a military hospital in Jhansi, about thirty-five kilometres from Babina. It was not the best solution, but we decided to make the best of the situation. The positive aspect was that I could go across to meet her on weekends and also at any other time in an emergency.

On successful completion of Madhuri's PG training, we prepared to transit to the Jhansi-Babina complex in May-June 1991 to begin our new quest of being together and yet apart. Mumbai had been exhausting for Madhuri, if not difficult. For me, it was a good experience as well, because I learnt the ropes of a static HQ. They have an important role to play in the field of military logistics in peace and war. I was able to imbibe several new inputs that helped me add to my military education.

The transition to the new duty stations was fairly complicated. Madhuri completed her specialist studies in February 1991. In March 1991, she was nominated to attend the four-month Medical Officer's Junior Command Course (MOJC), conducted in two parts. The first two months of technical training were carried out at AFMC, Pune, and subsequently at their training centre in Lucknow. I was to report to my unit in June 1991 at Babina. So, another logistics exercise ensued.

Initially, Madhuri moved to AFMC in Pune for the first phase of her course in mid-March 1991. Nikhil and I continued in Mumbai till his school closed for the summer holidays. Thereafter, I availed leave and proceeded to Pune with Nikhil, shifting in with my parents. With her training curriculum being busy, Madhuri preferred to stay within the AFMC premises and visited us periodically. She shifted to Lucknow for the second phase of her training in mid-May. In early June, Nikhil and I travelled to Babina.

The issue of Nikhil's schooling was a little tricky. Keeping in view that he would eventually shift in with Madhuri at Jhansi, we decided to admit him to a school there. The facility of a school bus from Babina to Jhansi and back on a daily basis was available under army auspices. Little Nikhil, just six years old, had to wake up every day at 5 a.m., get ready for school, carry a hastily prepared breakfast and lunch tiffin with him, and travel for more than an hour to reach his school in Jhansi. After attending classes till about 2 p.m., he travelled back, reaching Babina in the late afternoon.

We stayed in a small two-room complex in our Officers' Mess for the next two months and stuck to this daily routine. I tried to fill in the mother-father role in the best possible manner. But all credit goes to Nikhil. I cannot recall a single occasion of tantrums. He would often ask when his mother would return but never made a fuss about it. He was fond of outdoor activities and often accompanied me to the sports field in the unit lines. That kept us going, and he also learnt to be independent early in life.

To break the monotony, Nikhil and I decided to visit Madhuri in Lucknow over a long weekend. When I reached their institution, Madhuri was hauled up for not seeking permission to bring her spouse into the station. This looked like macabre humour in uniform! Despite this hiccup, the three of us had some nice moments together, and this incident became part of our bag of experiences to reminisce about and have a good laugh.

Nikhil and I returned to Babina the next evening and carried on until Madhuri reported to Military Hospital Jhansi. Having completed the MOJC at Lucknow, Madhuri was now ready to transition into the role of providing specialist medical care to children—her primary love. She reported to Military Hospital Jhansi in August 1991 for the next innings in her military career.

Postscript by Madhuri

Within five years of our marriage, we had to make difficult choices. Very early, we learnt that we needed to support each other—both from near and from afar. When it came to my opting for a PC in the army or pursuing postgraduate training in spite of the odds, Rajeev was very clear about supporting my growth. When I wanted to give up my training as I tried to juggle too many responsibilities, Rajeev wrote a letter with the words: 'Let's grow together without growing apart.' Without a second thought, Rajeev gave an adverse career certificate and was by my side to ensure I completed my training in paediatrics. When I would get frustrated trying to tightrope between home and studies, son and exams, kitchen and wards, he would coolly say, 'Try being less than perfect.' Thus were born the phrases which formed the pillars of our journey in the years to follow.

Another very important incident was the realisation that I was carrying our second child while on the MOJC course in Lucknow. After a son and a PG, which was more akin to a difficult pregnancy of three years, we were ready to welcome another member. I realised midway through the course that I was indeed pregnant but kept hush lest I be reverted from the course. I thought to myself that if I can complete the course now, I won't have to do it later with two kids home alone!

As for the Pune phase, it was fine, but the Lucknow phase had a fairly tough physical exercise component, including the Battle Physical Efficiency Tests (BPET) with a five-kilometre run and a long route march. Having decided to keep the pregnancy a secret, I was not one to opt out of the full training schedule and ran the full five kilometres. I also completed all the drills and marches that were part of the training curriculum, keeping my fingers crossed not to run into complications. With God's grace, I topped the course and delivered a healthy baby girl in Jhansi! When my instructor later learnt of this development, he actually visited me to see that the baby was all okay with ten toes and ten fingers! We were blessed to have a 'Jhansi ki Rani' born to us, who is today a confident, capable, and competent woman, settled in Seattle.

Part III

Learning the Art of Healing

Chapter 7

The Jhansi-Babina Tango

Having trained herself rigorously in the field of childcare within the intense academic environment of Mumbai's medical fraternity, Madhuri was now ready to deploy her newly acquired skills in the military setting of Military Hospital Jhansi.

This marked the beginning of a new chapter, one that would test not only her medical expertise but also her adaptability to the unique demands of military life. While she looked forward to serving in her professional role, the ground realities of settling into a new station brought with them their own set of challenges.

The Administrative Conundrum

By undertaking her specialisation studies in Mumbai, several advantages accrued to Madhuri. The great quantum and range of patients enhanced her theoretical and practical knowledge and also polished her clinical acumen. The MOJC at Pune and Lucknow added depth to her knowledge domain. She was full of energy and vitality and looked forward to utilising her skills to treat patients at Military Hospital Jhansi.

Once she arrived in Jhansi, the first issue she faced was finding accommodation. This aspect is always a little troublesome due to the general shortage of housing for married personnel. She was initially allocated a modest room in an old barrack. It took a week to make it adequately habitable. A makeshift platform based on steel trunks substituted for the cooking platform, and empty wooden boxes made up the beds. A few more arrangements for washing and ironing clothes were added to make the 'new house' functional. Nikhil moved in with her from Babina in the month of September 1991. Alongside, Madhuri also started her work in the paediatric department of the hospital.

The Paediatric Ward

Madhuri's immediate superior was a dedicated and sincere officer. However, his basic personality was at variance with Madhuri's cheerful and positive attitude. Due to this inherent dichotomy, there was an attempt to keep her away from the paediatric ward in the initial stages. It took a few months for interpersonal relations to smoothen out before Madhuri could settle down into her speciality with reasonable comfort.

Over a period of time, Madhuri became known for her clinical abilities. Care of children was often affected by the lack of modern equipment and medicines. Consequently, Madhuri innovated appropriate interventions to render better care. Shortage of oral rehydration solution (ORS) was often overcome by administering rice-water-based solutions. Intravenous needles and other such equipment in short supply were recycled after sterilisation. Special efforts to acquire scalp veins, IV cannulas, and other essential equipment were undertaken. As far as her patients were concerned, her empathetic behaviour endeared her to the children and their caretakers. In a short span of time, she became the go-to paediatrician.

It was during her time in Lucknow that Madhuri discovered she was expecting again. However, she did not complain on any account and finished the course at the top of her batch in her usual style. The new addition to our family was expected in the month of March 1992. So, while Madhuri and Nikhil hunkered down in Jhansi, I continued in Babina. As one of the sub-unit commanders, I kept a busy schedule, and it was only on weekends that I could spend time with Madhuri and Nikhil at Jhansi. It was as good as being posted in two separate stations. The only consolation was that, in an emergency, I could hop over to Jhansi relatively quickly. Also, many a time Madhuri would volunteer to do her share of DMO duties on weekends, as on other days it was not convenient to leave the children at home all alone. On those weekends, I would endeavour to be in Jhansi and give company to the children. Thus, on several weekends, our time together would be limited.

Nikhil started going to school from Jhansi. This was a big relief to him and also more convenient. Though only a child, he matured rather quickly. He started helping Madhuri at home with several household chores. He was a true foodie, with a particular fondness for eggs. No matter what he had eaten for breakfast, it would not be complete without two eggs prepared exactly to his liking—sunny side up! Often, he would push a small chair next to Madhuri near the kitchen platform and observe everything very minutely. Though he was not in a position to cook at the ripe age of six and a half years, he would often tell Madhuri that the proportion of salt or spices did not appear adequate. He would be right too. (Later in life, Nikhil persisted with his aptitude for cooking and adopted it as his hobby. His daal tadka and chicken are lip-smacking!)

Towards the end of the year, Madhuri was allotted an independent house and, after sprucing it up, the Jhansi house was finally set up. There was adequate space around it, and it was good for Nikhil as he loved to play outdoors. Also, the house was fairly close to the hospital and enabled Madhuri to move between the hospital and home quickly.

Madhuri's pregnancy was advancing with the passage of time, and as we stepped into the New Year of 1992, she found herself being overwhelmed with her hospital work. I tried to visit more often, but unit commitments made it difficult. The unit was preparing to celebrate 175 years of its proud legacy in February 1992, and this required extensive groundwork. I had key responsibilities in organizing the event, which meant I could only manage brief weekend visits to Jhansi. Madhuri, in essence, handled all her responsibilities largely on her own. I was often overcome by a sense of helplessness, but there seemed to be no resolution to the dilemma. Whenever possible, she would drive down to Babina with Nikhil, and she did this right till the ninth month, when she could barely reach the steering wheel!

In her seventh month of pregnancy, she was informed that she would have to proceed with an outstation assignment for a period of one month. This felt like a repeat of the Jodhpur days. Madhuri met up with the administrative officer and explained to him that her present medical condition was not conducive for this purpose. It would also entail moving Nikhil back to Babina, as he could not be left alone. As luck—or perhaps bad luck—would have it, the same evening she suffered a fall and sustained a minor fracture in the foot. She requested the surgeon to give her a plaster with a walking heel and continued with her duties. By evening, her ankle swelled up and she could barely walk. The treating doctor forbade movement and admitted her to the hospital. Despite this, her superiors insisted that she proceed with her outstation assignment the next day. This really upset Madhuri, but she decided not to complain. However, the treating doctor informed the hospital authorities that, given her condition, he could not permit her to be discharged or moved. Consequently, the unit administration relented.

In Jodhpur, the GOC of the formation had come to Madhuri's assistance on the intervention of her then CO. In Jhansi, it was her colleague who intervened and came to her rescue. Such experiences left a lasting impression on her. They only made her more resolute in tackling injustice whenever she spotted such instances during her service.

One day in the last month of her pregnancy, she suddenly realised that Nikhil was not around. A little later, she found him curled up in a dark corner of the house, wincing in pain. Further queries revealed that he had stumbled while playing and suffered a fall. On checking closely, Madhuri was aghast to note that he had a severe fracture and needed immediate medical attention. The fracture was a complex one, and the surgeon felt that hospital facilities were inadequate to operate at Jhansi. He recommended that he be moved to Lucknow for further care. Madhuri was in no condition to travel with Nikhil to Lucknow. As usual, Madhuri, with her quick thinking and decision-making, informed the surgeon that she might go into labour any day and Nikhil would have to be treated at Jhansi. With no further ado, Madhuri signed the parental consent and requested the doctor to do the best he could. It was a bold decision taken under duress. Soon, Nikhil was wheeled into the operating theatre. The surgeon did an extremely professional job with the limited facilities available to him. Madhuri spent the night with Nikhil in the hospital and continued with her duties the next morning and for the next three days until Nikhil could be sent home. I was in the midst of some training event and hence could not be of assistance. As it happened so very often, Madhuri handled the situation single-handedly with grit and determination. She summed up her situation by remarking that her tenure was turning out like 'Jhansi Gale Ki Phansi' (Jhansi, the noose around the neck).

Jhansi Ki Rani Arrives

At Babina, the 175th-anniversary celebrations of our unit concluded in mid-February and soon after, the annual training season began in full earnest. Madhuri continued to work in the hospital as usual. It was her aim to carry on with her duties till she went into labour—a difficult decision, but one she stuck to like a rock.

After my indoor training session was over in Babina, I went across to Jhansi for a day on the evening of 6 March 1992.

After dinner, the baby indicated that it was on its way into the big, wide world. At around 4:30 a.m. on 7 March 1992, our little angel was born—a rebellious girl, full of energy like her mother. Our happiness knew no bounds as our 'Jhansi Ki Rani' announced herself to the world (a perfect match for her brother who had made his debut as the 'Jodhpur ka Raja'). Her arrival helped Madhuri overcome the trials and tribulations of Jhansi.

A little later, I became conscious of the fact that I had to return to Babina for my ensuing morning training session. So, after a brief hug and a quick look at our new treasure, I returned to my unit. A few days later, our indoor training was over, and we were required to proceed with the outdoor session. I had to say my byes to Madhuri, Nikhil, and the little one. Madhuri's mother had suggested a beautiful name for our daughter: Vibhuti. The name indicates a person with amazing powers and prowess. Before I proceeded with my training event, we held a naming ceremony with both sets of grandparents in attendance. After they went back, Nikhil became the 'man of the house.' He had already started assuming responsibilities beyond his age, and with his baby sister alongside, he became Madhuri's star assistant. It was indeed commendable for a boy who had just turned seven.

Life Beyond Duty

Social life in the Babina-Jhansi complex was a blend of two different environments, each offering its own kind of gathering and camaraderie. At Babina, our main interaction was with families from my unit. The other officers in the unit also had children of Nikhil's age, and he really looked forward to having a fun time at Babina. Till today, he remembers those days of fun and frolic. The boys, in particular, were up to all kinds of mischief, playing in the small streams of water around our unit location or in the gardens surrounding the residential blocks. Madhuri shared a close friendship with the ladies of the unit.

Vibhuti was too young to remember her days with the regiment at that time, but she would often be at the centre of attention among the other kids.

Another important role that Madhuri continued to perform (as she had done at Jodhpur) was that of the honorary regimental medical officer (RMO) of the unit. She was the one person whom unit personnel and their families would turn to for both medical treatment and personal problems.

On the other hand, at Jhansi, there was a larger presence of medical officers and their families. They had a system of periodic visits to each other's homes and shared potluck meals. These were enjoyable and also ensured that no one person was unduly pressed for time and effort. These events left behind fond memories and forged lasting relationships.

Together in Spirit, Apart in Duty

The next two years after Vibhuti's arrival were a mix of being together and being apart almost all the time. My routine consisted of being in the station for a few months, followed by long training sessions in areas far away from the unit. Madhuri remained busy with her hospital commitments and, more so, with the children. They remained largely her responsibility. As had happened with Nikhil, I did make an effort to reduce her burden by availing leave periodically. After we had exhausted our respective leaves, Madhuri would often take Vibhuti with her to the hospital during her night duties. It was difficult, but the only way to ensure Vibhuti's safety and security.

Slowly, as she became a little older, Nikhil stepped in to help. Gradually, Madhuri actually started leaving Vibhuti in Nikhil's care at night after about a year, while she was away on DMO duties. He was told that if there was any issue he couldn't handle, he should ring up and inform Madhuri at the hospital. He handled his responsibilities with great care and indeed made us proud.

I was posted to the Kashmir Valley in May 1994 for an important operations-oriented assignment, and Madhuri was asked to report to the military hospital in Meerut. It would have been difficult for her to render her duties sincerely with two children in tow. So, she put in a request to be posted to the Pune complex, and fortunately, she came across an empathetic officer who understood her predicament. We heaved a big sigh of relief when her posting was diverted to MH Kirkee, where she had done her internship.

With both of us headed in opposite directions, it was time to pack up our belongings. Times of departure always weighed heavily on us. We tried to support each other by saying that these difficult times too would pass. In the meantime, we would continue to serve to the best of our ability. Once again, our guiding motto of 'Growing together, even while we were apart' took centre stage.

In April 1994, Madhuri, with the kids and baggage, moved to Pune and shifted into our common family home. The children were still very young and had to be admitted to school. Admission processes are always troublesome, and it took a major effort to admit Nikhil to a good school in Pune.

In May 1994, I too wound up my few belongings in Babina and moved to the Valley for an interesting tenure in a location where terrorist activities were at their peak. The opportunity to serve in an operational area helped me get back into the mainstream and contributed towards erasing the blot of a peacetime posting after the staff course.

We were now at our separate destinations, with Madhuri once again handling the major responsibilities in Pune. The Jhansi-Babina chapter had not been an easy one. For the record, we were posted together, being stationed within 35 km of each other. In functional terms, that did not really work out. In fact, my inability to be of greater assistance to Madhuri rankled me often, and for Madhuri, the responsibility of handling her official duties and two young children at the same time weighed heavily on her shoulders throughout her tenure in Jhansi.

Postscript by Madhuri

Getting to Pune felt good, but handling a job, two kids, and the construction of a house was a nightmare, to say the least. Though relatives were around, the everyday grind was all mine, and I remember times when I would sit on the steps in frustration, not knowing whether to laugh or cry. I would have loved to run away—but where would I go? Rajeev had promised to come to Pune on leave if things ever got completely out of hand, and I remember crying wolf once, just to avoid a total breakdown. The rest of the time, it was nonstop multitasking just to stay afloat. It was possibly one of the toughest phases—made bearable only by Rajeev's letters from Kashmir, written every day but delivered in bunches.

Chapter 8

Kirkee Calls Again

The Initial Days

There was a great sense of comfort in knowing that Madhuri had reached Pune, where she would be more secure. Nikhil was nine years old and Vibhuti was just a shade over two. The three of them settled down in our family home where, in addition to my parents, my elder brother Sanjeev, his wife Padmaja, and their two sons, Sandeep (eleven years old) and Ameya (seven years old), also resided. That was a full house, literally. The three boys were extremely happy to be with each other, being in a similar age group. Vibhuti, as the kid sister, was the cynosure of attention, particularly of the grandparents.

This situation was ideal in some ways and enabled Madhuri to settle down in her new workplace fairly comfortably. The construction of our new house had also commenced atop the terrace leased to us by my uncle. He had been monitoring the progress for the past few months, and Madhuri felt that she should start looking into the matter and relieve her uncle of the responsibility. To do this effectively, it was necessary to be on the spot. Hence, Madhuri requested the contractor to complete the exterior construction within an early time frame. She then planned to shift into the semi-finished house along with the children.

My parents were not very comfortable with this plan. They tried to reason with her that she should move out only after the house was completed. But she explained to them that it was important for her to oversee the construction closely, and that would be possible only if she stayed in the house. The children, who had settled down nicely in their new surroundings, were quite unhappy about their mother's insistence on shifting to the semi-finished house. A little bit of cajoling, combined with a little bit of firmness, enabled the move to the new location in August 1994.

I joined my new job in May 1994. The insurgency in Kashmir had reached a crescendo, and operations to neutralise anti-nationals were in full swing. I settled down into my assignment after a hectic familiarisation schedule. I visited almost all the posts along the Line of Control (LoC) in our area of responsibility (AOR) over a period of forty days. Each day I would walk 15-20 kilometres in the mountains, ranging from 8,000 feet and above. In the process, I greatly enjoyed my daily treks in the pristine surroundings of the Kashmir Valley.

Having been in that environment for about three months, I took a break to go down to Pune and assist Madhuri in shifting into our semi-ready house. She had made a plan to set up the house in typical army style. The idea was to use trunks and boxes to create a kitchen platform, storage racks, and make-shift beds in one portion of the house, while the interiors were completed in the other parts. With this as the basic backdrop, I joined Madhuri to set up our new home. It was an important moment for us, ensuring that we had our own home whenever we visited Pune.

Before the commencement of the construction, Madhuri had made detailed notes on the architectural aspects of the house. She sketched out many innovative ideas to incorporate an open design and maximise space utilisation. Madhuri also planned the entire kitchen layout to suit her height requirements. The placement of electrical gadgets and the plug-socket arrangement were planned to the last detail. Finally, when this plan was discussed with our architect, he smiled at the intricate planning that Madhuri had done and said there was very little left for him to do!

Accordingly, the contractor proceeded to implement the plan under Madhuri's hawk-eyed oversight till the completion of construction. That work has stood the test of time—thirty years down the line.

Madhuri–The Superwoman

Madhuri had taken a bold decision to move in with the children to our new house, which was finally completed by the end of 1994. Till then, she carried on with the make-shift arrangements. Her daily schedule would start at 5 a.m. While the clothes were set to wash, the preparation of breakfast for the children would start on a parallel track. Having got ready for the hospital, Nikhil would be given his breakfast and despatched. Vibhuti, just over two years old, would be coaxed to get out of bed, fed, and handed over to the maid who would arrive by 8:00 a.m.

After a quick breakfast, Madhuri would wheel out her scooter and zoom to the hospital to reach punctually—at the first bed in the ward—by 8:30 a.m. Her immediate work hours would go on till 2 p.m., after which she would return home to look into the needs of the children as they came back from school.

Fortunately, our maid Sunita, though not educated, was very simple and endearing. She would reach home before Madhuri left for the hospital and stay with Vibhuti the whole day until Madhuri returned in the afternoon. She would also take her to the playschool and back. She was truly a godsend, and even today, she feels more like the children's elder sister than anything else. Moreover, my uncle and aunt, who resided on the ground floor, would step in during emergencies, but with their advancing age, Madhuri did not wish to burden them unnecessarily.

After coming back from the hospital, Madhuri would attend to Vibhuti even before she could take her first break of the day. Nikhil would return a little later and also required some attention. So, once she had taken care of the children's needs, she would take out a little time for herself.

Throughout those difficult days, every evening, she would step out for an hour—away from all her daily concerns—and involve herself in an exercise and rejuvenation routine or do the groceries and other outdoor chores on her bicycle, treating it as part of her exercise. Once that was over, she would complete the rest of the home chores before getting dinner ready. She also made an effort to stay involved in the children's studies, even when tired, but it was hard to give it her full heart and mind. She told the children that she would try to help them as much as possible, but essentially, they had to learn to be independent. Nikhil, our ever-ready young warrior, handled himself rather well and contributed significantly towards the care of his sister.

After dinner, Madhuri would let out a big sigh of relief as she finally collapsed into bed—only to gear up and do it all over again the next day. And on top of everything, she still managed to squeeze in an hour of professional reading and writing at least three times a week. No wonder our goddesses are shown with multiple hands!

Apart from all this, Madhuri was often called in for emergencies after her regular working hours. With the hospital located 5 km away, each call meant commuting back and forth, plus the time spent caring for the patient, adding up to at least two hours each time. Instead of waiting for the hospital ambulance to fetch her, she would drive out alone, even in the middle of the night when required, so that she could attend to her patient at the earliest. Midnight calls, of course, made the whole routine even more strenuous. With her day generally ending at 10 p.m., Madhuri was working at least eighteen hours a day. But superhuman Madhuri that she was, she did not shy away from her responsibilities, especially towards her patients, who meant so much to her. In the larger scheme of things, Madhuri was a true one-woman army, holding the fort on multiple fronts every single day.

The Hospital Experience

MH Kirkee was bigger and better organised than MH Jhansi. It was set up in old World War II barracks and was long overdue for an upgrade but the much-needed reconstruction into a modern hospital only happened twenty years later!

At MH Kirkee, Madhuri was fortunate to have a mature and supportive immediate superior. Even better, the gynaecologist she regularly worked with—especially during the frequent arrival of new babies—was an absolute gem, always helpful, both professionally and personally. Additionally, the young doctors and juniors looked up to Madhuri with admiration, drawn by her strong professional reputation and competence. They were hungry for knowledge, and Madhuri was always willing to teach them. She became their mentor and guide throughout her tenure at MH Kirkee. Teaching her juniors brought her immense joy, and the teacher in her came to the fore at MH Kirkee, even as she continued honing her own skills in the art of healing.

MH Kirkee had a large clientele base. A major training institution in the vicinity meant that children of all ages formed a significant portion of the patients reporting at the hospital. On days when fewer than two paediatricians were on duty—due to leave or other assignments—the entire load often fell on one person. For Madhuri, this meant long, exhausting hours that ate into her time at home and added to the already considerable pressure she was under.

Based on her experience at MH Jhansi, Madhuri put in place a meticulous system for keeping patient records. For every patient, she maintained a dedicated diary or folder, carefully recording her daily observations with consistent attention to detail. These folders were always in the boot of her car. If she had to go to the hospital in an emergency, she could refer to the case without difficulty. Her method of preparing case sheets became a model for everyone to follow. Her neat and bold handwriting—rare for a doctor—combined with her ability to make clean sketches of the ailments affecting her patients, was key to her approach. She would then make her differential diagnoses and identify the most suitable treatment protocol. All this enabled her to treat her patients with clarity, sensitivity, and confidence.

She put great effort into developing her bedside manner in order to put patients at ease. As part of that effort, she would speak to the child's guardians with empathy to derive the best inputs from them. Taking down the history of a child's illness is as much an art as it is a science, and it is what leads to the most effective healing. This was Madhuri's forte, and it gave her deep satisfaction every single day.

Despite being a larger hospital, MH Kirkee also had its shortcomings. For example, at that time, it did not have a neonatal unit. As they say, necessity is the mother of invention and that proved true at MH Kirkee as well. She set up a makeshift neonatal ICU (NICU) by partitioning off one of the corridors of the paediatric ward. In the absence of adequate radiant warmers, she devised a progressive warmth-providing technique to cater to the needs of babies who outnumbered the available warmers. As for the shortage of nursing staff for this purpose, it was made up by training the mothers of the children. She found them eager and effective, driven by self-motivation. In addition, she started a mothers' milk-sharing system. Some mothers could not produce enough milk, while others had an excess, which could be painful if not relieved. Madhuri taught them how to express their excess milk and store it safely in the refrigerator. This milk would be given to children who did not receive a sufficient quantity from their natural mothers. Of course, this was done with the consent of both mothers, and the system worked to the benefit of everyone. Today, hospitals have formal breast milk banks.

She often reflected that the greatest welfare a soldier could receive was access to comprehensive healthcare for their children. It was only towards the end of her career that she succeeded in persuading her colleagues to establish an integrated mother-and-child care facility at the country's largest Army hospital. Today, AHRR proudly houses Vatsalya—the most comprehensive mother-and-child care unit in the country—just as she had envisioned.

Amidst all her innovative initiatives, one day she received an urgent call at home—a baby girl had just been delivered. She weighed only 600 grams and was born at 27 weeks, far short of the normal 40-week term. The attending gynaecologist believed survival was unlikely; at the time, babies under one kilogram and below 28-30 weeks' gestation were considered beyond saving. He had specifically asked for Madhuri to come in and make the final call. The mother had also been informed and, though heartbroken, had resigned herself to the outcome. Madhuri spoke to the attending nurse and told her that she would rush to the hospital immediately. She also told her not to declare the baby as 'dead' until she had seen the child.

When Madhuri reached the ward, she could barely make out the beat of the baby's heart. A baby small enough to fit into the palm of Madhuri's hand and yet, she took it upon herself to revive the little child. She quickly cleaned her up, warmed her, and started administering intravenous fluids and oxygen. Each moment was a challenge, but each passing day was also an indication that the tiny life was putting up a brave fight.

When Madhuri asked for the mother to be brought in, she was informed that due to a misunderstanding, she had already been discharged from the hospital. When a call was sent to her, she could not believe her good luck and was overjoyed. Slowly, the baby started gaining weight, and her grey pallor gradually turned to a pink hue. It was now clear that she was going to make it.

As the news spread of this singular achievement, the commander of the formation, under whom the hospital functioned, came to see the miracle baby. He made it a point to visit the hospital and congratulate Madhuri in person and ensured the story received its due recognition in the local newspapers. He also recommended Madhuri for an award by the chief of army staff. And so, for the first time at MH Kirkee, her tireless efforts were formally recognised—marking the beginning of many such honours to come. In addition, the commander also sanctioned some additional funds to the hospital to help make up for its shortages.

All in all, the crisis ended on a good note for everyone. The little baby was nicknamed Pinky by the ward personnel in view of her healthy colour. Later, she was discharged and, over the years, moved with her parents from one military station to another.

Twenty-five years later, Pinky called up Madhuri one fine day, when she was posted in Delhi as the deputy chief of Integrated Defence Staff (medical) and informed her that she was preparing for the Civil Services Exam. She visited us at home, and we were very happy to meet her in person. It is these moments that seem to give meaning to life, and Madhuri treasures them immensely.

While such events gave much happiness, some other incidents also acted as mood-dampeners. One such instance concerned our own daughter, Vibhuti. One day, she fell extremely ill and was running a high temperature. To look after her, Madhuri requested leave so she could care for Vibhuti at home. She was very upset when her request was turned down due to hospital requirements.

Madhuri then decided to admit Vibhuti into the paediatric ward and stayed in the hospital as her attendant. The next morning, she donned her uniform and continued with her official duties. Vibhuti questioned her mother as to how she had time for others but not for her own daughter. Madhuri had no answer to that query. But in passing, she did mention to her that she had not been granted leave as she had to look after many other babies.

As luck would have it, during his usual familiarisation round, the commandant happened to find our daughter in the paediatric ward. In his routine manner, he asked if there was anything he could do for her. Without missing a beat, she innocently scolded him for refusing leave to her mother despite her being unwell. An awkward silence followed before the commandant quickly moved on!

As time went on, Madhuri's responsibilities only grew. Her mother began showing signs of chronic kidney disease, and Madhuri often had to devote time and attention to her care. In fact, it was this personal experience that gradually sparked her growing interest in nephrology. She also realised that many kidney diseases in adults could be prevented if the initial signs were picked up in childhood. As her interest in the subject grew, she felt she should enhance her knowledge in the field by enrolling in a short course. So, she requested a short temporary duty to attend a paediatric nephrology course at AIIMS, Delhi.

Luckily, her superiors gave her the time, and she proceeded to Delhi for the same in early 1996. Since she was going to be in Delhi for some time, I too came down from my base in the Valley for a week. She was very busy with her course studies, but we found enough time in the evenings to catch up with each other. For this short duration, Madhuri's parents helped out by looking after Nikhil and Vibhuti in Pune. After completing the course in Delhi, she returned to Pune and seamlessly slipped back into her daily routine.

In Pune, there were always additional responsibilities—like attending parent-teacher meetings at the children's school.

Since it was our hometown, social commitments were plenty. All of this slowly piled up, adding to Madhuri's growing stress levels. To make matters worse, Vibhuti began showing signs of epilepsy. Madhuri, with her fine observational skills, had noticed that Vibhuti would suddenly go into a trance-like state even while speaking, or lose control of her hand if she was drawing or writing on a piece of paper. In her usual no-nonsense manner, she carried out the necessary checks and found that, indeed, Vibhuti would have to be placed on a long-term anti-epilepsy treatment regimen.

On the other side of the hill, I remained busy with the operational responsibility in Kashmir. Communications during those days were truly abysmal. Bad weather in the Valley also contributed to poor reception. In view of these restrictions, I could barely speak to Madhuri once a week.

By the end of 1995, Madhuri was really under a lot of pressure, and she told me that if I could not join her as soon as possible, it might not be feasible for her to continue serving on her own. Such a statement from Super-Madhuri meant she had truly hit her limit. I told her that I would put in a request for a compassionate posting once again and try to be with her at the soonest.

Having made up my mind to be by Madhuri's side, I immediately applied to be co-located with her in Pune. As luck would have it, a few things worked in my favour. The senior-most officer in the area happened to know me personally, and I was able to explain my situation to him. On top of that, several of my close friends were posted at Army HQ—the place where such decisions are made. Additionally, I was the senior-most officer of my batch and was due for promotion to the rank of Lt Col in early 1996, which strengthened my case even further. In response to my application, everything fell into place. My friends at Army HQ worked overtime to ensure that I was posted to Pune as per my request. They were nothing short of a godsend. I was to report in the first week of January and would be promoted immediately upon arrival.

This kind of good luck is sometimes unbelievable, and it kept our faith alive in the fairness of the system. Whenever we were at our tether's end, a miracle of coincidences would intervene and enable us to overcome our personal crises.

Together as a Family Again

I reached Pune from the Kashmir Valley in the first week of January 1996. It was a joyous reunion for us. Though I had been in a demanding role for the past twenty months, Madhuri's responsibilities were far more varied and relentless. I was just glad I could finally be there by her side.

I soon settled into my new job. It had a logistical orientation and was my first time in such a role, so it was a good opportunity to learn something new. The appointment was crucial not just for day-to-day peacetime functioning but also for operational readiness. Since I was the executive officer managing the day-to-day functioning of all logistics elements in our AOR, I remained pretty busy during office hours—and sometimes beyond—as a rule. However, there was adequate free time, and I could devote more attention to house chores as well as to the children.

Over time, Madhuri's stress levels eased. She began managing her daily routine—juggling office and home responsibilities—with much more balance. We also encouraged the children to explore outdoor sports and hobbies. Nikhil, being older, developed a keen interest in multiple games. Each morning, he would cycle to an indoor badminton court, play with great enthusiasm, and return just in time for breakfast and school. It was impressive for someone his age and gave us immense satisfaction.

Vibhuti was still just four, and I took on the task of getting her ready for school. Her epilepsy treatment had begun, and it was crucial to ensure that she took her medication regularly and on time.

On the social front, Madhuri and I managed to attend formal functions on both sides of our fraternity. At times, the schedule left us exhausted, but connecting with our colleagues was important, and we managed the tango reasonably well. The tenure also gave us a chance to reconnect with our extended family in a more meaningful way.

As often happens in such phases, time flew. My posting in Pune was for two years, after which I was to return to my unit. Madhuri's tenure was also coming to an end, so we requested a joint posting to Hissar, where my unit was stationed. However, the medical authorities had other priorities and plans.

Around early 1998, as we mentally prepared for another round of 'moving apart,' it struck me just how much this cycle was wearing us down. Madhuri, in particular, bore the brunt, carrying the major responsibility of raising the children. Their education was being disrupted each time we moved, and finding new school admissions was nothing short of a Herculean task. On top of that, housing shortages at every station only made things worse. It was a routine we were growing tired of.

It was during one of these moments of reflection that I raised the idea of retiring from the army. I felt it might be time to find work in Pune and start afresh in a new environment. I had just turned forty, and if I wanted to transition into civilian life, this seemed like the right moment to retrain or reskill. In fact, an opportunity had presented itself—a well-known IT company was expanding in Pune and looking for administrative officers. I went for an initial meeting with the concerned person, and the conversation ended on a positive note. Encouraged, I returned home for a final discussion with Madhuri. She, however, wasn't too keen on the idea of me leaving the army. I was doing reasonably well and was likely to be promoted to colonel within the year. This was an appointment every professional army officer aspires to—command of one's own regiment.

Madhuri believed that if either of us had to step away from our careers, it should be her. Between the two options, she felt that settling down in Pune to pursue her medical practice was a better choice than me leaving the army. Following this decision, she prepared and submitted her retirement papers. When some senior colleagues learnt of her decision, they called her in for a discussion. They urged her to withdraw her application, assuring her that this difficult phase would pass and that better days lay ahead. Convinced by their counsel, we decided to put our plans for leaving the forces on hold at least for the time being.

On the children's front, Nikhil had settled well in a reputed school in Pune and expressed a clear preference to remain there and complete his Board exams. Both children were especially fond of Padmaja (my brother's wife) and her two sons. In fact, their bond was so strong that one day, a frustrated Vibhuti—worn out by Madhuri's strict routines involving wake-up and sleep timings, structured study hours, and discipline—casually asked Padmaja if she could become her mother and assign Madhuri the role of *chachi* (aunt), just to settle things once and for all! At one point, Vibhuti even nicknamed Madhuri after a World War II dictator.

After careful consideration, we agreed on a temporary arrangement: Nikhil would stay back in Pune with my brother's family, Madhuri and Vibhuti would move to Pathankot, and I would join my posting at Hissar. It wasn't the most balanced tripod given the distances between each leg, but we resolved to make the best of it. Thus began our next chapter as a dispersed family, with the shared hope of reuniting eventually. I packed up my belongings and helped Madhuri assemble a minimal household setup for Pathankot, where she was to join the base hospital. She decided to take up a modest house—just enough for her and Vibhuti—to keep things simple.

Although Madhuri had already earned her lieutenant colonel rank while at MH Kirkee, she opted for a captain's accommodation in Pathankot, believing it sufficient for the two of them. Meanwhile, Nikhil moved into the house where my brother's family and our parents lived. I left for Hissar in April 1998, and shortly thereafter, Madhuri and six-year-old Vibhuti boarded the Jhelum Express to Pathankot. It was a gruelling forty-eight-hour journey, but Madhuri braved it with her usual quiet strength, little Vibhuti by her side. And so, our individual battles in three separate locations began again.

Postscript by Madhuri

During the initial months of my tenure at Kirkee, I was constantly on edge, juggling two young children, a demanding medical role, and the construction of our home, all on my own. Amidst this chaos, I vividly recall one particularly emotional moment.

Rajeev was posted in the insurgency-ridden Valley and could call me only once a week, through the military line. His brigade was allotted a narrow, fixed time slot for long-distance calls, and I would anxiously glance at the phone on my OPD desk while attending to patients, hoping it would ring during that window. The ten-minute call would pass in a flash, the line would abruptly go dead, and I would return home and tell the children, 'Dad called. He says be good and he is doing fine,' just to include them in the conversation.

Then one day, after I mentioned a call from Rajeev, three-year-old Vibhuti burst into tears. Her reason: 'Dad doesn't love me. He only calls mom.' She was too small to understand that we didn't have a military phone at home and civil lines to and from Kashmir were practically non-functional. After that day,

I stopped speaking about his phone calls altogether. Instead, I began reading his letters aloud to the children, trying to bridge the distance in the only way I could. It would be fair to say that each of us internalised our emotions and found our own way to cope with the new reality.

Chapter 9

The Unstable Tripod

Early Days at Pathankot

The first few weeks at Pathankot proved to be even more difficult for Madhuri, as she was there all alone with Vibhuti and had to do everything by herself. After the long, arduous journey on the Jhelum Express—which actually crawled in those days—she reached Pathankot in May 1998. She was a little wary of what lay ahead. All she knew was that it was an extremely busy hospital but severely understaffed. That, in itself, had significant implications.

To her pleasant surprise, her reception at the railway station was well-organised by the head of the paediatric ward, Colonel Arvind Gupta. He turned out to be a very thoughtful person and made great efforts to put her at ease. It would be appropriate to mention that he and his family turned out to be angels in disguise. Without them, it would have been well-nigh impossible for Madhuri to deal with her tryst at the Pathankot Base Hospital.

As usual, the first battle was on the accommodation front. Once again, Madhuri had to deal with the chronic shortage of married accommodation. After the first few days in the Officers' Mess complex, she was informed that she would have to vacate it, as families were not permitted there. That space was reserved strictly for bachelor officers. The hospital authorities offered her an alternative: a barrack in the vicinity of the hospital mortuary complex. Madhuri was stunned by the suggestion and made it clear that she could not accept such an arrangement.

Eventually, she was asked to approach the Station Housing Committee for a priority allotment of married accommodation. After some back and forth, the committee agreed to allot her a Captain's accommodation in the Nursing Officers' Colony. It wasn't an entirely fair solution, but considering her circumstances, Madhuri accepted it.

When she visited the assigned quarters, she found them to be in a state of disrepair. Several parts of the house had water leakages, and the walls were damp. She had to put in considerable effort to make the place liveable before they could move in. The apartment was on the first floor, and the sweltering North Indian summer made it unbearably hot. Apart from these trials, her daily battles had resumed in full force.

Fortunately, I managed to get a week's leave from Hissar and joined her to help tackle some of the initial challenges. We resolved the issue of the broken kitchen platform by going to the market and buying a marble slab of the appropriate size. We also purchased water coolers for the house and installed a battery inverter system to cope with frequent power outages.

However, the biggest hurdle was securing Vibhuti's admission into a good school. In Pune, she had attended junior and senior KG classes at a school that encouraged activity-based learning and did not rely on rote methods. In stark contrast, the admission process in Pathankot involved a challenging written test. Children were expected to read questions off the blackboard and write the answers on paper—an approach quite alien to Vibhuti's prior learning environment.

After the initial test, when we asked Vibhuti if she had answered all the questions, she cheerfully said yes. Relieved, we returned home, assuming all was well. A couple of days later, when we went back to the school to confirm her admission, we were horrified to learn that she had scored a perfect zero on the test. For a moment, we were completely shocked. When we asked Vibhuti what had happened, she innocently explained that she had copied everything written on the blackboard onto her answer sheet because she thought that was what she was supposed to do.

Madhuri then went in to meet the principal and explained the situation. She clarified that while Vibhuti wasn't yet accustomed to written tests, her conceptual understanding and practical knowledge were sound. Madhuri requested that the school conduct an oral assessment instead, to gauge her real abilities. Initially, the principal declined. But when Madhuri firmly argued that it would be unfair for a child to lose an academic year over a misunderstanding, the principal finally relented, although with conditions. Vibhuti would be given two months to catch up to the senior KG standards followed in Pathankot schools including Hindi, a language she had no exposure to. At the end of that period, she would have to appear for a re-test. If she passed, she could continue in the same grade; if not, she would have to repeat junior KG. So, while the first hurdle—provisional admission—was cleared, the real test had just begun.

The next two months were a whirlwind. After finishing her hospital duties, Madhuri would spend hours teaching Vibhuti the entire syllabus from scratch. The amount of material the little girl had to memorise and reproduce on paper was overwhelming. For Madhuri, it became nothing short of the battle of the decade. Every day after lunch, she would sit down with Vibhuti and patiently work through the day's lessons with her, step by step. It was an uphill task for both mother and child. Vibhuti, already unsettled by the move from Pune, was also grappling with loneliness, all while continuing her epilepsy treatment. The pressure on her was immense. But at the end of those two months, Vibhuti crossed the finish line with a flourish. Both mother and daughter heaved a deep sigh of relief. We often suspect that this early experience left Vibhuti with a deep-rooted aversion to academics. That trauma perhaps lingered for years, until she eventually found her true calling, nearly two decades later.

The Hospital and the Paediatric Ward

The Pathankot Hospital is one of the largest in the country, catering to the medical needs of a dense population of serving personnel, ex-servicemen, and their families. As a result, hospital work functioned like a relentless assembly line that had to be managed 24/7.

Its location was quite peculiar. The hospital stood on a plot of land bordered by an active air force airfield on one side, a busy railway line just 200 metres away on another, and a stone quarry on the third, leaving only the fourth side as the point of access. One of Madhuri's most vivid memories of this sound-heavy environment was having to pause mid-examination and wait for the noise of an aircraft, a passing train, or the quarry blasts to subside before she could properly assess her patients.

The paediatric ward was always running at full capacity. Fortunately, Col Arvind Gupta (who later retired as a brigadier), the senior advisor in paediatrics, was a kind and gentle man with deep empathy for his patients. He also had a strong sense of administration, which allowed him to serve the hospital community effectively. When Madhuri arrived, he patiently familiarised her with the complex working conditions of the hospital. He was also aware of the personal challenges she faced in raising Vibhuti on her own, and both he and his wife, Kiran, went out of their way to offer constant support.

Soon, Madhuri settled into her role in the ward. The OPD days were especially demanding. Her reputation as a skilled clinician spread quickly. Her meticulous record-keeping, compassionate manner, and her habit of treating every child as her own endeared her to all. She paid particular attention to those who had travelled long distances to consult her, ensuring their visits were not in vain.

As time went on, Col Arvind Gupta entrusted her with complete responsibility for the technical and clinical workload, while he focused on overall ward administration. This clear division of duties worked exceptionally well and became something of a model for the hospital. In due course, owing to her professionalism and competence, Madhuri was also given charge of the adult medical ward. This additional responsibility placed her under tremendous pressure, and there were moments when she was pushed to the brink. Yet, she also voluntarily took on the care of specially abled children. The work was exhausting but it brought her deep fulfilment.

The Hissar-Pathankot Angle

At Hissar, unit life for me was a mix of training routines and administrative duties. My promotion board was due to convene in early 1999. I was hoping to be promoted to the rank of colonel soon after and take over the reins of the unit. I wasn't particularly anxious about the promotion itself, as I believed my service record was solid.

But just a few days into the new year, I received word from a senior officer—someone in the know—that there seemed to be a hitch in one of my Annual Performance Reports (APR), and that this might affect my chances of promotion. I don't recall being overly disturbed by this revelation, nor did I make any attempt to investigate what had gone wrong. To the best of my knowledge, there was nothing adverse on record against me.

A few days later, the selection board met, and I received the good news: I had been selected for promotion to the next rank. It was only years later, after I had retired, that another officer—again someone with inside knowledge—told me that there had indeed been a snag during my selection process from lieutenant colonel to colonel. Apparently, one of the reporting officers had not been fair in his assessment, which had significantly impacted my merit standing. However, the screening officers noticed that this particular report was inconsistent with the rest of my performance record. They took corrective action at their level to address the discrepancy. Looking back, I marvel at how certain things seem to sort themselves out without our intervention. For the record, a similar pattern would repeat itself a few years later, as I will mention in due course.

In April 1999, I had the privilege of assuming command of The Poona Horse, one of the most prestigious and decorated regiments of the Indian Army. I took charge with full commitment. My motto was simple: 'Lead from the front,' in every aspect of regimental life. I aspired for my professional ability, personal conduct, and values of simplicity, sincerity, and integrity to remain beyond reproach. The principle I followed above all was: 'Men first, always and every time.'

As I was settling into my new command, reports began emerging of intrusions in the Kargil region in May 1999. As the situation escalated, it became increasingly clear that the Indian Army as a whole could be drawn into a serious military engagement.

The first 'casualty' of these developments was a long-awaited holiday that Madhuri and I had planned with the children—a break in Singapore in June 1999. We had secured the necessary approvals from the relevant authorities for leave abroad, booked our air tickets, and made accommodation arrangements. But with the unfolding crisis, it was clear that everything else had to take a back seat.

The cancellation of a much-anticipated trip—especially after a year spent apart across three different cities—was disheartening, if only briefly. But both of us quickly got back to our duties, as the seriousness of the threat in the northern sector became more apparent. As the operational tempo increased, we began preparations for possible mobilisation at short notice.

As casualties from the Kargil conflict began to rise, the ripple effects were felt at the Pathankot hospital too. Patients from hospitals located further north were moved southward to make room for incoming casualties from the conflict zone. In the process, Madhuri found herself increasingly occupied, helping manage the overflow of adult patients.

The Kargil conflict formally concluded around July 1999, but the heightened state of readiness continued for several more months. As things gradually began to return to normal, Madhuri and I decided to visit each other periodically. However, travel between Pathankot and Hissar was not straightforward. It involved a four-hour road journey between Hissar and Ambala, followed by a six-hour train ride to Pathankot. With the change in mode at Ambala, the journey would take anywhere between ten to twelve hours each way.

Since I was commanding the unit, it wasn't possible for me to visit Pathankot frequently. So, Madhuri took it upon herself to make the arduous journey along with little Vibhuti, now six years old. For these visits, Madhuri would take a Saturday or Monday off every month. She would board a train to Ambala on the day of departure and reach there by evening. From there, she would head to the bus station and travel by road to Hissar, arriving late at night. An exhausted Madhuri and Vibhuti would then crash out, and only the next day could we spend some time together.

Post-lunch the next day, the return journey would begin: a trip back to the Hissar bus stand for the four-hour ride to Ambala, followed by a transfer to the railway station to catch the 11 p.m. train to Pathankot. At around 4:30 a.m., she would arrive at the Pathankot station, hoping the train had run on time so that she could send Vibhuti to school and report to work at the hospital by 8 a.m. Fortunately, one of our regimental officers was posted in Ambala on a staff assignment and would often assist her in getting from the bus station to the railway station.

On one such visit to Hissar, Vibhuti fell ill and was running a high fever. However, Madhuri had to return by the next morning. So, after giving Vibhuti some medicine, she set out on the journey to Ambala as planned. Upon reaching the Ambala railway station, she discovered that the coach in which she had reserved seats had been declared defective and detached from the train. As a result, they no longer had assigned seats.

Madhuri requested the train conductor (TC) to allocate alternate seats, as the cancellation was through no fault of hers. He, however, said he couldn't help and asked her to speak to the station master instead. Thinking quickly, Madhuri realised that if she went to find the station master, the train would likely depart before she returned, leaving her and an unwell Vibhuti stranded in Ambala. So, instead of going to the station master, she asked Vibhuti to sit near the luggage and wait for her. Then, turning to the TC, she firmly told him that she would not allow the train to leave unless he made alternate arrangements—at least one seat—for her sick daughter. Without waiting for a response, she marched to the front of the train and jumped down onto the railway tracks. The TC was stunned and immediately requested her to return to the platform. Madhuri replied that he should call the station master to resolve the matter right there. Realising he had little choice, the TC checked his chart again and quickly allotted them a seat. That was all Madhuri needed—one seat was enough for both her and Vibhuti to travel with reasonable comfort.

Thanks to her quick thinking and decisive action, they were able to reach Pathankot on time. Vibhuti had to miss school the next day due to her illness, but Madhuri reported to work at the hospital on time. A small battle had been won through out-of-the-box thinking. The strategy had worked, and Madhuri would go on to apply similar thinking at key moments in her career in the years that followed.

Once the urgency of the Kargil War had subsided, I had to proceed with my unit to the deserts for collective training. This phase involves moving out with all our equipment and conducting outdoor exercises in near-combat conditions, both day and night. Nikhil and his friend had come to spend part of their vacation with me before they were to begin preparing for their Class 10 Board exams. I thought it would be a great experience for them to accompany me to the training area and witness how soldiers train and live in the open desert. They were thrilled to climb aboard the tanks and go wherever they went. They even learnt how to drive a tank and got familiar with a few weapons. To this day, Nikhil remembers those times with fondness and nostalgia.

While the children made lasting memories, the world around them was stepping into a new era. It was the beginning of the new millennium—Year 2K, as it was popularly called. Madhuri happened to be visiting Hissar at the time and was deeply involved in organising a social function with the other ladies. Suddenly, I received a call from Pune informing me that Madhuri's mother had taken seriously ill and was in a comatose state. She had been suffering from chronic kidney failure for some time, and now it appeared that her other organs were beginning to fail as well. Madhuri's father, who was at her mother's side in Pune, told the doctors that no critical medical decisions would be taken until Madhuri arrived. The nearest airport was in Delhi, from where a flight to Mumbai was available at 11 p.m., followed by an early morning connection to Pune.

We quickly set out for Delhi by road and, with some luck, reached the airport by 10:30 p.m. The airport manager was kind enough to delay the flight by a few minutes, enabling Madhuri to board the plane just in time. She reached Mumbai late that night and caught a connecting flight to Pune the next morning, arriving at her mother's bedside in record time. Her intuition told her that her mother would pull through if she could be with her for a few days. And she was right. A few days later, her mother awoke from the coma and began to recover. Only once she was out of danger did Madhuri return to Pathankot.

Meanwhile, Vibhuti couldn't be kept away from school for too long. After dropping Madhuri off in Delhi, I took a brief break and travelled with Vibhuti to Pathankot. There, the kind family of Col Arvind Gupta took it upon themselves to look after her until Madhuri could return. I, in turn, went back to Hissar to rejoin my unit.

In hindsight, each such experience only made us stronger. Vibhuti, in her own way, learnt to take things in stride. Since then, the Guptas have been her godparents. We remain deeply indebted to them for standing by us during those difficult times.

The Opportunity to Super-Specialise

By now, Madhuri had over seven years of experience as a paediatrician. Typically, those wishing to pursue super-specialisation do so soon after completing their initial training. But Madhuri had chosen to wait until the children were a little more independent. She had been inclined towards paediatric nephrology ever since her first stint of basic training in the subject at AIIMS, Delhi, in 1995. Watching her mother struggle with kidney disease made her realise that by specialising in this field, she could potentially prevent many children from facing a similar fate.

For years, she had been requesting Army HQ to consider creating a slot for this speciality, but without success. Ironically, it was just when she was stretched thin—juggling her time between Pathankot and Pune, between caring for her ailing mother, tending to our daughter, staying in touch with our son in Pune, and supporting me at Hissar—that she received news of being selected for training in paediatric nephrology abroad.

The timing placed her in a dilemma. With so many pressing responsibilities, Madhuri initially decided to forgo her study leave. However, the head of her establishment encouraged her not to let the opportunity slip by. He reminded her that she had a chance to become the first paediatric nephrologist in the armed forces. Instead of going abroad, he advised her to take an alternative route: pursue a one-year fellowship training at AIIMS, Delhi, along with periodic additional training to build further expertise and qualifications.

This option seemed more manageable, and Madhuri decided to follow his advice. The biggest challenge at this point was ensuring Vibhuti's care and education. I assured her that I would take care of Vibhuti in Hissar, where she could attend school as well. Though hesitant at first, Madhuri eventually agreed. We also had to factor in that undertaking a super-specialisation would mean extending her military service by several more years. But we reasoned that if we had already come this far, nothing ahead could be more difficult than what we had already faced. With this in mind, she opted for training in India instead of going abroad. Army HQ was kind enough to approve her request.

Madhuri then visited AIIMS in Delhi and approached Professor R. N. Shrivastava—the father of paediatric nephrology in India and head of the paediatric division at AIIMS—requesting to be accepted as his student. He graciously agreed. With all the arrangements in place, Madhuri returned to Pathankot to pack up and prepare for her move to Delhi, looking forward to returning to an academic environment after the demanding years at the base hospital in Pathankot.

It was now time for us to plan our next steps, as Madhuri was set to begin her training at AIIMS in July 2000.

The Hissar-New Delhi Story

Our focus now shifted to managing the transition on the personal front. The first task at hand was to settle Vibhuti in with me at Hissar. My aim was to try and take care of her on my own. One of my additional responsibilities in Hissar—apart from commanding my unit—was to ensure the smooth functioning of the army school in the military station. Thanks to this role, I was able to arrange her transfer to the Hissar school with relative ease.

Meanwhile, in Delhi, Madhuri arranged to stay within the campus of the Army Hospital Research and Referral (AHRR). Since the drive between Delhi and Hissar took about four hours, she decided to travel down on weekends to visit us and also help resolve any issues I might face while looking after Vibhuti. This was the first time I would be 'in charge' of my daughter completely on my own. She was barely eight but bursting with energy. After the structured, disciplined life she was used to with Madhuri, she found the relative freedom at Hissar exhilarating.

Over time, Vibhuti figured out that I had something to do with the school administration. One day, she saw a boy from her class misbehaving with another girl. Annoyed by his conduct, she marched up to him and, as I later learnt, probably gave him a good whack. Then she declared that if he continued with his rude behaviour, she would make sure he got thrown out of school since her father was in charge of discipline!

That afternoon, when I went to pick her up, the school principal informed me about this embarrassing episode. The boy's parents were understandably upset, and I had to assure them that I would look into the matter appropriately. It took some convincing to get Vibhuti to understand that she should report such incidents to her teacher rather than take matters into her own hands. But she stood her ground, insisting, 'He was wrong, and wrong is wrong!' That streak of righteous defiance has stayed with her to this day.

A couple of months later, I had to leave for outdoor training and realised I couldn't leave Vibhuti alone at home. At this critical juncture, my parents came to the rescue. To them,

Vibhuti was their little 'Rani,' and they soon joined me in Hissar. Their presence gave us much-needed support at a time when both Madhuri and I were pursuing demanding professional paths in different cities.

Madhuri's weekly visits to Hissar also became something of an SOP. It was no easy feat as she had to drive to and from Hissar and Delhi on her own. As winter set in, the dense fog that blanketed the plains made the journey even more treacherous. Yet she never missed a single date with us unless something pressing came up in Delhi.

On a lighter note, my skills as a caregiver came under close and constant review. Vibhuti's schoolwork, eating habits, personal hygiene, and manners were all subject to microscopic scrutiny. On most counts, I was found wanting! But I think Vibhuti enjoyed all the attention from my parents, from my officer colleagues, and from their families. She was, in short, spoilt but very happy. I knew Madhuri wouldn't be too pleased with this development, as it meant she would have to take on the task of disciplining her all over again.

Towards the summer of 2001, Madhuri received an opportunity to undertake a three-month fellowship in her field of specialisation at the National University Hospital (NUHS), Singapore. There, she trained under the world-renowned paediatric nephrologist Ms Hui Kim Yap and her team. It proved to be an excellent learning experience, and the professional bond that developed during this time has since grown into a personal connection that Madhuri continues to greatly cherish.

As I approached the final phase of my command tenure, our unit received routine movement orders to shift to Ambala. Fortunately, Vibhuti's academic year was drawing to a close, and my parents decided to return to Pune with her during the interim. In April 2001, while I moved with my unit to Ambala, my parents moved to Pune with Vibhuti, and Madhuri proceeded to Singapore for her training.

Around the same time, Nikhil graduated from senior school, having served as head boy and been awarded the 'Best Outgoing Student' of his batch. He joined a reputed junior college in Pune and was preparing to appear for his crucial 12th Board exams the following year. Keeping this in mind, I applied for a year's sabbatical in Pune, which was granted soon after.

After overseeing the move to Ambala, I took a short break and travelled to Singapore with Vibhuti to visit Madhuri. She was still in the midst of her nephrology training, and we had a wonderful holiday together.

A few days after we returned to Pune, Madhuri called from Singapore to inform me that she had received her new posting orders from Army HQ. She was to report to AHRR in New Delhi at the conclusion of her training, scheduled for the end of June 2001. And just like that, the game of 'Me here and she there' had resumed.

Madhuri felt I should request her superiors to reconsider and post her to Pune. Though I was unsure if this was appropriate, I decided to give it a try. I called the head of service and explained our situation that both Madhuri and I had endured prolonged separation and that it had taken a toll on our children's education. I added that I had taken study leave specifically to be in Pune for this reason, and it would make a world of difference if Madhuri could be posted alongside me. I believe he understood the weight of the situation. While he did point out that professionally, Madhuri was best suited to be at AHRR, I sensed him pausing to consider the personal implications. After a moment's silence, he assured me that Madhuri would receive revised posting orders within forty-eight hours. True to his word, her posting was diverted to Command Hospital, Pune. In that single moment, all our concerns were resolved, and we felt deeply grateful!

With this settled, I returned to Ambala to formally conclude my command responsibilities. At the end of June 2001, Madhuri returned from Singapore to Delhi, where she completed the closing formalities at AIIMS. She then joined me in Ambala for a couple of days over the weekend, where we were ceremoniously 'dined and wined out' by The Poona Horse. It was an emotional moment for both of us.

In the army, one always feels part of a larger family. When I had joined my unit in 1978 as a young second lieutenant, my immediate family consisted of the 17 men under my direct command. That number grew to 120 when I became a squadron commander, and eventually, as a unit commander, I came to see the entire unit of 600 soldiers—and their families—as my extended family.

With a heavy heart, I took leave of the regiment, and Madhuri and I set off on our journey south to Pune in our little family car—a Maruti 800. The car had no air-conditioning, and travelling in July 2001 was far from comfortable. But at that moment, our hearts were light. The simple thought that the four of us would soon be together was more than enough to chase away any discomfort. It took us three days and two nights to reach Pune. At the end of it, we were finally reunited with our children and ready to begin our next chapter together.

Postscript by Madhuri

The tenure at Pathankot, followed by the study leave, felt like a trial by fire. While juggling work and family, I found myself managing not one but three fronts—Pathankot, Hissar, and Pune. To add to that was the crisis of my mother's catastrophic illness, and then the long-awaited sabbatical to pursue my training in paediatric nephrology. It became a significant milestone in my journey and added a new dimension to my growth.

Until then, I had been a doctor-soldier. Now, as the wife of a commanding officer, I found myself dancing into family welfare meetings and coffee evenings with the officers' wives. Not once did I feel this wasn't my place. I took pride in embracing the role fully and enjoyed supporting Rajeev in his command responsibilities.

In a lighter vein, I remember Rajeev calling me one day after Vibhuti had moved in with him. He confessed that commanding an entire armoured regiment was easier than managing a young daughter on his own! This, of course, was before he called for backup from his ever-supportive parents, who stepped in and moved to Hissar to help.

On my end, passing the test and becoming the first paediatric nephrologist in the armed forces—while swimming against the tide, driven by conviction and passion—was a major milestone. The training laid the foundation for strengthening the triad of patient care, research, and education within me.

Part IV

A New Millennium, A New Avatar

Chapter 10

SHE STARTED IT ALL

The Home Front

IT WAS A JOY TO BE BACK IN PUNE WITH THE ENTIRE FAMILY together again, after three years of living a tripod existence. During this period, Nikhil had completed his 10th class Board exams and had now entered another critical phase—12th Standard (Junior College). In India, performance in these Board exams determines entry into professional streams, and typically, immense pressure builds up on students (with parents also feeling the heat as bystanders). So, it was a relief to be together during this important phase in our children's lives.

Vibhuti had entered the fourth grade of junior school. Compared to her previous school in Hissar, the curriculum in Pune was noticeably simpler. Vibhuti had developed a certain dislike for studies in general, so this lighter academic load turned out to be a blessing in disguise.

As for me, I had enrolled for my project work at the University of Pune. My area of interest was India-Pakistan relations. I was keen on examining whether our seemingly eternal hostility could transform into lasting peace, for the benefit of both nations. This meant delving deep into the history of independence, partition, and the efforts of various individuals and organisations over the years in order to explore whether fractured ties could be healed.

My daily schedule was flexible, with no strict time constraints. Madhuri, on the other hand, had to adhere to a fixed reporting time at the hospital. While her start time was firm, her closing hours stretched based on patient needs and teaching responsibilities. It was under these conditions that she began her new tenure at the command hospital in Pune.

Setting Up the First Paediatric Nephrology Unit

Madhuri had been eagerly looking forward to establishing a dedicated super-speciality unit at the hospital. She was full of enthusiasm and energy. However, she soon encountered several hurdles in turning her vision into reality. When she requested space to start a separate unit, she was told to collaborate with the adult nephrology department instead.

At the time, the concept of paediatric nephrology was still relatively new in India. As a result, the idea of setting up an independent paediatric nephrology unit within the children's ward was met with resistance. The senior nephrologists believed there was no real need for a separate setup.

Madhuri tried to convince the hospital authorities that treating kidney diseases in children required a completely different approach from that used for adults. In paediatrics, preventive care was more crucial than the tertiary-care approach generally used for adult patients. Moreover, close communication with the parents of young patients was essential and that was best done in the paediatric ward, not in the adult nephrology section. She succinctly argued that 'nephrology needs to come to paediatrics' and not the other way around.

Her time in Singapore, where she had seen a vibrant and child-friendly paediatric ward, had further strengthened her vision. She deeply wished to recreate something similar within a military hospital in India. Until Madhuri trained in paediatric nephrology, children with kidney-related ailments had largely been managed by doctors trained in adult medicine.

When Madhuri arrived at the command hospital, armed with her fellowship training, some of the senior nephrologists began to circulate the impression that she was not adequately qualified, since she did not hold a Doctor of Medicine (DM) degree. But Madhuri was not one to give up easily. She persisted in her request for a separate area within the paediatric ward to establish a sub-unit dedicated to children with kidney diseases.

After much debate and discussion, she won her first battle—she was allotted a modest two-bed space in the paediatric ward. It was a huge relief because the atmosphere in an adult ward is markedly different from that of a children's ward. The nurses in paediatrics tend to be gentler and more patient, and the approach of the doctors is also softer and more engaged. This helps put the young patients at ease and often improves their response to treatment.

Madhuri's persistence in advocating for the right environment for her patients vindicated her stubbornness. However, this did not endear her to certain colleagues in the adult nephrology department, some of whom remained sceptical of her efforts. At one point, there even seemed to be a subtle attempt to impede the growth of paediatric nephrology within the armed forces. This was a wholly avoidable stance that cast a shadow on professional collaboration.

Madhuri often wondered whether this resistance stemmed from psychological insecurities or perhaps envy of the recognition she was receiving in the national nephrology community. Whatever the cause, she resolved not to be weighed down by negativity and to bash on regardless.

Healing with a Smile

Command Hospital Pune, in those days, was located in sprawling old barracks spread across a wide area. Finding one's way to its various wards wasn't easy. The paediatric ward, in particular, was tucked away in the farthest corner of the hospital and, peculiarly, built below the general ground level. This made it prone to rainwater run-off and deprived it of natural sunlight due to its sunken structure and placement.

Madhuri made several attempts to brighten up the barrack structures through the Military Engineering Services (MES). When their response proved lacklustre, she turned to civilian philanthropists for support. The local Rotary Club came to her aid, and soon the children's wards were painted in bright hues and cheerful backdrops. Background music and a fish aquarium added a touch of liveliness. These changes lifted the spirits of the sick children, and their joy, in turn, brought happiness to Madhuri. These small interventions came with a big impact.

As luck would have it, on one occasion, a very senior officer from HQ Southern Command visited the hospital. During his rounds, he stopped by the paediatric ward and asked Madhuri if she had any suggestions for improvement. Without hesitation, she raised the issue of the ward's structural deficiencies and urged the need for MES attention in the interest of the children. Notes were taken, and upon returning to his office, the officer swiftly issued instructions for corrective action. The usually sluggish MES was suddenly galvanised into activity and soon delivered the long-overdue maintenance and improvements. And while everyone in the ward was pleased, some within the hospital administration felt that Madhuri had overstepped her brief by speaking so candidly.

On another occasion, while Madhuri was attending her OPD, a senior officer from the hospital hierarchy visited the paediatric ward as part of his routine familiarisation rounds. On discovering she was not present, he expressed his displeasure. When informed she was in the OPD, he dismissed the explanation and made some disparaging remarks.

Upon hearing about the incident, Madhuri requested a one-on-one meeting with the officer. Once in his office, she politely but firmly stated that if there were any concerns about her conduct, she would prefer to hear them directly, rather than through remarks made in her absence. She outlined her work schedule and explained why she had not been present in the ward during his visit.

After having expressed herself clearly and respectfully, she took her leave. Her straightforwardness had the desired effect. From that point on, she faced no significant problems during her tenure at the hospital. In fact, the same officer went on to acknowledge and appreciate her work, even after his retirement. Every such 'moral battle' only made her more resilient for the next challenge.

As part of her efforts to make the ward more comforting and cheerful, Madhuri also initiated celebrations of various Indian festivals and special occasions. Diwali, Christmas, Children's Day, birthdays—all became reasons to organise lively musical parties in the gaily decorated ward. These events delighted the young patients and also contributed to a more positive work atmosphere for the staff.

Then one day, to her complete surprise, the army commander of Southern Command in Pune made an unscheduled visit to the hospital. During his round, he visited the paediatric ward and formally awarded Madhuri the General Officer's Commendation Card in recognition of her dedicated efforts to bring joy and comfort to the young children under her care. For Madhuri, the commendation was more than a medal; it was a tribute to the joy she had fought to bring into those little lives.

Establishing Stability in Paediatric Nephrology

After the initial hiccups, Madhuri focused on stabilising the work processes of her nephrology unit. The challenge here was that she had to start from scratch. There were no clear logistical channels to ensure the regular availability of medicines required by children. The equipment essential for their treatment was either improvised from adult-use models or simply unavailable.

Madhuri soon realised that pharmaceutical companies were more inclined towards catering to adult patients who needed long-term treatment involving expensive medication. In contrast, kidney-related ailments in children were largely preventable and treatable if diagnosed early. Early intervention not only allowed these children to lead healthier lives but also reduced their need for intensive treatment as adults. However, this didn't align with the profit margins of pharma firms, making them reluctant to supply paediatric medicines at affordable rates.

Faced with this challenge, Madhuri began reaching out to the civilian sector for support. Over time, she managed to secure additional funding through corporate social responsibility (CSR) initiatives as well as assistance from the local military hierarchy. Slowly but steadily, she brought a sense of structure and stability to the paediatric nephrology unit at Command Hospital Pune.

She introduced simple innovations that enabled mothers to manage their child's treatment at home, reducing the need for frequent hospital visits. She also devised practical treatment protocols that allowed children to attend school without embarrassment—an important psychological boost for children who often, due to their condition, struggled with confidence and hesitated to go to school. Her approach—practical, compassionate, and focused on the bigger picture—had a significant impact on the mothers of her young patients. She laid strong emphasis on the preventive aspects of care, urging them not to lose heart when setbacks occurred. Her ability to offer hope was just as valuable as her medical expertise, giving families a sense of reassurance that their children could grow into healthy adults.

While prevention was her first line of defence, Madhuri did not shy away from making tough decisions. When necessary, she recommended kidney transplants even in small children. Her combined approach, which was conservative in prevention and aggressive in tertiary care, proved to be an ideal blend that stood the test of time.

Her greatest joy now comes from hearing from those very children—now grown into capable, successful adults—who call her from time to time to share updates about their lives and health, and to express their gratitude.

The Home Side

During this period, we were staying in our own house on the other side of town. Since I was on study leave, I could help with the morning chores before Madhuri left for the hospital. The downside, however, was the long commute. She had to drive ten kilometres each way, every day. While the morning drive would take around twenty minutes, the return journey in evening traffic often stretched to an hour.

There were many days when she had to go back to the hospital after reaching home either to attend to an emergency or for an official or social function. On such days, knowing her schedule would be tight, she would carry a change of clothes and essentials with her, returning home only late at night after all her responsibilities were over. Her car boot gradually turned into an eclectic mix of clothes, groceries, and folders of patient records!

By now, Nikhil had grown into a self-reliant young man with a structured daily routine. After school hours, he would attend coaching classes for subjects he wanted to explore further. He also had a strong passion for sports. Despite it being his board exam year, he managed to strike a healthy balance between academics and athletics.

Vibhuti, on the other hand, was still quite young and needed more attention. Her epilepsy treatment was ongoing. While hospital visits were infrequent, her medication needed to be administered with absolute regularity. Madhuri kept a close watch on her progress, with the alertness of a hawk. Fortunately, Vibhuti responded well to the treatment.

However, her attention span in class was a bit of a challenge. Whether it was due to a lack of interest in studies or simply her curiosity about the world, she often got distracted. Teachers would frequently have to call her back to focus on what was being taught instead of gazing out the window. When Madhuri once asked her why, she simply replied that there were more interesting things happening outside the classroom! Despite her lack of enthusiasm for conventional studies, her natural intelligence ensured that her academic performance remained fairly good.

My research project work was also an ongoing activity. I would visit Pune University after the children had left for school or college to read and make notes in my area of interest. Alongside my research, I also began learning a foreign language as a value addition. At times, it felt like I was putting in more hours of study than Nikhil! In good humour, Nikhil would often tell his friends that his dad followed a stricter study schedule than him and that he was the one making sure dad had his meals on time and got his cup of tea.

Normally, study leave is granted for a period of two years. However, I opted for a one-year sabbatical to keep open the possibility of attending the next Higher Command Course, should I be selected. As luck would have it, my nomination came through in February 2002. It was good news, reflecting well on my professional standing.

Around the same time, Madhuri was offered a fellowship course at the Great Ormond Street (GOS) Children's Hospital in London, for a duration of four months beginning in March 2002. GOS is a world-renowned institution and offered her an excellent opportunity to further hone her skills in paediatric nephrology. She had been selected for the only vacancy allocated to candidates from all Commonwealth countries—a truly commendable achievement.

These developments, however, came with implications. My HC Course would require me to move to Mhow in the first week of July 2002, where the course is conducted over one year. Separation from the family loomed once again. In this world of dualities, good fortune often carries with it a parallel inconvenience. But such was our life and by now, we were used to adjusting to its recurring patterns.

In the first week of March, Madhuri flew out to London while Nikhil, Vibhuti, and I continued in Pune. I was glad that my presence at home had made it possible for her to take up this opportunity. Nikhil completed his exams in the first week of April. Vibhuti finished her fourth standard exams, and I, too, wrapped up my project work by the end of the month. Madhuri's course was to conclude at the end of June, and since there was a brief gap in between, I decided to join her in London for a short visit in May. I made arrangements with her parents to keep a watchful eye on the children and proceeded to London.

A few days after I reached, there was a politico-military flutter back home in the wake of the terrorist attack on the Indian Parliament in December 2001. However, the developments did not warrant an early return. After two pleasant weeks, I returned to India, and Madhuri followed at the end of June. While we were away, Nikhil and Vibhuti got a little breather from us, living for a while in independent mode.

Before I left for Mhow, Nikhil's board results were declared. He had done reasonably well and now faced the question of what career path to pursue. Having seen his mother always busy, he concluded that medicine was not for him. He also briefly considered joining the army but ruled it out after witnessing our own struggles with being posted apart. A true foodie at heart, Nikhil expressed interest in pursuing a career in the hospitality industry. We felt that option was a bit too narrow to begin with and suggested he first undertake undergraduate studies in a mainstream field. If his interest in hospitality persisted, he could explore it later. He agreed and chose to pursue engineering.

That year, the admission process for engineering colleges was conducted in a semi-online format for the first time. The process was fairly streamlined, and by the end of the day, Nikhil had secured admission to a good college in Pune. We were pleased as it meant he would be settled in Pune for the next four years.

Soon after, I left for Mhow to begin my year-long tryst with the HC Course. It was an excellent training platform for military planners, and I looked forward to it with great enthusiasm. Meanwhile, Vibhuti moved up to the fifth standard, and her treatment for epilepsy was gradually drawing to a close.

Against this backdrop, we settled down in our respective locations by July 2002. Upon her return from the UK, Madhuri applied her newly acquired expertise to her small nephrology unit with renewed energy. Her focus remained on the innovations she had already introduced for the benefit of her patients. She continued to emphasise reducing the cost of medical care, simplifying home-based treatment for mothers, and empowering children to take responsibility for their own care wherever possible.

At Mhow, I had an interesting back-in-the-game phase after my ten-month sabbatical. The academic curriculum was primarily military in nature, designed to broaden our professional horizons. Given India's diverse geography—mountains in the North, dense jungles in the East, sweeping deserts in the West, and vast maritime responsibilities in the South—the military implications of terrain were far-reaching and complex. As a result, our schedule included extensive visits to various military institutions, formations, and operational bases. These were immensely educative for all of us. I was grateful that the military authorities allowed Madhuri to accompany me on many of these trips. She would take short leave and join me for these journeys.

Being an army officer herself, Madhuri was entitled to travel with us in military aircraft and attend the briefings and discussions that were part of our itinerary. This gave her the opportunity to visit several forward areas across the country and gain first-hand operational exposure. Later, when she assumed a senior position overseeing medical support in Northern Command, this experience proved invaluable in quickly building her operational acumen.

During my time at Mhow, the children also visited occasionally and enjoyed exploring some of the locations in Central India. These periodic visits offered them new experiences and perspectives. Even though they ultimately chose not to join the armed forces, this exposure helped them grow into citizens with a pan-Indian outlook.

Since I was aware that a return posting to Pune after the course was unlikely, I volunteered for a posting to the insurgency-affected Northeast. I hoped to build further on the operational insights I had gained during my earlier tenure in the Kashmir Valley. So, in June 2003, I was pleased to be posted to a formation tasked with operations in the Assam Valley, along with concurrent responsibilities along the India-China border. My tenure in the East was deeply engaging and rich in learning. Madhuri was able to join me for some time, along with Vibhuti, and together we had the chance to explore some untouched, beautiful regions.

As I was completing a year in this assignment, I received an unexpected posting order to the Career Management Branch at Army HQ in July 2004. Ordinarily, I would have expected to serve in the East for two years, and understandably, my superior officer at the time was not pleased with the abrupt move, especially given the operational commitments of the formation. However, he was a mature and thoughtful leader and eventually agreed to relieve me as per the official schedule.

Meanwhile, Nikhil and Vibhuti had completed another academic year, and Madhuri had further strengthened her standing in her field. In the paediatric ward, a new head of department (HoD) had taken over from the previous one. A competent professional, she and Madhuri shared a good rapport, especially in the initial phase of their association. The new HoD was also keen to improve the functioning of the ward, and Madhuri proved to be an effective collaborator in this effort.

As Madhuri's patient base continued to grow, the need for more space for her nephrology work became pressing. The HoD made some changes to add space in the ward, and Madhuri was pleased to have more comfortable and functional surroundings for the treatment of her young patients. Soon, patients from across the state began arriving, as paediatric nephrology care was not available anywhere else in Pune at the time.

Other Important Occurrences

While all this was unfolding, we had a new addition to the family in March 2004. I had come down on short leave from the East to be with Vibhuti on her birthday. That year, she wanted only one gift—a soft, cuddly puppy. We tried to dissuade her, knowing it would mean added responsibilities. Madhuri was especially concerned that once the initial excitement wore off, the puppy's care would fall to her.

Despite our best efforts, we couldn't change her mind, and soon we found ourselves the proud parents of a black-and-white Cocker Spaniel. Thus began our adventures with four-legged children. We named the little girl Pixie, a name that matched her quizzical expression and lively nature. She was quite a handful from the beginning. As expected, Madhuri gradually became the primary caregiver. Nikhil served as the backup, and Vibhuti would—sometimes—share the responsibility!

In 2006, Pixie became the proud mother of a litter of pups. Two of them were gifted to families in Pune. By then, I had settled into my assignment in Delhi and asked Madhuri to fly the remaining three puppies to me. The moment I laid eyes on the three delightful bundles of energy, I was smitten. I gave one to an acquaintance and kept the other two with me for company. The girl was named Peppy, and the boisterous boy was called Coco. With their long, droopy ears and playful antics, they made a charming pair, especially as they accompanied me on my evening walks. So now, I had two children with me in Delhi, while Madhuri had Vibhuti, Nikhil, and Pixie with her in Pune.

I remained in Delhi from July 2004 to September 2006. During this time, Madhuri and the children would visit me during their holiday breaks. I had acquired a new car for my daily commute, which we made good use of, exploring various spots in and around Delhi. These outings became our way of bonding and staying connected despite the distances.

By mid-2004, Madhuri was nearing the end of her three-year tenure in Pune. We considered the possibility of requesting a posting for her in Delhi. Around this time, a senior officer, who was due to take up an assignment at AFMC, expressed a desire to have Madhuri side-stepped to AFMC from the command hospital. She believed Madhuri would be an excellent addition to the institute's faculty and serve as a role model for young medical cadets. This placed Madhuri in a dilemma. After years of managing long-distance coordination, we were eager to finally be together. Yet, the offer had its merits—remaining in Pune would provide continuity in Vibhuti's schooling, and with Nikhil entering the final phase of his engineering degree, her presence would be beneficial.

Then, an unexpected event tipped the scales. My uncle, who lived with us in Pune, passed away following a cardiac complication. My aunt was suddenly left alone and in need of daily support. These circumstances led Madhuri to accept the offer of moving to AFMC, which meant postponing, yet again, our hope of reuniting in Delhi.

Soon after my promotion to brigadier, I was posted to Bhatinda to command a prestigious formation. In terms of time, Pune wasn't too distant as after an overnight train to Delhi, a short flight would get me there within a day. And so, in September 2006, Coco, Peppy, and I began our stint in Bhatinda, while Madhuri, the children, and Pixie remained in Pune.

Postscript by Madhuri

Fresh from Singapore and now the first paediatric nephrologist in the Indian Army, I felt on top of the world. The occasional pricks to my soaring gas balloon didn't dishearten me; they only made me paddle harder against the tide. The postgraduate residents in the department became my greatest allies, and I encouraged them constantly to aim for excellence. I was firm, but nurturing. It was during this time that I learnt one of my most valuable lessons: Rule with your head but lead with your heart. Today, I feel like a proud mother hen watching her chicks flourish. Each of them is doing remarkable work in their field, and I continue to draw joy from their achievements.

The story between Rajeev and me, however, wasn't always smooth sailing. We often had to deal with the emotional strain of prolonged separations. Even when one of us managed to take leave to visit the other, we rarely got uninterrupted time together. We had decided not to take leave at the same time, so that we could space out our visits and meet more frequently. But the result of that choice meant that during my visits to Rajeev, I would often sit alone at the field mess, eating by myself while he was away on operational duties or out at the firing ranges.

When he came to see me in Pune, there would be a long list of household chores demanding attention, or he would be left waiting outside the hospital until late at night while I attended to patients. We had little choice and would often console each other with the hope that things would eventually get better.

Rajeev often credits me for managing the home, the children, and my profession with minimal help. But I believe his resilience—his ability to stay strong and motivated while constantly relocating and living alone—was no less than a herculean feat.

Chapter 11
A Triad of Roles

As Faculty at AFMC

For Madhuri, being posted to AFMC as faculty was a dream come true. Her first love—besides her reverence for the uniform as a soldier—was being a clinician, especially for children. The second was to be a teacher. Now, she had the opportunity to smoothly shift gears, and she grabbed it with full zest. She had a bagful of ideas to make teaching an exciting proposition and was keen to enthuse her students into a self-driven learning mode by making the teaching-learning methodology more engaging. However, she soon realised that bringing about change in a system was not easy.

The first directive she received from the head of her department was that, as one of the junior faculty members, she would have to concentrate on administrative matters rather than teaching and patient care. This was a bit discouraging. She assured him that she would fulfil all her administrative responsibilities, but in addition, she wished to continue interacting with the students and attending to her clinical work. Soon, however, she found herself being allotted numerous duties that kept her away from what she truly considered her real job—teaching her students through patient care.

Luckily, the head of the institute—who had been instrumental in having her posted to AFMC—was well aware not only of Madhuri's organisational capabilities but also of her brilliant academic record. There were some major projects the institute had in mind that required aesthetic finesse woven into their conception and execution, and she knew Madhuri was the right person to undertake those responsibilities independently on her behalf. As a result, Madhuri was given relatively more freedom to organise her teaching schedule alongside the execution of her additional tasks.

AFMC is an institution that is arguably the best in the country in terms of teaching faculty and infrastructure available for instruction. The student-teacher ratio is excellent, and the faculty comprises brilliant doctors with wide-ranging experience. Administrative facilities for the students include comfortable hostels with good dining arrangements, along with infrastructure that supports physical well-being. The institute as a whole has an excellent ethos, blending academic and moral values that stay with students for life.

Madhuri was keen to use this backdrop to train her students not only to become good doctors but also good human beings—both inseparable parts of what it means to be a competent doctor, especially in the armed forces, where the sensitivities of soldiers and their families are crucial. The institute caters to the training of undergraduate students (referred to as cadets), who are required to serve in the armed forces for five years upon completion of their course at AFMC. Postgraduate training is also conducted at the institution.

These undergraduate students are essentially civilians and need to be mentored and guided into becoming strong and sensitive men and women as they transition from adolescence to adulthood. It is a time when their minds are highly impressionable, and they seek role models. Madhuri was exemplary in this regard. Her brilliant performance during her own undergraduate days was documented on numerous display boards across the college, especially in the library. Besides her academic excellence, she had been a good sportsperson and had an attractive personality. Altogether, she was a rare combination of brain, brawn, and smartness.

She was also clear-headed, had an excellent memory for medical facts and figures, and possessed strong clinical acumen. Over time, she had refined her bedside manners to reflect kindness, patience, and a deep sense of considerateness towards patients and their caregivers. Making good use of information technology, she adapted her teaching and presentation techniques to make them engaging and interactive—this was one of her core focus areas. Rote teaching was not for her. She would begin her sessions with witty introductions to the day's topic and maintain interest levels by ensuring all-inclusive participation.

Clinical rounds with students were her favourite. A day prior to any clinical session, she would select a case study that the students were expected to read up on and analyse before her arrival at the bedside. She would then assess their technique of history-taking, which she always emphasised was the most critical part of examining a patient. Gradually, she would guide them through the differential diagnoses of the case before encouraging them to suggest appropriate treatment plans.

Many a time, she employed what she called the 'blind-teaching method.' Here, students were asked to select what they felt was a particularly difficult case—one that Madhuri herself had no prior knowledge of—and work it up fully on their own. The next morning, Madhuri would examine the patient in front of them and explain, in an open-book fashion, how she arrived at her conclusions. She seldom made a mistake, and her methodical approach would often lead to the identification of rare diseases. Over time, an aura built up around her as both a doctor and a teacher.

While the undergraduates were her primary interest, Madhuri also guided postgraduate students in a highly organised manner. Postgraduates are expected to study and work independently, particularly for their theory component. Just as she helped undergraduates structure their learning and develop clinical acumen with patience, she focused on honing the postgraduates' critical thinking skills and grounding their arguments in sound logic.

As specialists, they would eventually work independently, offer important clinical opinions, and help formulate treatment protocols. Drawing from her own experience, Madhuri often devised simple solutions to complex problems, and she encouraged her students to do the same. She urged them to think boldly and break away from conventional approaches. She also pushed them to take up basic but original research for their theses, discouraging the production of standardised, cut-and-paste submissions. This nudged them into reading more deeply and absorbing the fundamentals of research methodology.

Indeed, such was her impact as a teacher that during her tenure at AFMC, she was honoured as the 'Best Teacher in the State' by the Maharashtra University of Health Sciences.

The Seniority Conundrum

In 2006, Madhuri was considered and approved for promotion to the rank of colonel. Until then, her name had consistently figured at the top of her batch merit list, as she had graduated first in her class in 1982. However, when the seniority list of her batch was published following her selection to colonel, Madhuri was shocked to find her name pushed to the bottom. In effect, she had lost seniority to officers who had ranked below her when they passed out of AFMC.

Madhuri had not been aware that selection to a permanent commission at this stage would affect her seniority. Recognising the seriousness of the matter, she formally initiated a case for rectification of the anomaly. The initial letters that had granted her the President's Commission were revisited to check if anything had been overlooked. The spirit of those instructions clearly suggested that short service officers who were granted permanent commission upon due consideration were not supposed to lose their original seniority. It was understood that the seniority of such officers would be aligned with their inter-se merit at the time of graduation from AFMC.

The logic behind this policy appeared to rest on two key factors. Most importantly, both SS and PC officers underwent the same study period. Therefore, the only rational basis for inter-se seniority was the merit at graduation. The second factor applied particularly to lady officers as due to organisational constraints, only one woman cadet was offered PC at the time of entry into the institution, not after completing her undergraduate studies. This made the system inherently unequal and skewed against women cadets.

Keeping these considerations in mind, Madhuri appealed to her departmental authorities to review and correct the anomaly. It took some time for the hierarchy to deliberate before she received a standard reply. The message essentially stated that, after considering all relevant factors, her seniority had been finalised in accordance with the existing rules. To us, it seemed that the authorities had inadvertently applied the seniority model used for SS officers in other arms and services. In their case, the training duration for SS and PC officers differs. Hence, upon being granted PC, SS officers are typically placed lower in seniority. However, applying the same logic to SS medical officers, whose training is identical, appeared both inaccurate and inappropriate.

At that juncture in Madhuri's career, we felt that reopening the case and escalating it further would trigger a chain of undesirable administrative actions, especially at a sensitive turning point in her professional journey. We concluded that the issue could be revisited at a more opportune time, if required. In service life, sometimes it is wiser to allow matters to resolve themselves. On that hopeful note, the issue was set aside, and Madhuri returned her full attention to her two enduring passions: teaching and treating.

The Professor's Dilemma and Delivery

After being promoted, Madhuri continued with her responsibilities as a member of the faculty. She had enjoyed her tenure thus far, though the seniority setback had briefly upset her. But now that we had decided to set it aside for the time being, she was back to her usual self-confident and full of zest. Since she had already served as faculty for a couple of years, we assumed that a posting was likely in the near future. I was halfway through my command tenure at Bhatinda, and we both felt the need to be together, especially since it had been almost five years since we were last posted in the same station.

It was against this backdrop that Madhuri mentioned to me an upcoming visit of the head of medical services to AFMC for the annual review of the institution. This is an important event during which medical research proposals are evaluated before final approval. Madhuri was part of the audience and not directly involved in the proceedings. It would be her HoD, as the professor, who was expected to speak if required.

As the discussions progressed, the topic of paediatric research came up. At that moment, the senior officer unexpectedly turned towards the audience and asked for comments from Professor Madhuri Kanitkar. There was pin-drop silence in the hall. Everyone was aware that Madhuri was not yet a professor and that the current HoD was someone else. When this was pointed out to the senior officer, he calmly responded that he knew who the current incumbent was but that he was referring to the incoming HoD. A brief silence followed as the entire auditorium absorbed the implication. Madhuri's elevation to professor and HoD was being announced albeit in a most unorthodox manner!

It was a completely unexpected development. Just as we were discussing our future course of action at home, this announcement changed the game for us—partly in our favour, and partly not. Madhuri had not anticipated this promotion, as there were several paediatricians senior to her in the AMC, all of whom had strong aspirations for the position of HoD at AFMC. The role carried prestige and honour, making it highly sought after.

The decision to bypass more senior colleagues generated considerable buzz and intense discussion within the fraternity. Madhuri was set to become one of the youngest HoDs in recent memory. Those who recognised and appreciated her commitment and capability were genuinely thrilled and gave her wholehearted support. However, others were critical of the move, feeling that this disregard for seniority set a worrying precedent, and their discontent was palpable. This undercurrent of negativity meant that Madhuri would now need even greater reserves of motivation and resilience to stay afloat and thrive.

We had to adapt quickly to this unexpected turn. The upside was that Madhuri would likely continue at AFMC for at least two more years. This would give Vibhuti time to complete high school and Nikhil to finish his engineering studies while still having their mother close by. The downside was that I would have to continue living away from them for a while longer. Yet, in the larger scheme of things, we concluded that maintaining continuity was the better choice.

Her new appointment gave Madhuri the chance to shape the paediatric department in line with her vision. She was excited by the possibilities that lay ahead. And thus began her journey in leadership.

Vision Plan 2020

Madhuri had been reflecting deeply not only on various aspects of teaching and training at AFMC but also on how the field of paediatrics should evolve within the armed forces. There was a growing need to introduce additional sub-specialities in line with advancements in childcare. Equally essential was the formulation of a long-term plan for their phased introduction, development, and structured training of future trainers in each sub-speciality. In cases where facilities were not available within the country, select training would have to be undertaken abroad. This, in turn, would enable subsequent training to be conducted in India and help expand the pool of specialists within the organisation.

Another key area was research. It was important to establish a more rigorous and relevant research framework, one that addressed real-world medical challenges and contributed meaningfully to treatment outcomes. The establishment of research laboratories and the creation of a dedicated pool of researchers were vital to this vision. Equally important was the integration of information technology to advance research, training, and treatment methodologies. She also envisioned developing an integrated mother and childcare concept, which she believed could be implemented in select nodal centres of the armed forces hospitals.

All these initiatives were consolidated into a formal document that outlined the concept, vision, mission, phases, and timelines for specific deliverables at each stage of implementation. In 2007-08, she released this document into the public domain under the title *Vision Plan 2020*. When she returned to AFMC as the dean in 2017, she gave the final push to realise this plan—and even went beyond it—achieving the goals well ahead of schedule.

Snippets from Bhatinda

After completing a two-year tenure in Delhi, I was posted to a formation in Bhatinda. It was a prestigious command, and I had the opportunity to independently emphasise various facets of professional training. My underlying philosophy was simple: train hard, train true. I insisted on high standards of both theoretical understanding and practical excellence in the art and science of warfare, especially with regard to mobile, mechanised operations. Our formation could be tasked with operations anywhere along the Western Front, so it was essential to know the terrain thoroughly and ensure that we were always an overmatch for our adversary. This required a high level of readiness in both training and leadership. That was the thrust of my time in Bhatinda.

Madhuri joined me briefly when I assumed command and quickly endeared herself to everyone she met, in her inimitable style. Her easy conviviality, natural ability to put people at ease, empathy for the troops, and the quiet confidence she exuded were—and still are—remarkable assets. I never had to worry that she was a short-duration visitor. In social interactions, she was always the centre of attention, effortlessly so and never overbearing, which can often be a pitfall in a hierarchical setup. Her presence had a lasting effect as well. Even when she wasn't physically around, people felt her influence. In many ways, her warm personality rounded off my quieter nature and made me seem less officious, perhaps even more approachable, as a commander.

In 2006, Nikhil completed his engineering degree and moved to Delhi for his first job. He had secured a placement as a business analyst and was based in Gurugram. One of my fondest memories from the Bhatinda days was our weekend time together. I was then living alone in the Commander's House—along with Coco and Peppy, my loyal companions since Delhi—and Nikhil's visits were always something to look forward to. He would take the overnight train from Delhi and arrive early Saturday morning, spending the weekend with me before taking the late-night train back on Sunday to be at work Monday morning.

A keen sportsman, he made good use of the excellent sports facilities within the cantonment. My own social life became livelier during his visits. We would also occasionally head out to the countryside which were truly enjoyable outings. These Bhatinda-special memories remain vivid and continue to bring smiles whenever we recall those father-son days. They helped carry us through the times we had to be apart.

Our 25th Marriage Anniversary

An important landmark of the Bhatinda days was our 25th wedding anniversary on 16 November 2007. I had been at Bhatinda for over a year by then. As is customary in the army, the winter months are often earmarked for outdoor training. Accordingly, most of the formation units had moved out for their respective training schedules. I would visit each unit or subunit periodically to assess the standard of training and provide guidance for further improvement. Much of my time was spent in the adjoining desert terrain, where we conducted manoeuvre-based training exercises. All these efforts had to be coordinated into a single large-scale exercise under my supervision, with the aim of creating synergy in the application of force and manoeuvre on the battlefield. In pursuit of these objectives, I remained deeply engaged with the professional calendar.

One fine day, Madhuri called to say that she was considering taking a week's leave around the time of our anniversary. Since it was our 25th, she felt it was the perfect occasion to celebrate with close family and express our gratitude for their steadfast support through the years. It was this support that had kept us together, even though circumstances often kept us apart. In times of need, each one of them had contributed to stabilising our home front, and it felt like the right moment to say a heartfelt 'Thank You' by hosting them in Bhatinda.

I was initially a little apprehensive about the logistics, as it involved coordinating travel for most of our family from Pune to Delhi, and then from Delhi to Bhatinda and repeating the same for their return. Both our sets of parents were in their seventies or early eighties, so it was important to ensure safe and comfortable arrangements. Fortunately, I had a large independent bungalow with a lovely garden as my residence in Bhatinda, and there was ample guest accommodation nearby for everyone else. After some hesitation, I agreed to the plan. Madhuri offered to handle all travel arrangements from Pune onwards, while I would take charge of their reception and stay in Bhatinda.

On my part, I reorganised the training schedule to ensure I could remain in Bhatinda for those few days around the anniversary. Madhuri began coordinating with all our close relatives and friends for a three-day get-together. It was a hectic task for her as she had to make rail reservations to Delhi, manage their reception there, and then arrange for their onward journey to Bhatinda by overnight train. Nikhil, who was based in Delhi, proved to be a huge help, coordinating logistics both there and later in Bhatinda.

A day before the rest of the family travelled, Madhuri reached Delhi. She personally received the senior members of the family at the railway station, ensured they were comfortable, and helped them transition to the next train for Bhatinda later that night. Back in Bhatinda, I was able to take a break as planned. Thankfully, all the logistic arrangements made by Madhuri went off smoothly, and soon everyone was settled comfortably in and around our residence.

The following few days were filled with joy and warmth. For the younger lot, there were water sports and a chance to explore some of our military equipment. Bhatinda Cantonment is among the best organised in the country, and visits to various parts of it, as well as to nearby locales, added to the experience.

Time passed quickly, and before we knew it, it was time for everyone to head back. Once again, Madhuri managed the return arrangements seamlessly. With Nikhil assisting her, the return journey was executed with the same efficiency that defines her. She had accounted for every detail. It was a celebration truly befitting the occasion, and the memories of those days remain etched in our minds.

During my tenure in Bhatinda, I had put all my energies into preparing the troops for the ultimate eventuality—war. I derived immense satisfaction from executing the large-scale manoeuvres I had long envisioned, training my entire formation to the standards I had aspired to. Our focus was on achieving operational efficiency by day and night, maintaining sustained momentum, and excelling in accurate firing and sound tactical drills. I believe we made significant strides.

It was time to bid farewell to the formation in March 2008. By then, my request for co-location with Madhuri in Pune had been accepted, and I was assigned a key post at HQ Southern Command. While I felt a tinge of sadness in leaving behind my formation, it was accompanied by a deep sense of joy as I looked forward to reuniting with my family once again.

Together Again

Meanwhile, Madhuri continued with her work as the HoD. In recognition of her meritorious service, she was awarded the Chief of Army Staff Commendation once again in early 2008. This reaffirmation boosted her momentum in implementing the Vision Plan she had outlined for her department. Her teaching methodology, along with the emphasis she placed on original research by her postgraduate students, began to reflect in their improved academic performance. The articles they published in medical journals carried more substance and relevance.

She also streamlined the department's administration to ensure that PG students were not burdened with mundane administrative tasks. This allowed them to focus more intently on their studies, without unnecessary distractions. The resulting academic environment fostered stronger bonds between faculty and students, making the department a more vibrant and academically conducive space.

Madhuri was fortunate to have the support of excellent colleagues, all of whom were inspired by her forward-looking ideas. Each had their strengths, and Madhuri had mastered the art of recognising and highlighting those. She allocated responsibilities based on temperament and capability, which led to an exceptionally amiable work environment. This, in turn, translated into enhanced productivity in both teaching and administration. Over time, she nurtured a winning blend of professionalism and social camaraderie that encouraged positivity for faculty and students alike.

It would not be out of place to say that the students who were part of this outstanding paediatrics family benefitted immensely. Today, many of them are accomplished doctors in various paediatric sub-specialities, just as Madhuri had envisioned. It gives her immense satisfaction to know that she and her team were able to elevate the field of paediatrics within the armed forces to an altogether different level.

After I joined Madhuri in Pune, we decided to shift to military accommodation closer to our workplaces, as this offered greater administrative convenience for both of us. The only downside of this move was for Vibhuti. She had just graduated from high school in March 2008 with a fair score and had secured admission to a good college for her further studies. However, our relocation to the cantonment meant she would now have to travel daily to the other side of town for her college routine.

She had just turned sixteen, and Madhuri was not in favour of her using a mini two-wheeler to navigate the dense city traffic every day. Vibhuti, on the other hand, felt she was old enough to handle things on her own and that an independent means of transport was essential. It became a classic adolescent-versus-parent standoff. Madhuri told her that I would make the final decision after weighing the pros and cons.

I wasn't fully aware of the undercurrent between the two of them until Vibhuti raised the issue with me that evening. She assured me she would be very careful if allowed to use a two-wheeler for her daily commute. Madhuri was not present during this conversation, and from what I heard, it seemed like a reasonable and time-saving option, especially when compared to the discomfort of bus travel. Perhaps I didn't fully register the safety concerns that were uppermost in Madhuri's mind. After listening to Vibhuti, I gave her my consent.

As soon as Madhuri returned from work, Vibhuti triumphantly announced that she was about to get her new two-wheeler. Madhuri was clearly taken aback. She felt that the decision had been taken a little too hastily, without due deliberation. It was a mild rap on the knuckles for the father-daughter duo. However, she agreed that since the decision had already been made, we could try it out for a while. If at any point it was felt that her commute wasn't safe, Vibhuti would switch to travelling by bus. Thus, the issue was resolved with a fair amount of adjustment and compromise. In the process, we got a firsthand experience of how an adolescent mind works and resolved to tread more carefully in future such situations!

The months that followed remained busy for both Madhuri and me. My assignment at HQ Southern Command was operational in nature and involved a constant flow of work, often extending into late hours. Madhuri, too, remained engaged, especially with her PG students. While we were now together geographically, our respective work schedules left little room for quality time with each other. Still, the comfort of being in the same city, and a sense of quiet contentment, made up for that absence in their own way.

As for Vibhuti, the first year of junior college was a refreshing change after the grind of the high school Board exams. It was a time of newfound freedom and independence and also of learning. With her new scooter, she quite literally took to the streets and thoroughly enjoyed her first year. She had a wonderful circle of friends, and we often had fun interacting with them and listening to their lively conversations.

Nikhil, meanwhile, continued with his job as a business analyst in Delhi. His work involved long hours, and at times, we could sense a trace of weariness in him. Still, he was learning quickly and had made new friends at his workplace. His mature outlook, combined with his easy-going nature, helped him build close associations with those around him.

As is usually the case, time seemed to pass swiftly, and we were approaching the end of the year. Around this time, I received news that my recent performance report had not been very encouraging. This could potentially affect my future promotion prospects. In the army, such assessments are often further reinforced—or mitigated—by whether an officer is nominated for the prestigious National Defence College (NDC) Course. Quite unexpectedly, in the first week of November 2008, I received a phone call informing me of my selection for the NDC. I was taken aback and waited for the official confirmation to believe it.

Madhuri, ever the optimist, had always maintained that someone, somewhere, would look out for us and ensure no harm would come my way. Her belief, once again, proved prophetic. As she said, good people in the right places had done what was fair and just. The official letter arrived the very next day which was an encouraging sign for the road ahead.

A few days later, Madhuri and I hosted a small social gathering at our residence. Our time in Pune had been a busy one, and the evening gave us a chance to thank friends and colleagues and express our gratitude. I was scheduled to leave for the NDC Course in the first week of January 2009. The running joke that evening was that it was a 'normal delivery.' Meaning, I had reported to HQ Southern Command in April 2008 and was departing after a full term of nine months. Even in uniform, humour finds its place!

The Delhi-Pune Split

I reached Delhi in the first week of the new year. All NDC students are allotted excellent accommodation in the heart of the city. Although I would be living alone for the most part, I opted for family quarters so that Madhuri could stay with me during her leave. Around this time, I also spoke to Nikhil about the possibility of him moving in with me. This would mean he would need to commute daily to his workplace from Central Delhi. After considering it, he agreed to shift in. And so, we ended up with a two and two split across the two cities: the father-son duo, with Coco and Peppy, in Delhi, and the mother-daughter duo, along with Pixie, in Pune.

The NDC Course has a unique and enriching curriculum. It focuses on geo-political, economic, diplomatic, and military issues, both at the national and international levels. The participants include high-performing officers from all branches of the Indian Armed Forces, officers from the armed forces of friendly foreign countries (FFCs), and representatives from the All India Civil Services. The result is a diverse and experienced cohort drawn from various walks of life, making for high-level discussions and interactions rarely found elsewhere.

Over the course of a year, participants engage in a robust exchange of ideas and perspectives. As part of the programme, three international visits are organised, enabling attendees to explore foreign policy, strategic partnerships, and global institutions first-hand. These experiences significantly widen participants' horizons and are especially valuable, since many go on to occupy key policy-making roles in their respective domains. The relationships built during the course also pave the way for mutual understanding and collaboration in future endeavours.

During my NDC tenure, the pace of academic work was demanding but well-balanced, allowing for effective learning without being overbearing. A particularly enjoyable aspect of the course was that Madhuri was permitted to accompany me on all three foreign visits. After each official visit, we had the opportunity to take a short spell of leave, allowing us to explore nearby regions before returning home. Thanks to this, Madhuri and I were able to travel through a wide range of countries across the Middle East, Europe, and some Indian Ocean island nations. These visits were not only professionally enriching but also immensely enjoyable for both of us.

Nikhil too had a rather interesting and enjoyable time while staying with me. There were many youngsters of his age in the residential complex, and he quickly formed a new circle of friends. Fortunately, he also found a colleague who commuted daily from Delhi to Gurugram for work. They arranged a shared travel setup, which made the daily commute more manageable.

Nikhil, sincere by nature, continued to put in long hours at his firm. However, over time, a sense of restlessness began to creep in. Occasionally, we would discuss whether he should consider a change—perhaps switch jobs or broaden his outlook. One option was to pursue a management course to deepen his knowledge and open new avenues. By then, he had acquired a fair amount of work experience, and it seemed like an appropriate time to contemplate a sabbatical.

He had stayed in touch with many of his engineering college friends, most of whom were also employed in various companies. The common refrain among them was that, while the work was demanding, personal fulfilment was often lacking. Over time, the idea of launching their own start-up began to gain traction within his close-knit group. When Nikhil mentioned this to Madhuri and me, we felt it was a promising option, provided they had clarity on the direction and viability of their venture.

Back in college, Nikhil and his friend Rohit had collaborated on an automation project, which had earned them recognition. They now wished to build on that foundation and were willing to quit their jobs to pursue this venture, planning to establish it in Pune as it was well-suited for technology-driven start-ups. Madhuri and I felt that if this experiment was to be undertaken, this was indeed the right time. They were young and energetic, and better equipped to navigate the inevitable hurdles ahead. Of course, they would also have to contend with the challenges of limited business experience and unfamiliarity with regulatory processes. While we knew this idea was being seriously considered, we were unaware of the exact timeline for its launch.

Then, one day in October 2009, Nikhil returned home from work in high spirits and announced that he had been promoted. We celebrated the news in typical bachelor style. The next morning, he left for office in an upbeat mood. However, that evening, he came back with another announcement. Curious, I asked what it was and was told that he had resigned from his job. It took me by surprise, and for a moment, I was speechless. Not quite sure how to react, I figured a glass of beer might be the best response and that is exactly what we did. We raised a toast to the beginning of a new phase in his life. Nikhil and his friends had made the bold decision to relocate to Pune and formally register their start-up later that month.

So, before I could complete my NDC Course, Nikhil—after an instructive and formative stint as a business analyst—set off to start his own venture with his close friends. It was their dream to be job providers, not jobseekers. Honestly, Madhuri and I were proud of their decision to chart their own course, and we assured them of our full support in whatever way we could contribute.

My course was scheduled to conclude in late November. I had hoped that I would be posted within Delhi after its completion, which would have allowed us to request the medical authorities to transfer Madhuri there as well. She could then have taken the opportunity to establish a new paediatric nephrology unit in the capital. However, that request was not accepted. I informed Madhuri of the development and advised her to continue her work in Pune for as long as possible.

When the postings were announced at the end of the course, I found myself assigned to an appointment in Leh, while several of my course-mates received postings in Delhi. I must admit, this came as a disappointment. I did feel dejected for a while. But eventually, I came to terms with it, telling myself that something good would come of it in due course.

After the course concluded, I returned to Pune for a month-long break. I was then to report to my new headquarters in Leh in the first week of January 2010.

The Pune Panorama

It was good to be back in Pune for a while. Vibhuti was in her second year of junior college and was scheduled to graduate after the upcoming semester, after which she would move on to her career-oriented studies. She had dropped mathematics as a subject in the 12th standard and was now leaning more towards the liberal arts. For several years, she had also been training in Bharat Natyam (a classical Indian dance form) and had now reached the level of *arangetram*. This was the culmination of the initial phase of formal training in the art. But the daily rehearsals were taking up much of her time, and we began to worry that it might be affecting her academic performance. When we suggested that she pause her dance practice for a while, she firmly declined. She assured us that she would complete her arangetram in December and then dedicate the next three months fully to her studies in preparation for the final exams. We were sceptical of this plan, but seeing her conviction, we decided to let her follow through.

Given her creative disposition and her natural flair for sketching and painting, it seemed that the National Institute of Design (NID) in Ahmedabad would be a good fit for her higher studies. She too was interested but eventually told us she preferred to pursue a course at a similar private institute that she felt offered greater freedom of expression and encouraged original thinking, in contrast to NID's more structured approach. She had her eyes set on a place called Shrishti in Bangalore. We hadn't heard of it before, but a quick online search revealed that it did seem aligned with Vibhuti's interests and aspirations.

But before any of that came her final exams and before even that, her arangetram. A great deal of effort goes into preparing for such a performance. The teacher-student relationship follows the traditional *guru-shishya* (teacher-disciple) model, and the days leading up to the event were packed with rehearsals and preparations. Her childhood friend performed alongside her, and together they gave a splendid performance before a large audience. Vibhuti looked visibly joyful and relieved that everything had gone off almost perfectly. Her teacher, above all, radiated satisfaction. Vibhuti could be temperamental at times, and her teacher had occasionally wondered whether she would see the training through. But Vibhuti was deeply fond of her teacher, and perhaps it was for her that she chose to complete the journey to prove to herself and to her teacher that she could do it.

True to her word, once the arangetram was over, Vibhuti turned her focus to academics. While her performance in the preliminary exams wasn't particularly encouraging, she held fast to her commitment and, in the final exams, performed creditably. Her results were declared in May 2010. Determined to secure admission into the Shrishti Institute of Art, Design, and Technology, Vibhuti took matters into her own hands. She cleared the online written exam and travelled to Bangalore to appear for the interview stage. She did well and earned admission to the institute. Through it all, Madhuri and I played no part. A fiercely independent girl, Vibhuti was confident in handling this new chapter of her life on her own. She even finalised her accommodation and returned to Pune feeling highly accomplished. We were happy for her, and it felt like she had truly found her calling.

Madhuri helped Vibhuti prepare for life in a hostel and later accompanied her to Bangalore in June to help her get oriented with her new surroundings. When the moment finally came to say goodbye, Madhuri felt a tug at her heart. But she knew that Vibhuti was more than capable of handling things and so, with a quiet au revoir, she returned to Pune.

All through Vibhuti's transition, I hadn't been of much help since I was stationed in Leh. All I could do was hope that she would settle into her new way of life and, more importantly, that she would enjoy the field of study she had chosen. Meanwhile, Madhuri received her posting orders; she was to report to Base Hospital, Delhi, by the first week of July 2010.

And just like that, life came full circle once more. Our small family was splitting up in four different directions. Nikhil and his friends had established their technology-based company and were working hard to build a solid foundation for their venture. The new configuration meant Nikhil would now be the lone ranger in Pune, with Vibhuti holding the fort down south in Bangalore, Madhuri at the central pivot in Delhi, and I manning the northern frontier in Leh. It was, in military terms, a linear deployment of our family, each one roughly two hours of flying time from the other. Not bad at all! All independent, each living their own lives, free from interference. And so, in

July 2010, our little clan deployed itself in its latest avatar to take on life head-on.

Throughout the first decade of the new millennium, we were constantly playing catch-up as a family. Still, Nikhil and Vibhuti were fortunate to enjoy a stable schooling phase in Pune for the most part. Madhuri made her mark by establishing the first paediatric nephrology unit in the city, and her professionalism earned her a place on the AFMC faculty. When the children reached a crucial stage in their education, she was selected—out of turn—to head the department of paediatrics at her alma mater. It was a time when she could apply her full range of skills as both a doctor and a teacher. In many ways, it was a fitting recognition of her expertise and a reward for years of consistent, solid work, often carried out in isolation. Before she moved from Pune to Delhi, she was awarded the Chief's Commendation Card for her exemplary service as head of paediatrics. This marked the third time her contributions were formally recognised by the chief, and it felt like a sign of greater things to come.

Postscript by Madhuri

The nine long years from 2001 to 2010—summarised in this section—were the most meaningful for us, both professionally and personally. During this entire period, Rajeev and I were together for barely two years. That demanded a great deal of adjustment from all four of us. It was, without doubt, the most productive phase of our professional lives and also the time when the children most needed guidance and support for their own futures. Being split into three or four geographical outposts was tough. Looking back, perhaps that very hardship helped our children grow into fiercely independent, confident, and successful individuals, but it came at the cost of a missed family atmosphere and the daily struggle of what often felt like a single-mother existence.

For me, it was emotionally exhausting to shoulder every responsibility alone. What made it harder were the occasional unkind remarks from some insensitive colleagues about our long-distance relationship. Over time, we learnt to take such jibes in stride and simply keep marching on. The running joke was, 'Money can buy everything. For the rest, there is the army!' Or, when asked why we were never posted together, my tongue-in-cheek response would be that the policy stated, 'Spouses will be posted together as far as possible.' In our case, it was always interpreted as 'as FAAAR as possible!'

Humour in uniform also came in unexpected ways, like when either of us was asked by a colleague, 'Do you happen to know the other Kanitkar in uniform from the Armoured Corps or the Medical Corps?' Over time, we learnt to respond to that question with a smile, even though the strain of being apart weighed on us from within.

Madhuri at age 2, October 1962

The teen *deviyas* (goddesses) growing up in Japan, 1970s

Madhuri's parents

With my parents and siblings

Speedy the sprinter at AFMC

Madhuri dons my first saree gift, June 1980

My first buy (a Yezdi) with a loan of five thousand rupees, 1985

Award for topping first MBBS, 1980

With top honours at NDA, June 1977

Freshly minted officer,
Lieutenant Madhuri Khot

Madhuri with her best friends,
Neena and Sunita, at AFMC

Young Officers' Course, 1979

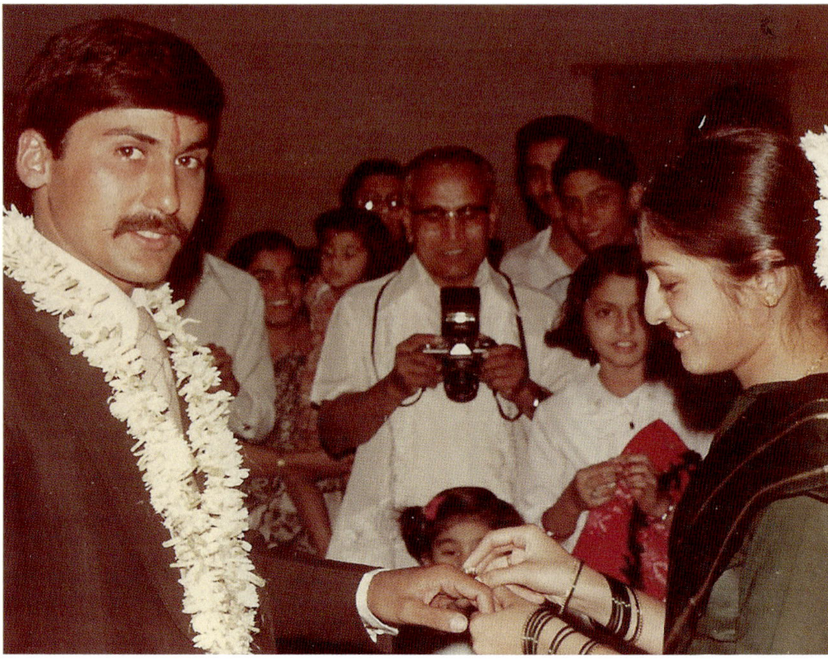

Our engagement, January 1981

Our wedding, November 1982

Madhuri passing out of AFMC with top honours, December 1982

Nikhil made us parents, 1985

Blessed with our Rani of Jhansi,
Vibhuti, March 1992

As budding officers, 1994

Commandant and first lady, 2000

Madhuri at NUHS, Singapore, 2000

Professor and HOD, AFMC, 2008

During fellowship training at
Great Ormond Street, London, 2001

Paediatric nephrology team, AFMS

As the first paediatric nephrologist in the armed forces with her young patients

Renovated ward, Delhi hospital

On the greens at Bhatinda

First lessons in horse riding

Brigade commander and better half

While in Delhi as QMG

I become a major general

As a brigadier and lieutenant general in Delhi, 2016

With Peppy

With Coco

Our 25th anniversary, Bhatinda, 2007

Nikhil and Tejas getting hitched in Bhopal

Vibhuti graduates from the University of Michigan

Madhuri being awarded the PVSM

Madhuri at Siachen

Madhuri's promotion to major general, 2017

The Kanitkar clan together, 2008

Growing together without growing apart

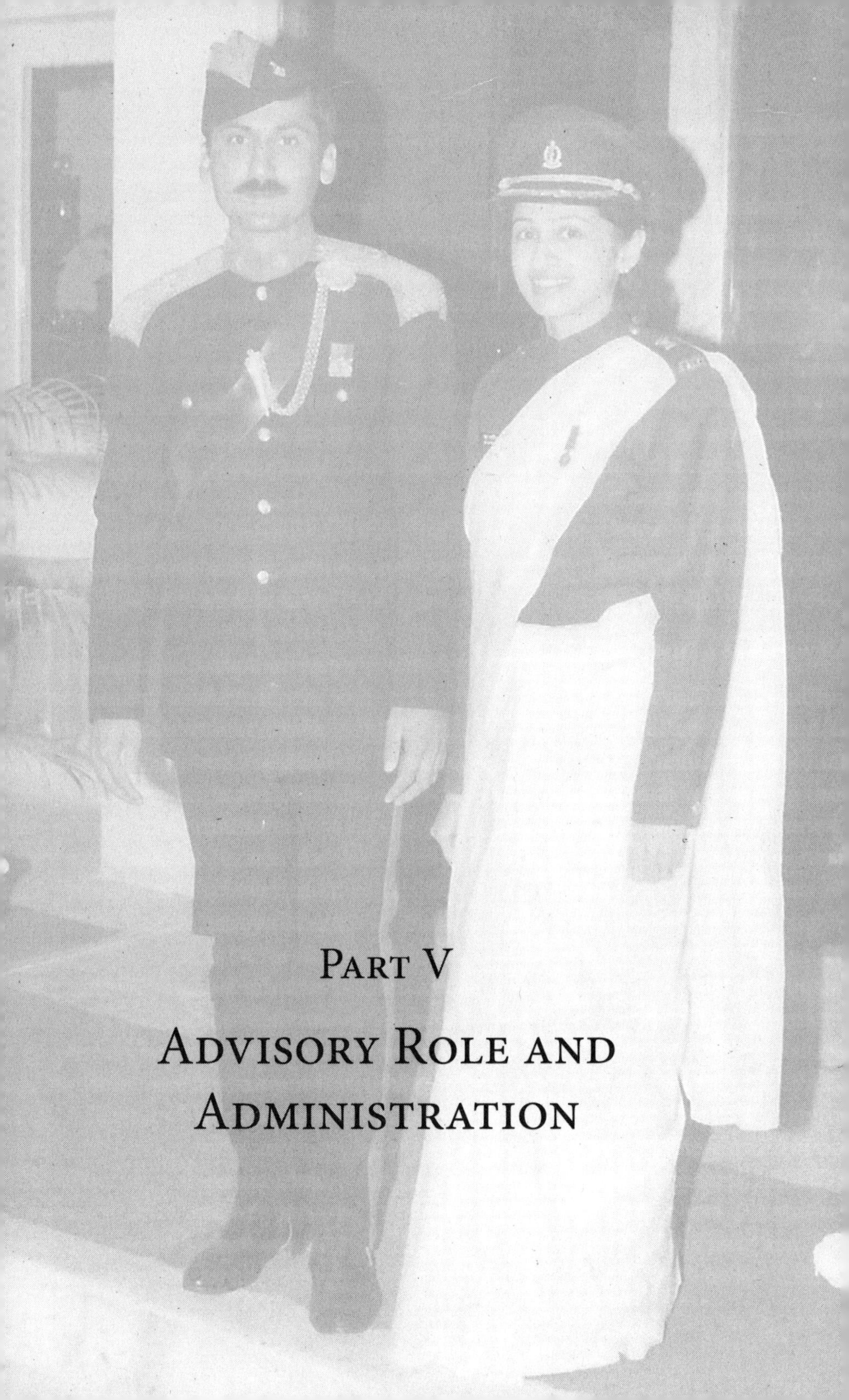

Part V
Advisory Role and Administration

Chapter 12

Four Locations, One Family

The North-South Axis

Life began anew for all of us as the family found itself spread along a 3,000 km axis from Leh to Bangalore. I was stationed up north in Leh, forming the head; Madhuri, posted in Delhi, was the heart; Nikhil, in Pune, stood strong as the spine; and Vibhuti, at the southern tip in Bangalore, was all set to strike out independently. While the downside of this arrangement was the sheer vertical spread of our physical separation, the upside was that any point along this axis—especially Pune or Delhi—could be reached within a few hours, thanks to improved and more economical air connectivity. We decided to make the best of this evolving infrastructure and vowed to remain connected and continue our journey of staying together while being apart.

Madhuri Anchors Herself in Delhi

As always, the first hurdle to cross was finding suitable accommodation. Thankfully, the situation was far simpler this time as our children had grown up and were now managing independently. Since I was posted in Leh, Madhuri had only herself to worry about for the time being. She was allotted a single room at the Officers' Mess near the base hospital in Delhi, her new workplace. It was reasonably good accommodation, and the location was convenient and ideal for the moment.

At the same time, since I was in a field posting, I was entitled to apply for separated family accommodation in Delhi. I exercised that option, and we were allotted a small family apartment. Madhuri shifted there and, as always, got the house up and running with her trademark efficiency. A few months later, she was allotted upgraded accommodation in her own right—a lucky break that was most welcome. She moved into the new quarters with a huge sigh of relief. The place was neat, comfortable, and modern and just right for her needs.

Posting to Base Hospital

Ideally, with her qualifications and professional record, Madhuri should have been posted to the Army Hospital Research and Referral or AHRR, in Delhi, where her skills would have been most effectively utilised. However, there was no vacancy at AHRR, and she was posted instead to the base hospital.

In Delhi, AHRR and base hospital are comparable to AIIMS and Safdarjung Hospital, respectively. The base hospital has an excellent team of doctors to serve the substantial volume of patients who first report there for tertiary care. When a case exceeds the base hospital's capacity, it is referred to AHRR, where the most critically ill are treated by specialists with advanced qualifications. Naturally, there is a sense of pride and prestige in being posted to AHRR. That honour, however, was not Madhuri's this time.

But true to form, Madhuri did not dwell on this minor setback. Her professional reputation had already reached Delhi before she did. Once she settled in, her presence began to be felt across the medical community in the city. Her patient list began growing rapidly, and soon, many of the VIP referrals concerning paediatric cases started getting directed not to AHRR but to the base hospital. I still remember her matter-of-fact declaration: 'I don't need AHRR. But BHDC and the patients need me!'

Challenges and Opportunities at Base Hospital

The base hospital at Delhi was located in old barracks, much like the Command Hospital at Pune. Space was at a premium, with several portions under prolonged repair. Even the neonatal intensive care facilities were inadequate. In addition, Madhuri needed space to establish a nephrology unit for children in Delhi. She surveyed the areas in need of repair and soon drafted a plan to revitalise the entire layout of the paediatrics department. Fortunately, she had the support of commandants who were open to her ideas. Her plans got a timely boost when some senior officers visited the base hospital. During their interactions, they were greatly impressed by her suggestions for improving the infrastructure and promptly sanctioned significant resources to initiate the upgrades. They also expressed a desire to revisit the hospital once the proposed changes were in place. This proved immensely helpful, as it provided both motivation and a deadline for the administrative and construction teams tasked with implementation.

Within a year, much of the foundational work had been completed. Madhuri had created a phased plan for execution, and subsequent officers continued the work, eventually establishing the kind of department she had envisioned. A new paediatric intensive care unit (PICU) was set up with modern equipment, including a state-of-the-art monitoring system. Adequate facilities for a nephrology unit were also developed. All the wards were renovated in bright colours to make the environment cheerful—an important factor in aiding children's recovery. The wards were reorganised to separate the more serious cases from those less ill, allowing better treatment protocols to be followed. Even the needs of the caregivers—mostly mothers—were taken into account.

This compassion-filled, patient-centric approach brought immense satisfaction to Madhuri and was deeply appreciated by the families under her care. In recognition of her tireless efforts, she was once again awarded the Chief's Commendation Card for outstanding service.

The Teacher Role and ACMS

During this time, Madhuri also continued her role as a teacher and mentor to several postgraduate students working in her ward. It was a role she cherished deeply, and her students greatly valued her clinical insight and sharp analytical and decision-making abilities. This facet of her work came into sharper focus due to the base hospital's affiliation with the Army College of Medical Sciences (ACMS), located adjacent to it. Her experience and training at AFMC were now being extended to a broader audience, many of whom were children of service personnel.

Her strong association with ACMS would prove crucial later when the institution faced existential challenges. When those challenges finally arrived, they were in the form of bureaucratic hurdles and inter-service differences of opinion that threatened its very continuation. However, after extensive discussions at the highest levels, ACMS was retained for the larger good of the armed forces. Madhuri's role in preserving it was both timely and significant.

The Leh Sideshow

I arrived in Leh in the second week of January 2010 to take charge of a new assignment—overseeing all logistical issues across the Ladakh region. It was a challenging but fascinating role that offered a steep learning curve from day one.

When I took off from Pune, the temperature was a comfortable 25°C. After transiting through Delhi, I landed in Leh early the next morning, only to be hit by a wall of freezing, rarefied air. The temperature outside was -19°C. In the space of twenty-four hours, I had experienced a 44-degree temperature drop. Thankfully, the formation HQ I reported to followed excellent standard operating procedures for coping with extreme cold. The first week was dedicated entirely to acclimatisation, essential for operating effectively at Leh's altitude of over 11,000 feet. At such elevations, every activity has to be done slowly and deliberately.

Soon, I immersed myself in learning the finer points of logistics management in Ladakh. For any practical soldier, the first task is familiarisation with the area of responsibility (AOR), understanding the terrain, the harsh weather, and how both impact men and material from a logistical standpoint. Our AOR covered a vast stretch of rugged mountain ranges and barren valleys with little vegetation. It was connected to mainland India by only two roadways: one from Srinagar to Leh via Kargil, and the other from Manali to Leh via Rohtang Pass. With no rail connectivity and just a single civilian airfield at Leh, logistics were heavily dependent on air transport. However, even this was constrained by the high-altitude environment, which significantly reduced aircraft lift capacity. All of this had to be factored in while planning and executing logistics operations in the region.

Over a period of time, I travelled to every nook and corner of the AOR and developed a sound understanding of the intricacies of logistics in particular. These journeys were undertaken both by road and by air, each offering a different perspective, both essential to comprehending the full operational implications. On some of these familiarisation tours, Madhuri was able to accompany me and had the rare opportunity to visit areas where very few women of the Indian Armed Forces had ever set foot. During our visit to the Siachen Base, she even tried her hand at ice-wall climbing and gained first-hand insight into the medical challenges faced by soldiers at extreme altitudes—18,000 feet and beyond. We also visited the breathtaking Pangong Tso and several other lakes in Eastern Ladakh. Alongside these natural wonders, the serene and mystifying gompas and monasteries were truly captivating. The broad bed of the Indus flowing through the valley, river rafting through its gorges, and the multi-hued mountains added to the unforgettable experience of nature's bounty that Madhuri shared with me.

On several weekends, when the loneliness of separation made itself felt, I would pack a small hamper and drive along the banks of the Indus River. Sometimes, I would stop by a bend in the river, sit quietly, and take in the majestic peaks around me—my constant companions and silent confidants.

In the monsoon of 2010, Leh Valley was struck by a severe natural disaster in the form of a cloudburst. This phenomenon involves an intense downpour in a short span of time, leading to sudden and destructive flooding. Given the barren terrain and lack of tree cover to absorb or slow the water flow, the deluge caused massive destruction, both in terms of human lives and material loss.

I woke up in the middle of the night to find myself quite literally floating on my bed as floodwaters had entered residences built on lower ground. Sensing the gravity of the situation and aware that communications could fail at any moment, I immediately called Madhuri to assure her of my safety. I told her I was evacuating my quarters, which were rapidly filling with water, to assist others in need. Wading through the rising waters, I made my way to the military hospital, which, fortunately, was located on higher ground and remained unaffected. But I knew it was only a matter of time before casualties from the civil areas would begin arriving in large numbers. My logistics team quickly mobilised to ensure safety and damage control across all military installations. Early the next morning, I moved out with the engineer officer to assess the scale of destruction, and it was extensive.

Over the following days, our top priority was saving lives. All of us in the logistics branch worked tirelessly to set up relief camps for civilians whose homes had been destroyed.

We provided shelter, food, and basic supplies until the affected families could begin rebuilding their lives. A few days later, the National Disaster Relief Organisation was activated and flown in to take over the formal relief operations. However, for us in logistics, a larger crisis was unfolding. The road network had suffered heavy damage. Many bridges had been washed away, cutting off supply routes and halting the daily movement of essential goods. Worse, the interior roadways were also rendered unusable, isolating several local communities. This disruption severely impacted what is known as the winter stocking process—a critical logistics operation undertaken for both the armed forces and civilians of the region.

Each year, the Ladakh region remains cut off from the rest of the country for nearly seven to eight months—from November to June—due to heavy snowfall and extreme weather conditions. To sustain life during this period, all essential supplies—food, fuel, clothing, and more—must be stocked in advance during the road-open season between July and October. The cloudburst occurred in early September 2010, and it took nearly a month to restore road connectivity. As a result, we lost precious time during the already narrow window for stocking supplies. By re-engineering alternate routes and mobilising additional air resources, we were finally able to complete our stocking operations just in the nick of time.

In a surprising turn of fortune, Mother Nature seemed to relent after the initial devastation. November brought relatively mild snowfall, buying us some extra time. We made the most of this reprieve and managed to complete the logistics arrangements needed to see the region through the long winter ahead.

Sometime in early 2011, the promotion board results for the rank of major general were declassified. The happy news of my approval for the next rank was a welcome morale booster after our intense engagement with the floods of 2010. There was a general indication that I would have to move out on promotion to take command of a formation around June 2011.

My tenure at Leh had been most interesting and rewarding. Fortunately, I enjoyed an amiable relationship with my superiors, and the posting offered real-life exposure to operational and logistic matters in some of the highest and most challenging battlefields in the world. In due course, I received my new assignment as a divisional commander and was required to report to the formation HQ at Ranchi to take over my new responsibilities in mid-June 2011, bringing my approximately 18-month stint at Leh to a close.

The Pune-Bangalore Highlights

Nikhil and his friends had launched their enterprise in earnest in November 2009. Though all of them were novices when it came to the intricacies of establishing a private company, we were proud that they had embraced the entrepreneurial path and taken on the challenge of building something from the ground up. Together, they defined a vision, a mission, and their individual roles within the team.

Their broad aim was to apply technology across various domains, particularly in enhancing security, managing assets, and improving customer value through their products and services. They began by developing automated solutions for different establishments and institutions. I still remember the grand celebration they had when they received their very first pay cheque—INR 10,000—after several months of effort. Before giving up their fairly lucrative corporate jobs, each of them had been earning more than ten times that amount. But the happiness of having earned it independently, through something they had built themselves, was a joy beyond comparison.

Over time, they realised that to be competitive, they needed to sharpen their focus and develop truly unique products. They came to understand that the technology space demanded constant innovation and that standing still was not an option. Eventually, they narrowed their focus to the niche area of applying RFID technology in the high-value jewellery industry—a sector with tremendous global demand. They also recognised that adoption of such technology might take longer in India due to the availability of low-cost labour. To address this, they decided to establish an additional base abroad, in a market where business processes were streamlined and governed by transparent rules. Nikhil's business partner, Rohit Karnik, who had completed his master's in Singapore, suggested they explore opportunities there and leverage the city-state's world-class infrastructure. Thus, Singapore emerged as a second base alongside Pune.

We were genuinely proud to see Nikhil and his friends take on this challenge with such dedication and determination. Throughout their initial struggles, our encouragement remained unwavering. Today, it is a pleasure to see them confident in their business environment, having learnt the ropes and mastered the nuances of their trade and navigating their chosen path with increasing ease and comfort.

At Bangalore, Vibhuti had begun her new life with full zest. She found herself among a very different set of people who were deeply immersed in creative design, art, and technology. The unique selling point of the institute she had joined was its emphasis on originality, freedom of expression, and flexibility in the choice of subject and workspaces. Freed from the pressures of technical subjects like maths and physics, she began to blossom into a person of ideas and ideation. She made new friends and was soon painting the town red with them. Bangalore's vibrant pub culture was a favourite with her group, and she would often share stories about the new life she was enjoying.

At times, we were naturally apprehensive about her safety, especially in a new city. However, Vibhuti had always been someone with a clear head and sound values. Over time, we came to meet some of her friends, and their warm personalities and camaraderie put us at ease.

On one occasion, Madhuri managed to coordinate a trip with the children to Leh. For military personnel posted in the difficult terrain of Ladakh, air travel on military aircraft is extended to their immediate families. I made arrangements for all of them to assemble at Chandigarh Military Station. From there, they boarded an IL-76 military aircraft—one of the largest aircraft in the world, of Russian origin—and flew into Leh one bright morning.

Because of the strong sun and rarefied atmosphere at Leh, all flights operate early in the morning, typically around 4 a.m., to allow for a return leg before the day gets too warm. So, after the initial thrill of boarding a service aircraft at such an unusual hour, both the children settled in for what would turn out to be an unforgettable experience. The seating arrangements in the aircraft allowed for sweeping views of the landscape, and the vast, majestic panorama outside likely left a lasting imprint on their minds.

In Leh, Nikhil and Vibhuti were overjoyed to reunite with Coco and Peppy. Both pets had taken a real liking to Leh and were by now an inseparable part of life in the Officers' Enclave. In particular, they loved romping around in the snow-covered areas around my hut during winter.

After proper acclimatisation, Madhuri and the children were able to visit several picturesque sites in and around Leh. The highlights included driving through some of the highest motorable passes in the world, like Khardung-La and Chang-La. They also visited the excellent Military Museum, which records the valour and history of our soldiers on the icy battlefields of Ladakh. All in all, I believe they had an experience that was truly unforgettable.

Such visits bring families face-to-face with the terrain, conditions, and sacrifices that military personnel endure, and in doing so, they create a deep and lasting sense of 'Nation First, Always and Every Time.' It is a dividend that is both intangible and irreplaceable.

Time to Move On

It had long been my parents' wish to visit me in Leh before I moved on to my next assignment in Ranchi. Accordingly, arrangements were made for them to travel from Pune to Delhi. From there, Madhuri was to accompany them on the final leg of the journey to Leh. Both parents were in their early-to-mid eighties, so we had to be mindful of their health parameters. My mother, in particular, was a little concerned about my father's ability to cope with the high altitude, but he was determined to make the trip.

The plan was for them to fly to Srinagar and then drive to Leh. However, just before their scheduled departure, the security situation in Jammu and Kashmir—and particularly in the Kashmir Valley—deteriorated due to operational reasons. Road movement became restricted, and even air travel was deemed inadvisable. As a result, the visit had to be cancelled.

Despite all our preparations, they were unable to see the place I had called home for the past year and a half. It left me with a lingering sense of incompletion as I took leave of the Ladakh region in June 2011.

Despite this one regret, I carried with me very fond memories of my time in that region. The operational and logistic lessons I learnt were immense, and they proved to be of great value to Madhuri later during her tenure as the officer in charge of medical care in Northern Command. Nikhil and Vibhuti, too, had been fortunate to visit me in Leh and savour the stunning tapestry of the Ladakh ranges. As I flew out over those majestic mountains one fine morning—along with Coco and Peppy—all these memories flooded my mind. I heaved a sigh that was equal parts joy and melancholy as I braced myself for the next innings at Ranchi. While I would now move to a new location, the rest of the family would remain in their respective places for the time being—Madhuri in Delhi, Nikhil in Pune, and Vibhuti in Bangalore.

Postscript by Madhuri

Rajeev has put it mildly, but for me, saying I was heartbroken would still be an understatement when I got posted to Delhi just after Rajeev moved out! Life was ironic; it felt like we were playing an endless game of kho-kho (a traditional South Asian sport). This time, we had truly hoped to be together. After all, many officers from the NDC batch had managed to remain posted in Delhi, but Rajeev had to move to Leh. It felt like fate was being unkind.

This turned out to be an extremely difficult period for me personally. I had never lived alone before, and for the first time, I truly realised how hard it must have been for Rajeev all these years to do just that. But with Nikhil starting his business in Pune and Vibhuti pursuing her studies at Srishti in Bangalore, I had little choice. I had to make an empty nest feel like home.

Thankfully, the Joshis became my extended family. Air Marshal Joshi and Manju went out of their way to make me feel at home. Their children—Arun, Arti, and Minal—and their grandkids truly became family. The professional satisfaction of enhancing patient care in one of the busiest hospitals in the country offered some much-needed solace.

Chapter 13

The Ranchi-Delhi Relay

Settling at Ranchi

Ranchi is the capital city of Jharkhand, a state carved out of the former Bihar (Ranchi used to be the summer capital of undivided Bihar). With an average elevation of 2,140 feet, it forms part of the Chota Nagpur Plateau. Thanks to its altitude and generous tree cover, Ranchi enjoys a pleasant climate, almost akin to that of a hill station. The cantonment area is greener and more well-planned than other parts of the city. My first impressions on arriving in Ranchi were positive, and I looked forward to my tenure there.

Besides this scenic and climatic backdrop, Ranchi also holds historical significance. During World War II, the legendary General William Slim—army commander of the 14th Army during the Burma Campaign—was stationed here for jungle warfare training. Interestingly, every divisional commander of the formation has since had the privilege of staying in the same residence once occupied by General Slim. The house, in truth, is just a long barrack divided into functional sections. One end houses the kitchen, followed sequentially, like compartments in a train, by the dining room, the living room, and finally, two bedrooms at the opposite end. An impressive garden stretches along the front of the house, forming a beautiful promenade. Nestled within the garden is a remarkable bonsai collection, arguably one of the best in the country in terms of quality, quantity, and age.

As a divisional commander, one is given great latitude in the training and administration of one's formation. In my case, the division was located far from its higher HQ, which meant fewer senior-level inspections or unplanned visits. This allowed me the freedom to focus on operational preparedness and administrative issues without frequent external interruptions.

There were, however, some peculiarities in the command and control structure. For instance, visiting my superior HQ, or even one of my sub-formations, required transiting through Delhi. This turned out to be a hidden blessing, as it gave me the opportunity to meet Madhuri during these travel breaks in and out of the capital.

Madhuri's Move to Ranchi

By June 2011, Madhuri and Pixie, who had accompanied her from Pune had spent a year in Delhi at the base hospital. On my way from Leh to Ranchi, I stopped at Delhi during my joining time. It was during this stopover that Madhuri and I decided to request the concerned medical authorities to consider posting her to the military hospital in Ranchi.

As a divisional commander, I could see the many advantages of having Madhuri by my side. In the armed forces, as one rises in seniority, the hierarchical gap between a senior officer and his subordinates also increases. Social interactions become more formal, and this distance can sometimes affect morale. The spouse of the commander plays a crucial role in bridging this gap, particularly in fostering camaraderie among the ladies of the station. The divisional commander's wife is considered first among equals in the ladies' circle, and the tone she sets has a cascading effect on the station's overall atmosphere. A sense of inclusion and warmth among the families often translates into a more harmonious and productive working environment. I believed Madhuri's presence would contribute meaningfully to this ethos and help me keep the formation well-aligned with its operational responsibilities.

We made our case to the director general, who jokingly raised an eyebrow and asked why I was keen on bringing another 'terrorist'—referring to the always-energetic Madhuri—into an insurgency-prone area like Ranchi. Before I could respond, Madhuri, ever quick on the uptake, replied with a grin: '*Kate ko kate se nikalne ke liye*' (To remove a thorn, you need another thorn). The DG burst out laughing and agreed to our request. He informed us that while the process might take some time, our case had been approved in principle. That alone was enough for us to feel hopeful.

As I settled into my responsibilities in Ranchi, Madhuri resumed work in Delhi with renewed energy, knowing that a transfer was on the horizon. She had already kept her commandant informed that she was pursuing a posting to Ranchi and now updated him about the DG's approval. While happy for her, the commandant made a fair point that, owing to the heavy workload in Delhi, he would only be able to relieve her once a replacement was posted. This was a bit of a dampener but understandable.

So, although Madhuri's posting orders were soon issued as per the DG's instructions, the actual move was delayed by the usual bureaucratic hurdle: the unavailability of a paediatrician to take her place. Days of waiting turned into weeks, and weeks into months. Finally, after a delay of nearly four months, Madhuri was able to join me in Ranchi in October 2011.

Tango During Command

It was the first time that the two of us were together during a command tenure. In my earlier stints as commanding officer—first at Hissar and Pathankot, and later while commanding a brigade in Bhatinda—Madhuri had been based elsewhere, most recently in Pune. But now, in Ranchi, she was finally able to join me, and that brought me great joy and comfort.

Madhuri reported to MH Namkum (near Ranchi) and quickly settled into her role as advisor in paediatrics. This was similar to her previous position in Delhi, although the patient load here was lighter, making the job somewhat less demanding.

Her commandant at MH Namkum was someone she had previously worked with at AFMC in Pune, and the mutual familiarity helped them establish a good working relationship from the outset. Madhuri's professional prowess had always gone beyond just her subject expertise, and she was also well-versed in the nuances of other specialities. Her teaching skills were widely acknowledged and admired. As the second-most senior officer in the hospital, she effectively functioned as the second-in-command. Meanwhile, the commandant had a strong administrative bent. It was decided that he would focus on the hospital's day-to-day operations while Madhuri would oversee its teaching and training initiatives. This arrangement proved to be an ideal partnership and contributed to a professionally rewarding and personally enjoyable tenure for both.

As GOC of the formation, I was able to support them with administrative and financial assistance. Madhuri also worked with the units through the ladies' welfare channels, launching several initiatives to improve patient care. This fostered a sense of ownership between the field units and the hospital, leading to more empathetic treatment protocols, improved ward upkeep, and a better healing environment. All this ultimately benefitted patient recovery.

On a broader level, I was able to restructure healthcare access for troops stationed at two different military locations under my command. While Ranchi had MH Namkum nearby, the other station depended on MH Bareilly, nearly two hours away. In consultation with Madhuri, I reallocated medical resources to improve access to the more remote station. Madhuri also reached out to MH Bareilly to sensitise them to the needs of our personnel in their area. Her efforts led to better coordination and understanding, resulting in improved healthcare services for both troops and their families. These changes, though seemingly minor, made a significant difference. They reduced travel and waiting time for medical attention, thereby boosting troop morale. Additionally, Madhuri initiated several health awareness and care programs for women and children, further enhancing the formation's overall well-being. In every sense, Madhuri's presence during my command was an invaluable asset.

When Madhuri first joined me in Ranchi, she was given a briefing on how the GOC's wife was expected to interact with the ladies of the station. The structure of these interactions appeared overly formal and bureaucratic, even among the ladies themselves. There was also a surprising amount of paperwork required to document welfare activities, which seemed at odds with the spirit of community and care.

Madhuri was not one to operate by the book when it came to empathy and human connection. As a seasoned medical professional, problem-solving and analysis came naturally to her, and her innate warmth enabled her to connect with people, be it the wife of the senior-most officer or the youngest soldier. She had done this throughout her service without needing a rulebook. With her natural leadership, strong value system, and vibrant personality, she was perfectly suited to the role of first lady of the formation.

My only advice to her was: 'Just be you.' And with that, everything fell beautifully into place.

Life at Ranchi and a New High for Vibhuti

At Ranchi, my professional life was exceptionally demanding. The formation under my command was tasked with training support for Central Police Forces deployed in the region.

However, our core responsibility remained focused on operational preparedness for the Western Front. In early 2012, this culminated in an extended and intensive training schedule in the deserts of Rajasthan.

During this prolonged field deployment, Madhuri stayed back in Ranchi. Despite continuing her duties at the hospital, she went out of her way to remain actively engaged with the families of the formation, particularly the ladies and children. Her presence and care were a source of immense reassurance for the troops, who could now concentrate fully on their tasks, knowing that their families were in good hands. This kind of support system is crucial in sustaining morale during prolonged separations.

Once we returned to the barracks at the end of our desert training stint, there was finally a window of respite for everyone. It was during this welcome break that we had the pleasure of hosting both our children and our parents at Ranchi. Known as the 'City of Waterfalls,' Ranchi offered many scenic locations, and we took the opportunity to show them around. The visit held special significance for our parents as well, as staying in the same quarters once occupied by the famed General Slim of World War II lent a sense of history and pride to their trip.

Time seemed to pass swiftly, especially after Madhuri's arrival in Ranchi and the busy nature of my duties. But amidst all this, another heartening development unfolded; this time concerning Vibhuti's education in Bangalore. Her institute, Srishti, had a system of international exchange programmes with peer institutions in the United States. Vibhuti's work during her initial years there had drawn positive attention. As a result, her application for an overseas experience was approved, and she proceeded to the University of Michigan as an exchange student for a six-month programme.

Vibhuti embraced the opportunity with full enthusiasm. So much so that, at the end of her term, the University of Michigan offered her an extension of six more months for further specialised training. Her home institute in Bangalore agreed to the continuation, and she gained a full year of exposure to the outstanding infrastructure and academic environment that Michigan had to offer. That one year turned out to be a launchpad for future prospects. With clarity of purpose and sustained effort, Vibhuti had laid a strong foundation for herself. We were delighted and proud to see her thrive.

Back to Delhi

Following her impactful tenures at AFMC and the base hospital in Delhi, Madhuri was approved for promotion to the rank of brigadier. Her superiors advised her to be ready for a move from Ranchi at short notice. Since my own tenure was also nearing completion by the end of the year, we conveyed that it would be logistically helpful if she could be posted back to Delhi. There was a fair possibility that I might be sent there too.

Fortunately, the authorities were receptive to the idea. Soon enough, Madhuri received her posting orders to return to the base hospital as a consultant in paediatrics. The consultant's position carries expanded responsibilities, ensuring the quality and consistency of paediatric services across the region and providing supervisory guidance to advisors in the field. While the role had a strong administrative component, Madhuri remained deeply committed to the clinical side, especially her passion for paediatric nephrology. So, after completing a metaphorical 'full term of nine months' in Ranchi, Madhuri donned her new rank and resumed duties in the familiar surroundings of Base Hospital, Delhi, in August 2012.

A few months later, in November 2012, I too received orders for a posting to Delhi, this time to the finance directorate at Army HQ. My principal role involved assisting with the formulation of the army's annual budget—a significant shift in domain, but a welcome challenge.

At the base hospital, Madhuri had been allotted temporary family quarters, and I joined her there, accompanied as always by Pixie, Coco, and Peppy, our ever-faithful companions. Thus began our next chapter together in December 2012, with both of us looking forward to spending the new year—2013—in each other's company, after years of intermittent togetherness.

Postscript by Madhuri

Being a GOC's wife was an interesting experience. Supporting Rajeev in the same station while continuing as an officer at work was a novel dynamic. I often felt like I was playing a double role, just like in the old Hindi film, *Sita Aur Gita;* Sita at divisional functions, and Gita at work.

One amusing anecdote comes to mind. During my daily rounds in the ICU, I noticed that the father of one of the commanding officers had been admitted to our hospital. His daughter-in-law introduced me as the GOC's wife. He responded, quite matter-of-factly, 'That can't be. We see her every morning and evening working in the wards!' For him, a GOC's wife was someone who showed up occasionally to distribute sweets on Diwali and the like, not someone seen in scrubs every day!

Another personal milestone from that time was learning to play golf. For the first time in years, I had a little time on my hands, and I decided to put it to good use. Ranchi had an excellent golf course and a very skilled coach, so I gave it a shot and discovered a new interest. I also made a serious commitment to expanding my professional capabilities. I applied for and was selected for a two-year fellowship in Medical Education and Research—the FAIMER Fellowship—offered at CMC Ludhiana. The programme involved three on-site contact sessions with online modules in between, as well as a project component. It turned out to be one of my most valuable decisions. The fellowship not only helped me develop new skills but also prepared me for the future roles that destiny had quietly lined up for me.

Chapter 14

Together Through Trials and Tribulations

Just-In-Time Accommodation

Upon taking charge of my new assignment in Delhi, I applied for family accommodation. Fortunately, at senior ranks, the army gives priority to allotting alternative quarters in the absence of authorised ones. Within a couple of weeks of my arrival, I was allotted a reasonably located residence. The quarters needed a bit of sprucing up, and I had just begun the process when we received distressing news: Madhuri's mother had taken seriously ill once again in Pune. She had suffered a brain stroke that left her partially paralysed. One side of her face was immobile, and she was unable to articulate her thoughts clearly. This, on top of her existing kidney issues, made the situation more complex. Madhuri rushed to Pune and admitted her to a private hospital close to our home, easing the logistical challenges.

Her father, now in his eighties, was already showing signs of Parkinsonism and early dementia. He was also responsible for the care of his elder sister, a spinster immobilised by polio. It became clear that he could not manage everything on his own. Madhuri could not stay in Pune indefinitely, and her two sisters—based in Mumbai and Pune—were not in a position to offer sustained help at that time.

After her mother stabilised, the doctors cleared her for air travel. Madhuri decided to shift her to Delhi and requested her sisters to regularly check in on their father in Pune. In the first week of January 2013, she wheeled her mother straight from the hospital to the airport and flew her to Delhi. I received them at the airport, and we took her directly to the base hospital, where Madhuri was posted. We hoped that her condition would improve with better medical care in Delhi and with Madhuri keeping a close watch on her treatment. Needless to say, it wasn't the happiest of New Year's for us, but we were grateful that we could be there for our parents when they needed us the most.

In Delhi, her mother's health fluctuated between periods of improvement and relapse. Her kidney function declined further, and she had to begin dialysis. Other health complications added to her fatigue, and she grew weary of the constant hospital visits. Nevertheless, after some recovery over the next two months, she expressed a strong desire to return to Pune and be with her husband. She even voiced, on occasion, her unwillingness to remain alive tethered to machines.

In February, Madhuri flew down with her mother to Pune and settled her back in. She and her sisters resolved to take turns staying with the parents and doing the best they could under the circumstances. However, the prognosis for both parents remained bleak. After some persuasion, her mother agreed to continue dialysis, and Nilima—the middle sister, also a doctor—offered to shift her to Bangalore for closer care.

Then, around April 2013, her father's dementia worsened to the point where he could no longer care for himself, let alone his bedridden sister. It was once again action stations for Madhuri and her sisters. After detailed discussions, they concluded that each of the three elders—father, mother, and aunt—would need to be cared for separately.

The first step was to identify a reliable assisted living facility in Pune for their aunt. The extended family and the youngest sister from Mumbai agreed to check in on her from time to time. Their father was to be flown to Delhi, where Madhuri and

I could care for him. Their mother would move to Bangalore with Nilima. Having coordinated all the arrangements in Pune, Madhuri returned to Delhi with her father. For a brief moment, it felt like we had managed to stay just ahead of the unfolding challenges.

It was truly providential that Madhuri and I had been posted to Delhi together just in time, and that, due to our seniority, we had been allotted suitable accommodation before the need arose to move our parents in with us. It felt like a blessing we didn't take lightly.

With the support of the base hospital in Delhi, we were able to care for Madhuri's father, while her mother underwent dialysis at the Air Force Command Hospital in Bangalore. We were deeply grateful to our organisation, which enabled us to meet our responsibilities—both professional and personal—with dignity and care.

Working and Caring –The Twin Responsibility

It was against this backdrop that both of us continued to perform our military duties in our respective spheres. On my end, I was among the key executives responsible for managing the army's budget, an especially crucial role given the financial climate at the time. The army's budget is vast and complex, but like the rest of the country, we too were navigating a period of financial constraint. We were instructed to implement maximum savings, and as we moved into the final quarter of the financial year, several portions of the budget had to be frozen. It was a unique learning experience, one that allowed me to witness the process up close. At the Financial Directorate, our task was to find workable solutions without compromising the army's daily functioning. Tough decisions had to be made on occasion, but in the end, we successfully managed to weather the monetary storm.

At the base hospital, Madhuri continued to function with her usual immaculate efficiency. She reinforced academic rigour in teaching and training and worked to initiate a collaborative effort with the faculty of the AHRR, which was just a stone's throw from her workplace. This coordination proved immensely helpful for the postgraduates, and Madhuri remained steadfast in her mission of shaping better doctors and future leaders in her own distinctive way.

On the social front, our time at DK1—Dhaula Kuan Officers' Colony—was full of fond memories. We had a few close friends living nearby, all senior officers like us. Most of us were dealing with demanding roles at work while also caring for ageing parents. Despite these heavy responsibilities, we made time for moments of shared joy. Madhuri, having picked up some golf during our Ranchi days, often joined me on the course in Delhi as well. We formed a regular four-ball with a couple of friends and spent many happy hours out on the greens.

Parents' Health Deteriorates

Madhuri's father's health continued its slow decline. Over time, he became more moody and obstinate. His food intake reduced significantly, and he grew frail. Occasionally, he would ask about Madhuri's mother, forgetting that she was not in Delhi but in Bangalore. Eventually, he even stopped recognising his own sister, whom he had lovingly cared for his entire life. We did our best to keep him comfortable, despite the emotional toll of watching him fade.

Meanwhile, her mother's condition worsened as well. Dialysis sessions became more frequent. Although the Air Force Command Hospital in Bangalore provided good care, she gradually began refusing to attend her sessions. A deeply spiritual woman, she had always been in tune with the rhythms of life . . . and death. One day in June 2013, she quietly told Nilima that she knew her time had come. She found it heartbreaking that her husband no longer recognised her on video calls. The endless cycle of dialysis had become unbearable for her, and she often pleaded to be allowed to leave the world while her husband was still alive.

Nilima, who shared her mother's spiritual outlook, understood what she was asking. She spoke with Madhuri and Rashmi over the phone, and after collectively speaking to their mother, they agreed that it was time to let her go with dignity. She had lived a full and loving life with a devoted husband, three daughters who adored her, and a warmth that touched all who knew her. There was nothing more she wished for in this lifetime. It was time to let go.

On the full-moon night of 23 June 2013, Madhuri's mother passed away, bathed in soft moonlight, as if gently escorted by the heavens to her next destination. Madhuri flew down to Bangalore the next day to witness her final rites. At the same moment, Rashmi, the youngest sister, was on a pilgrimage to Kailash Mansarovar. She later recounted a strange and powerful sensation—an intuitive realisation—that her mother had said her last goodbye. Such are the mysterious ways of nature.

Madhuri's mother was a gem of a person. I have not come across a kinder soul. She was simple, deeply spiritual, humble, gentle, with a heart of gold, and generous beyond measure. She cared for her family with unmatched devotion and shouldered responsibilities with grace and quiet strength. We all owed her debts that can never truly be repaid. Perhaps even the Gods loved her too much and called her back sooner than we would have wished. Surely, she attained moksha in her own inimitable way.

Saying Goodbye

We did not inform Madhuri's father immediately of her mother's passing, given his deteriorating health. Yet, in some inexplicable way, he seemed deeply connected to her even in absence. On the very night of her death, his condition worsened significantly, and he had to be hospitalised once again. A few days later, Madhuri gently broke the news to him. His quiet acceptance made us wonder whether he had fully registered what had happened. But as the days passed, he withdrew further into himself, and one day in August 2013, he slipped into a coma. When he regained consciousness, he was severely weakened and unable to eat on his own. A PEG (percutaneous endoscopic gastrostomy) tube was inserted into his stomach, allowing a caregiver to feed him directly.

Around the same time, Madhuri received her new posting as deputy director general, postgraduate training (DDG P&T) in the office of the director general armed forces medical services (DGAFMS). It was a significant appointment, offering her the chance to shape the policies and processes that governed postgraduate training and utilisation of doctors in the armed forces. It aligned well with her strengths: clarity of thought, creativity, and a strong sense of purpose.

While the new role was gratifying, her father's declining health weighed heavily on her mind. Soon after Madhuri took charge, the hospital informed us that they could no longer provide palliative care, citing a shortage of paramedical staff. We felt disappointed but also understood the constraints of a busy hospital.

In the days that followed, we converted a room in our home into a mini-ICU and arranged for round-the-clock caregiving. Madhuri trained me in the basics: how to feed him through the PEG, how to monitor his vitals, and how to administer saline when required. We kept a strict communication protocol with the caregiver. Madhuri would drop in during lunch breaks to check on him, and I would relieve her in the evening to spend time by his side. Between August and November 2013, we took care of him ourselves, without placing the burden on anyone else. Thanks to Madhuri's enduring bond with her students and nursing colleagues, someone or the other would stop by every now and then to see if we needed assistance.

In the second week of November, Madhuri had to travel to AFMC Pune on official duty. Father had grown extremely frail and spent most of his time sleeping, possibly a natural energy-saving response. He appeared oblivious to the world around him. On 14 November, Madhuri called from Pune to check in. When I told her there had been no significant change in his condition, she gently suggested I come down for a day on the 16th to be with her as it was our wedding anniversary. I hesitated, unsure whether it was wise to leave Delhi just then. But Madhuri insisted that I, too, needed a short break and that a day away wouldn't make much of a difference.

We made arrangements for one of Madhuri's trusted colleagues to check in on her father during our brief absence, and I flew down to Pune on 15 November. On the morning of our anniversary, Madhuri and I visited my parents in Pune to seek their blessings. That afternoon, a call came from the doctor in Delhi who had gone to check on her father. He was gasping a little, and the doctor felt he might need to be moved to the hospital again.

Madhuri made a difficult but resolute decision; she didn't want her father to suffer anymore. She asked her colleague to stay by his side and hold his hand for her. She assured him that we would take the earliest flight back and be with him by night. But before we could leave, her phone rang again. We knew what the call would say. Her father, in his own quiet and mysterious way, had chosen to bless us on our wedding anniversary and then take his leave.

We flew back to Delhi, our hearts heavy. It was painful to think that, after having been with us for over six months, he passed away during the brief moment we were away. At the hospital, we found everything in order. His body had been respectfully moved to the mortuary, and the necessary formalities completed. We informed our extended family and close friends. Her father was deeply revered in both family circles and among his professional peers.

Nilima and Rashmi arrived in Delhi the next day for the last rites. After the cremation, the three of us sat down to reflect on all that our parents had endured in their final years. We reminded ourselves that the Creator has His own design for sustaining, dissolving, and reviving the universe. Perhaps, in that cosmic rhythm, the reunion of our mother and father was just another act of grace. And for us, it was time to honour their memory by moving forward.

Postscript by Madhuri

The year 2013 will always remain etched in my mind as one of the most difficult periods of my life. I was battling on three fronts. The first was personal—the declining health of my parents, and then the unbearable loss of both of them in the same year. Being a daughter, a doctor, and a caregiver all at once was emotionally and physically exhausting. Letting go of them was the hardest part. Supporting them through their final moments drained me deeply.

The second was professional—a transition from clinical work to administration. After years of working in a cheerful paediatric ward surrounded by children, I now found myself confined to a closed office, surrounded by files. The shift felt depressing and daunting.

The third front was the most unexpected. In my new role as DDG, I encountered a few seniors who lacked empathy and expressed dissatisfaction with my limited knowledge during the early days of my tenure. It was disheartening. I was still learning the ropes and grappling with a new world of files and noting sheets, but instead of mentorship and support, I found the environment cold and non-conducive. What disturbed me most was the resistance to new ideas and the dismissal of innovative thinking. For the first time, I began to wonder if gender played a role. The male-dominated setup felt particularly isolating.

Under the weight of all this, I developed hypertension. My once happy-go-lucky nature took a serious hit. It took me more than three years to recover from the trauma of that phase. What helped me eventually was learning yoga and meditation, particularly the practice of Yoga Nidra. Bit by bit, I began to find balance again. Gradually, I immersed myself in my new field of policymaking and eventually found the drive to make meaningful contributions to higher-level administration within our organisation.

Chapter 15

Mastering Administration and Policy Making

Change of Job Profile

In August 2013, Madhuri underwent a significant shift in her career. It was a momentous milestone. She had practised the science and art of medicine for over three decades with complete dedication. In the early years, she had to fight her way to become a paediatrician. Later, she had to persist and persevere before finally being permitted to train in paediatric nephrology. Over time, she distinguished herself and gained both national and international recognition for her consistent achievements.

Despite the many personal hurdles she faced while trying to balance a demanding career and responsibilities at home, she managed both exceptionally well. The children had largely remained her responsibility, and she raised them almost single-handedly with unwavering resolve. While she was a firm disciplinarian, she also gave them the freedom to follow their instincts, particularly at key junctures in their education and career choices. It was this combination of firmness and flexibility that helped Nikhil and Vibhuti grow into independent individuals.

Through it all, she remained deeply committed to her patients during her years of clinical practice. Having poured herself wholeheartedly into her work for so long, it seemed fitting that she now takes the next step in her professional evolution: moving into higher administration and policymaking. This opportunity came when she was appointed deputy director general, postgraduate training (DDG P&T) in the office of the director general armed forces medical services (DGAFMS). It was a natural progression for someone who had served with such dedication to now help shape the very system she had long upheld.

Appointment as DDG P&T

The role of DDG P&T is a pivotal one. It oversees the entire spectrum of clinical training within the Armed Forces Medical Services (AFMS) and is responsible for providing qualified medical personnel to all three wings of the armed forces. One of its key responsibilities is managing the annual selection of undergraduates for AFMC. The policies for their selection, retention, and subsequent postgraduate and super-speciality training are all framed under this department. It also oversees the selection of teaching faculty for AFMC.

Beyond medical doctors, the role extends to the Army Dental Corps, nursing officers, and the training of paramedics. In many ways, it sits at the very core of the AFMS's operational efficiency. The officer in charge must possess a rare mix of maturity, balance, strong communication skills, and above all, a clear head and an empathetic heart. Madhuri, with her stellar record as both a clinician and an administrator, was well suited to this demanding role. She took it on with the intention of revitalising the system and enhancing the overall effectiveness of the AFMS.

It is likely that her outstanding track record was one reason she was moved from her clinical role at the base hospital to the more strategic domain of policymaking at the DGAFMS office. When she assumed her new responsibilities, Madhuri was hopeful that she could initiate meaningful reforms in her department. However, just prior to her appointment, a change had been made to the department's hierarchical structure. This altered the chain of command through which policy proposals had to travel before reaching the head of the service. As a result, files from her desk now had to pass through additional levels, slowing down decision-making. Madhuri was sceptical of this change but chose not to contest it, as the decision had been taken at the highest level. True to form, she remained undeterred. She was committed to fulfilling the role as it was meant to be performed. With characteristic humility and determination, she began by learning the workings of the department from her junior colleagues as well as her immediate senior.

During her tenure as DDG, she interacted with a variety of superiors, each professionally competent but differing in style. Some were sincere and open, others preferred to move things forward quietly, avoiding conflict. A few would shape their views only after sensing the mood of their own superiors. With the more mature officers, Madhuri would discuss matters in depth, making a persuasive case for her stand. When disagreements arose, they would respectfully agree to disagree. In every instance, she would send in her detailed analysis and recommendations, clearly prioritised and well-reasoned, leaving her superiors free to add their own remarks. This system, while not perfect, functioned reasonably well in most cases. Yet, Madhuri soon realised that the default approach in many quarters was: don't disturb the existing order. This ran counter to her idea of what a vibrant headquarters should be. Still, she resolved to do her best within the constraints of the system.

On several occasions, her proposals—crafted with care and insight—were dismissed or stalled in favour of maintaining the status quo. It was disheartening, especially because she was investing her full energy into this role, even as she managed the emotional toll of caring for two ailing parents at home.

Enhancing the AFMC Selection Process

As DDG, Madhuri was closely involved in the annual selection process for new entrants to AFMC. She observed that the entire process was prolonged and administratively burdensome for both the institution and the aspirants, as well as the parents who accompanied them. The triple-tiered process comprising medical evaluation, physical fitness assessment, and the all-important interview would stretch over almost a month. For the 120 available seats, nearly four times that number of candidates were called each year.

The various components of the selection were conducted sequentially, which caused significant delays. After closely analysing the existing system, Madhuri proposed that the different verticals of testing could run simultaneously, akin to parallel processing in computer systems. This would require some adjustments in the deployment of doctors and administrative staff across different points in the process. It was logistically feasible.

Though the organisation was initially hesitant, Madhuri persuaded the authorities to conduct a pilot run, and it worked! The entire selection process was now completed within seven to ten days instead of the earlier three to four weeks. Not only did this make the process more efficient, but it also optimised resource utilisation and eased the burden of administration. Additionally, it gave aspirants more flexibility to appear for selection processes at other institutions across the country.

Madhuri also recognised that attracting meritorious candidates required more than just streamlined logistics; it needed effective communication. To this end, she made it a point to address the aspirants and their parents at the outset of the selection each year. She spoke of the many advantages of a career in the armed forces: dignity, security, a sense of purpose, challenges, adventure, and pride. Her talks left a strong impression, and over the years, the word began to spread, both through word of mouth and social media.

The impact of these efforts soon became evident. The cut-off marks for admission steadily rose each year, reflecting the growing appeal of AFMC as a preferred choice. What began as an experiment became an institutionalised trend.

Restructuring the Specialist Pool

Madhuri also took a deep interest in reassessing the system for managing specialists and sub-specialists within the Armed Forces Medical Services. She identified several areas that needed review.

First, there was a need to assess the actual strength of specialists across the three services to determine whether the current pool was sufficient to meet operational and clinical demands. If the distribution was skewed, a more equitable redistribution plan had to be formulated. If the overall numbers were inadequate, then a time-bound strategy was required to bridge the gap. She also recognised that gaps often arose due to specialists transitioning into administrative roles upon reaching senior ranks or retiring due to various reasons. Therefore, a long-term (10-15 years) strategy was essential to maintain a robust pipeline of well-trained specialists. Additionally, with rapid advancements in medicine, new sub-specialities had emerged. There was a need to take stock of these, train a nucleus of experts—both within India and abroad where necessary—and have this group train others within the AFMS. To this end, Madhuri developed a comprehensive plan to restructure the specialist cadre and improve its long-term sustainability.

In the years that followed, she contributed significantly to broadening and deepening the specialist pool. However, when it came to the actual deployment and employment of these specialists, her efforts met with mixed results, largely due to differing perspectives on inter-service resource-sharing.

While the Armed Forces Medical Services are technically integrated under the DGAFMS, allowing for equitable distribution of medical personnel across the army, navy, and air force, the reality on the ground was often different. Assignments were not always based on actual workload or patient needs. Instead, specialist placement was sometimes influenced by local administrative preferences or legacy practices.

Madhuri worked diligently to correct this imbalance. On occasion, her persistence yielded results. But overall, she felt that the system still had significant room for reform. She remained convinced that streamlining deployment practices would benefit the AFMS as a whole, and she continued to push for change for the greater good of the services.

Selection and Counselling of PG Trainees

Madhuri also led significant reforms in the policy and procedures related to postgraduate (PG) training, specifically in the selection and counselling process. Initially, a separate examination was conducted for the selection of PG trainees. While a structured system of examinations and counselling had been in place for years, it was largely manual in nature. As a result, it was occasionally prone to disruptions, which sometimes led to unwelcome complications.

Madhuri and her team undertook the task of automating the formulation of exam papers, drawing from a vast and regularly updated question bank. The process of evaluating answer sheets and recording results was also refined to ensure greater fairness and transparency. Her primary objective was to ensure a level playing field for all aspirants and in this, she was largely successful. Moreover, she introduced an online counselling system, based on real-time data of available vacancies across specialities. This made the process of nominating PG trainees quicker, more efficient, and demonstrably fair. Madhuri's ability to think innovatively and her knack for improving existing systems helped her implement these reforms with characteristic flair.

She also advocated a broader vision that every officer in the AMC should ideally specialise in a medical field during their service. She believed that specialisation not only offered a sense of personal fulfilment but also enhanced professional utility, helping mitigate officer shortages. Some of her ideas gained acceptance; others, however, could not be taken forward due to systemic constraints.

Madhuri also contributed to the induction and training framework for specialists in the Dental Corps. She noticed that the staff officers at the Dental HQ were deeply committed to attracting top talent into the service. Their cohesiveness as a team enabled close coordination, and Madhuri was able to work effectively with their leadership to elevate professional standards across the corps.

Nursing Corps and Paramedics

Madhuri was equally focused on improving the training and specialisation pathways for the corps of nursing officers. She streamlined the study curriculum and restructured training schedules at nursing schools and colleges to create a better balance between nurses pursuing specialist training and those engaged in active hospital duty.

This balancing act was not without its challenges. There was a constant tug-of-war between academic aspirations and operational needs, and firm decisions had to be made on dividing the nursing workforce across these two priorities. Madhuri navigated this complex terrain with effective communication and persuasive dialogue, managing to align the leadership of the Nursing Corps towards a common goal.

Though it was a quiet area of reform, largely unnoticed by others, Madhuri drew personal satisfaction from it. She saw it as an essential step towards enhancing the quality of care available to armed forces personnel. In addition, she paid close attention to upgrading the skills of para-medical staff, recognising them as an indispensable extension of efficient nursing services.

The Issue of Teaching Experience

One of the most critical areas Madhuri dealt with during her tenure as DDG was the issue of teaching experience for medical officers. This became particularly relevant for those officers seeking academic appointments in the civilian sector post-retirement.

A change in Medical Council of India (MCI) regulations had led to the derecognition of military hospitals as official teaching institutions. As a result, many senior officers found themselves ineligible for faculty positions, despite having spent years teaching within the armed forces.

Madhuri took this up proactively. Through sustained engagement with the relevant civilian authorities and backed by her own professional standing in both military and civil medical circles, she was able to resolve the issue. Most significantly, she succeeded in getting the recognition reinstated with retrospective effect.

This single reform enabled many officers to receive official certification of their teaching experience in a format recognised by the MCI. It not only expanded the pool of qualified teachers for postgraduate institutions but also greatly benefited the welfare and dignity of retired personnel who had been previously overlooked.

Pharmacy and Sports Medicine

As part of her larger vision for the AFMS, two subjects held special interest for Madhuri: pharmacy and sports medicine. At the national level, the field of pharmacy was beginning to receive serious attention. Tighter regulations were being enforced to curb the operations of unqualified or fly-by-night pharmacists.

The mishandling of drugs by ill-trained personnel had, in many instances, led to life-threatening consequences. In the armed forces, the issue was compounded by the fact that, in 2003, the Pharmacy Council had derecognised the training programme being provided to military pharmacists.

Madhuri foresaw the gravity of this problem. She believed that pharmacy needed to be recognised as an independent discipline within the Armed Forces Medical College (AFMC) and that qualified pharmacists must be inducted into the services. She presented a three-pronged plan to her seniors: first, to establish a pharmacy department at AFMC; second, to allow personnel under the three directorates to receive formal training through local pharmacy colleges; and third, to initiate direct recruitment of certified pharmacists.

Unfortunately, her suggestions were not met with enthusiasm. There was limited awareness of the seriousness of the issue. At one point, during a formal conference, she was even reminded that she was 'operating beyond her brief.' Nonetheless, she remained undeterred. While the matter did not receive immediate traction, corrective action was formally initiated a few years later along the very lines she had earlier proposed.

A similar situation unfolded in the case of sports medicine. With the growing emphasis on sports and physical training across the services, Madhuri saw an urgent need to begin structured training in the various sub-specialities of sports medicine. This, too, was feasible but required a shift in mindset and the ability to navigate bureaucratic roadblocks. Despite her best efforts at the time, she could make limited headway. However, later, in her role as the dean of AFMC, she was finally able to establish both the pharmacy and sports medicine departments despite hurdles at various levels.

These instances highlight Madhuri's far-sightedness. In my view, she was easily a decade ahead of her contemporaries in imagining a more capable, future-ready AFMS. She often hoped that one day she would be in a position to push through the broader structural reforms she had envisioned. In our conversations, she would occasionally express her frustration at the lack of institutional vision. She felt that new ideas were often met with resistance, and that innovation was too frequently dismissed as rocking the boat. Her perseverance, however, ensured that the seeds of reform were sown which had a lasting impact.

Visit to the Pentagon and PACOM, USA

One of the standout memories from Madhuri's tenure as DDG P&T was her official visit to the United States, specifically to the Pentagon and the Pacific Command (PACOM) in the Hawaiian Islands, alongside the DGAFMS. The purpose of the visit was twofold: to foster professional collaboration and to exchange knowledge with the medical arm of the US Armed Forces.

The DGAFMS had chosen Madhuri to accompany him, convinced that she was well-equipped to represent the AFMS with competence and dignity. However, when the proposal was initially sent for approval, it was rejected on the grounds of 'exercising due economy.' The DGAFMS then indicated that if she were not permitted to join the delegation, the visit might be called off altogether. This led to a reversal of the earlier decision, and Madhuri was eventually cleared to travel.

The visit turned out to be a great success. As anticipated, Madhuri forged meaningful relationships with key individuals; connections that would later play a significant role in strengthening professional ties between the two military medical communities to the benefit of both.

The Seniority Issue

Madhuri had first encountered the issue of lost seniority during her promotion to the rank of colonel. At the time, she had hoped that the matter would be reviewed, but no resolution had been forthcoming. As time passed, it became clear that this discrepancy had also delayed her promotion to brigadier and would likely affect future career milestones as well.

It was around this time that she decided to take up the issue again. Together, we examined the case closely, going over its nuances and referring to the original commissioning documents. We believed there was merit in requesting a formal review, as some of the existing provisions appeared to contradict the foundational terms of her commission. Madhuri submitted a succinct and well-reasoned representation to the relevant authorities. Several months later, she received a brief, impersonal reply stating that, after in-depth consideration, the restoration of her seniority was not possible.

Some well-wishers advised that the matter could be taken to court and that she had a strong legal case. But Madhuri was not one to challenge the very organisation that had given her so many opportunities. A confident and principled officer, she chose to let the matter rest, anchored in her values and her deep respect for the institution.

It would be appropriate to conclude by noting that Madhuri's persistent efforts—whether in sustaining a steady flow of excellent undergraduates to AFMC, ensuring transparency in the selection of postgraduate trainees, automating critical processes in the DDG's office, or introducing a host of forward-looking initiatives—were formally recognised. In early 2016, she was awarded the prestigious Vishisht Seva Medal (VSM) for her outstanding service.

The Delhi-Bhopal Express

In the months of October and November 2013, while we were coping with Madhuri's father's illness, my batchmates and I were under consideration for promotion to the rank of lieutenant general. In many ways, this is the pinnacle of a military career. Beyond this, appointments such as chief of army staff hinge on extraneous factors—such as age, residual service, and seniority within the batch—often beyond one's control.

Competition for the rank of lieutenant general is intense. Even minor variations in the quantitative assessment can tip the scales. Fortunately, following the turbulence in one of my earlier command tenures, I had the opportunity to serve with exceptional superiors. While I may not have been the most articulate communicator, I believe my sincerity and hard work were recognised and appreciated.

The results of the promotion board were declassified in December 2013. We were still reeling from the grief of Madhuri's father's passing, and the news of my approval for promotion brought a small measure of solace during that time.

In January 2014, we suffered another loss; this time of Pixie, our first pet. Over the years, she had lost her vision and eventually succumbed to multi-organ failure. I was alone at home when she passed. Watching her life fade away was deeply moving. With a heavy heart, I performed her last rites in our garden, planting a hibiscus shrub over her resting place. The plant bloomed beautifully and, in my mind, continues to stand watch over Pixie even now.

In early February 2014, I was informed that I would be taking command of a formation based at Bhopal by the end of the month. However, the formation's area of responsibility (AOR) extended across a large expanse of the country. I knew this would mean a demanding travel schedule and a very busy calendar. Still, being based at Bhopal was something of a lucky break as it was well-connected to Delhi by both rail and air. Madhuri and I discovered that several convenient overnight trains operated between the two cities. She could arrive early in Bhopal for a weekend visit and return to Delhi within a suitable timeframe. This gave us hope that, despite the distance, we could stay in regular touch and manage our lives around the long-distance nature of our relationship, which we had now grown accustomed to.

Bhopal Military Station had evolved impressively over time. The formation's HQ is perched atop a hill, beautifully landscaped in typical army fashion. The GOC's residence—an old colonial-era bungalow—is nestled amidst gardens and natural water channels. Living in such a serene and picturesque environment felt like a privilege. However, the house needed a woman's touch to turn it from a well-kept residence into a warm and functional home. That transformation was made possible during Madhuri's flying visits. Each time she brought a little more order, warmth, and her unmistakable presence into my temporary home.

A Breath of Fresh Air at Bhopal

Madhuri's arrival at the military station brought with it a breath of fresh air. She had an infectious smile that never left her face, and her laughter and cheerfulness lit up every space she entered. From the outset, she made it clear that there would be no hierarchy among the ladies. She went out of her way to interact with even the most junior members of the community, and her informal, energetic approach served as a great morale booster to all she met. She reached out equally to the families of non-officer ranks in ways that were sincere and unaffected by her own status. Her warmth and ease in their company reflected genuine compassion. That she was also a doctor helped dissolve any potential social awkwardness.

My first few months in Bhopal were extremely busy. I spent a great deal of time visiting my subordinate commanders and troops posted across different parts of my area of responsibility. I would often plan my itinerary in a way that allowed Madhuri to accompany me on as many of these visits as possible. As an army officer herself, she was permitted to fly with me in army helicopters whenever that mode of transport was being used. This made it easier for her to interact with the families of troops in various stations within a limited time. Her presence and insights after these visits were immensely valuable. She offered realistic and empathetic feedback, both from the perspective of human relations and through the lens of her medical expertise.

Madhuri had developed a strong fondness for golf, which had taken root during her time in Ranchi and was nurtured further in Delhi. In Bhopal, she took it to another level. She would usually arrive in Bhopal by train from Delhi around 6 a.m. on Saturdays, come home, freshen up quickly, and head straight to the golf course by 7 a.m. I would often join her, and we cherished those mornings together, recharging ourselves on the lush, serene greens of Bhopal. Sundays followed the same happy routine.

For Madhuri, these weekends were more than just a break; they were a chance to detox from the intensity of her work in Delhi. The peaceful environment of the Bhopal Military Station gave her exactly the kind of escape she needed.

Another cherished memory from our Bhopal days was the grand get-together we organised for all the past commanders of the formation and their spouses. We took it upon ourselves to invite them to relive their years of service, reconnect with one another, and inspire the current generation of officers with their legacy. Except for a few who couldn't attend due to age or personal reasons, most of the 'old and the bold' gathered in the tranquil setting of the cantonment. The warmth of that gathering continues to bring us joy to this day.

My tenure in Bhopal, with Madhuri by my side—if not physically present then always in spirit—culminated in joyful moments in March 2015.

A Proposal and a Surprise

We had been gently nudging Nikhil for a while to consider settling down. Then, in January 2015, I visited Mumbai to receive the Vishisht Seva Medal (VSM) at an award ceremony hosted by the Southern Army commander. We used the occasion to quietly coordinate a meeting with the parents of the girl Nikhil had been dating—Teju—to see if we could help move things forward.

The children, we suspected, had begun to sense that both sets of parents were growing a little impatient. During an informal conversation, Nikhil suddenly caught everyone by surprise. He proposed to Teju then and there, right in front of all of us. There was a stunned silence for a moment, and then sheer joy as Teju accepted. It was a beautiful and spontaneous moment, and we celebrated the occasion in Mumbai with happiness in our hearts.

Back in Bhopal, Madhuri—who loves orchestrating such special events—felt it was our turn to plan a surprise. Under the pretext of my tenure nearing completion, she invited Nikhil, Teju, Vibhuti, Teju's parents, and her sister to visit us over a weekend in March 2015. In collaboration with my personal staff, Madhuri devised a delightful treasure hunt for the young visitors. The game would take them across various spots within the cantonment, with the final treasure being none other than their engagement rings, hidden and waiting to be discovered. To maintain the surprise, house decorations for the engagement ceremony were put in place only after the couple had left for their hunt. Teju's parents were in on the plan and wholeheartedly supported the idea. Nikhil and Teju, on the other hand, had no clue what was about to unfold.

While they were away, our home was transformed into a beautifully decorated venue, ready to host an engagement celebration. When the treasure hunt concluded, and the two returned—tired and thrilled from the game—they were completely taken aback by the transformation. Only then did they realise they were about to get formally engaged.

It turned out to be a magical evening, filled with fun, laughter, and heartfelt emotion. For us as parents, watching our children glow with happiness was a deeply fulfilling moment—a memory we continue to cherish.

My tenure in Bhopal was coming to an end, but not before one final round of war games was completed. Professionally, it had been a very fulfilling posting and concluded on a high note for me. A few days later, I received the posting order for my relief. I was required to hand over the charge to him by mid-April 2015 and proceed on leave until my next assignment was finalised.

Madhuri's last act of social interaction in Bhopal was a lively farewell with the ladies of the station. She had decided to make it a joyful event rather than a routine formal affair. So, she proposed a 'Run for Fun' in the scenic premises of our HQ complex. All those who were interested could join her for the run, which was to begin atop the hill on which the HQ was located. The route sloped downhill along the winding driveway leading to the main road junction, covering a couple of kilometres.

To make things more interesting, she took a circuitous route and attempted to re-enter the HQ complex through the rear gate. Dressed in sports attire, she was stopped by the military police, who informed her that no one was permitted inside as an event was underway, attended by the corps commander's spouse. It was only after they realised who she was that they let her through for the very event organised in her honour! That was humour in uniform in its truest form.

The event was thoroughly enjoyed by all. At the end of the run—where Madhuri finished first, thanks to her regular fitness regimen—she quickly slipped into a changing room, got into a fresh set of clothes, and surprised everyone by joining them for tea, perfectly turned out as always. I believe that day remains etched in the memories of all who were present during those joyful days in Bhopal.

After completing some formal handover activities, I joined Madhuri in Delhi, with no clarity yet on my next assignment. One fine evening, I was informed that I was being considered for the post of principal staff advisor at Army HQ. A few days later, I was officially appointed as the quartermaster general (QMG) of the Indian Army. It would be my final assignment before retirement. The two-year residual service clause meant that I would not be eligible to command an army, but I was determined to give this new role everything I had.

Amidst these developments came another joyful milestone: Vibhuti's graduation from Srishti. She had thoroughly enjoyed her years in Bangalore, acquiring skills in subjects that truly excited her. Now, she was ready to spread her wings and fly. Madhuri and I flew down to attend the ceremony. It was a proud moment for her and for both of us. There had been times when we weren't sure whether we had guided her in the right direction. But she had grown up with strong values, and that gave us immense satisfaction. We had always wanted her to be an independent and confident woman. That journey had begun when she chose Srishti back in 2011—an unhesitating, bold step that showed she knew what she wanted. Over the years, she matured into someone with clear opinions and growing self-assurance. Just before her graduation, she was selected by Flipkart to join their design team in Bangalore—a perfect beginning, allowing her to start her independent life in a city she had come to love. We celebrated the occasion with a small but happy gathering, proud of the person she had become. And now, with Madhuri by my side—both physically and emotionally—I was ready to take on my final responsibilities as the QMG before I called it a day.

It would be remiss of me not to mention the loss of Coco during our time in Bhopal. He had succumbed to a severe bout of jaundice. Madhuri had rushed down from Delhi to help me take care of him at home, but twenty-one days later, the Almighty summoned him. With a heavy heart, I laid him to rest within the corps commander's house premises. Coco had been a mischievous little fellow, full of pranks and endless joy. I like to believe he is at peace in his eternal resting place in Bhopal. For my final stint in Delhi, Peppy remained with us—a quiet, loyal companion and our little lone ranger.

The Delhi Compact

I reported to Army HQ in late April 2015 and assumed the appointment of the quartermaster general (QMG). The role encompassed a wide range of responsibilities: provisioning rations for the entire army, formulating infrastructure policy, creating assets, and managing military lands, farms, and animals, to name a few. The budgetary resources at the disposal of the QMG were enormous and needed to be handled with integrity and dedication to ensure the armed forces received the best value for money. It was an onerous task that demanded focused attention, and I was determined to do justice to every aspect of my charge, without fear or favour.

Before long, I settled into my assignment. Madhuri and I moved into a comfortable bungalow located close to both of our workplaces. She was already immersed in her professional responsibilities, but my arrival in Delhi added a new layer to her busy schedule, with additional commitments emerging from my side of the organisation. As the spouse of a senior officer in Delhi, she found herself involved in various initiatives aimed at the welfare of our troops' families, many of which were coordinated through the Army Welfare Office at the highest level. In addition, she had to attend numerous social functions that were considered obligatory, along with fulfilling her own medical community engagements.

Life in Delhi soon evolved into a packed calendar of duties and social engagements. Yet we both recognised how important it was to support each other through the complexities of our roles and their daily ripple effects. We were grateful to be together and to have the space to talk things through, rather than feel isolated in our respective worlds.

Following Nikhil's engagement ceremony in Bhopal, we had fixed the date of his wedding for 7 June 2015 in Pune. Given the availability of excellent facilities within the military complex, the pre-wedding and main wedding functions were held in those serene and dignified surroundings. After returning to Delhi, we hosted a reception for the newlyweds, allowing them to meet our friends and colleagues. Both events were wonderful experiences, though a bit stressful due to the frequent travel between Pune and Delhi for the arrangements.

In 2016, Vibhuti left for the United States to pursue her master's degree in information sciences at the University of Michigan. After working for about a year at Flipkart, she felt ready to qualify herself further before settling into a long-term professional path. Though her formal education at Srishti had been in design and visual graphics, her real interest lay in becoming a UX/UI designer, something that required a background in scientific subjects. The Indian education system, unfortunately, didn't allow much flexibility in switching academic streams. So, she explored international options and found that the University of Michigan offered exactly the kind of cross-disciplinary programme she was looking for. Soon enough, she was accepted into their Information Sciences programme, with the course scheduled to begin in September 2016.

The tuition fees were considerable, but we encouraged her to seize the opportunity. We knew she would work hard and eventually justify the investment. However, Vibhuti was firm on one point: she wanted to self-finance her education. And so, in September, she left for the US on her own. She had proactively coordinated with the university authorities and independently navigated the formalities involved in relocating. Having secured a place in a student hostel on the beautiful campus, she gradually settled into her new routine.

One of her biggest challenges was returning to mathematics, something she had gleefully discarded nearly five years earlier. But with renewed vigour and the support of some good friends, she managed to tackle it head-on. Not only that, within six months of starting her master's course, her academic record and creative strengths earned her a faculty position in the undergraduate programme. With that, her tuition fees were fully waived, and she also began receiving a respectable monthly stipend for her teaching role. In addition, she actively contributed to the cooperative student housing she lived in.

Like mother, like daughter, she managed multiple responsibilities in parallel, met every commitment, and earned her academic credits on time. She completed her degree without taking any student loans or placing any financial burden on us. Her clarity of thought and sheer determination had paid off, and we felt a deep sense of pride and contentment.

With Vibhuti now independent and settled into her new life, Madhuri and I could turn our attention to our own professional responsibilities with renewed focus.

The Departmental Enigma

As mentioned earlier, during her tenure as DDG, Madhuri worked under several immediate superiors over time. She maintained amicable relations with most of them, but her strong drive to get things done occasionally brought her into conflict with the hierarchy. Madhuri had introduced a number of initiatives in the field of information technology aimed at automating the processes of PG examinations, PG counselling, and forecasting specialist requirements for the armed forces. These new ideas sometimes led to differences of opinion.

She also sensed that her innovative proposals wouldn't gain traction unless they appeared to have originated from a senior officer. For the greater good, she factored in this dynamic and aligned her initiatives accordingly to ensure progress on important issues. Despite this strategic compromise, a certain atmosphere of disruption began to set in.

However, Madhuri was not one to be deterred. She continued to pursue her policymaking and implementation efforts with determination and sincerity. At no point did she believe that her earnest efforts would be misunderstood by her colleagues or even her seniors. This belief came naturally to her, and she firmly held that actions taken in the best interest of the Armed Forces Medical Services would ultimately be recognised and appreciated.

She remained unwavering in her commitment and performed her responsibilities with excellence till the end of her tenure as DDG. When the time came to move on to her next assignment, she left with a content and cheerful heart, unaware that personal biases would later attempt to undermine her professional contributions.

The Last Days and Homecoming

Time once again flew by, as it often does when one is fully absorbed in meaningful work. As the quartermaster general, I had the opportunity to implement several reforms. We managed to close down the uneconomical military farms. The provisioning system was streamlined and partially automated, leading to greater transparency and reduced scope for discretionary decision-making. The Land and Works Department was restructured to enhance productivity, and we laid the groundwork for improved management of military lands. In all these efforts, I received steadfast support from my colleagues in the QMG's branch, which gave me a deep sense of professional fulfilment during my tenure.

Amidst all this, a deeply personal loss struck. My father passed away. He had been unwell for a couple of years, suffering from a slow-growing cancer of the throat. Though he received care from the best doctors at the Army Cardiothoracic Centre in Pune, the illness eventually affected his voice box, leaving him unable to speak. As his condition deteriorated, he slipped into a quiet depression. In July 2016, he left us.

He had been a kind and earnest father, someone who worked hard with integrity all his life. He had dreams of seeing his children well settled and indeed, one of his sons became a doctor, another a soldier, and the youngest an engineer from an IIT. He had much to be proud of, and I believe he made his final journey in peace.

As for our days in Delhi, they were filled with cherished memories and the company of friends. Our love for golf—which had started in Ranchi in 2011—continued through Bhopal and flourished fully in Delhi. Madhuri remained my constant partner, and we shared many refreshing moments together on the greens, often surrounded by good company and light-hearted camaraderie.

As we approached the new year of 2017, I was nearing retirement. In October 2016, Madhuri's promotion board for the rank of major general had convened, and the results were declared in mid-December. We had received informal indications that all was well, but receiving the official confirmation just before the New Year made the celebration all the more joyous.

Though the issue of seniority would continue to shadow Madhuri's long-term prospects, we chose to set that aside for the moment and revel in the happiness of her promotion. The head of medical services graciously offered her a choice of posting.

Without hesitation, Madhuri requested to be appointed dean of AFMC—her alma mater.

Soon after, her appointment orders came through. She was to report by the end of January 2017. As for me, I was due to retire at the end of February 2017, completing more than thirty-nine years of service. It felt almost surreal that this chapter of life was drawing to a close.

In the last week of January 2017, Madhuri assumed the mantle of dean, AFMC, as the first lady dean of the college in the rank of major general. She received instant acclaim within her professional circles, and the event was widely reported in the press. Looking back, that moment of media attention marked the beginning of what would become a long and evolving relationship with the media, one that would truly blossom during the COVID era, when she was entrusted with many important responsibilities.

My 60th birthday fell on 15 February 2017, and Madhuri organised a wonderful celebration at AFMC to mark the milestone. It also symbolised the beginning of a new chapter for me. Just a few days later, I would become a free man, no longer needing to request anyone to post me with Madhuri. She joined me in Delhi briefly for the formal retirement function. Most of our household belongings had already been packed and sent to Pune in advance, and we flew out of Delhi on 28 February 2017.

The only one missing was Peppy, who had left us sometime in mid-2016, having grown frail with age. She rests peacefully in the garden of the last residence I occupied as QMG. We now looked forward to the new responsibilities Madhuri had taken on as dean of AFMC—a fresh chapter in her military odyssey, and a new life for me.

Postscript by Madhuri

My transition into administrative roles—walking the corridors of power, learning to adapt, and as the saying goes, 'an old dog learning new tricks'—was also the first time I truly grasped the deeper implications of a decision we had made long ago: 'Let us grow together without growing apart.' At that point, Rajeev was already a two-star general, and I was still a one-star.

The journey was far from easy. We had to manage multiple responsibilities on different fronts, which included caring for ageing parents, adjusting to new roles, navigating the loss of seniority, and dealing with the onset of hypertension brought on by stress. But as they say in the forces: 'When the going gets tough, the tough get going.'

In hindsight, I am grateful to all those who made my path challenging. They presented me with obstacles that ultimately became opportunities to grow stronger. I have no doubt that my senior colleagues must have also found it difficult—and perhaps even frustrating—to work with a younger woman officer who was determined to bring about change quickly.

The Indian Armed Forces is among the most reliable and respected institutions in our country. Its strength lies in its hierarchy, and its stability stems from a cautious approach to change. I had to learn to work within that system . . . a system that, despite its rigidity, taught me resilience, the courage of conviction, and the confidence to carry on regardless.

I owe a great deal to the armed forces.

Part VI

Higher Leadership and Management

Chapter 16

Dealing from the Dean's Den

A Dream Come True

Ever since her first visit to AFMC in 1978, Madhuri had fallen in love with the institution. From that day on, she had nurtured a quiet dream: that one day, she might have the chance to be at the helm of this revered academic establishment. That dream came true at the end of January 2017, when she took over as the dean and deputy commandant of AFMC. Her joy knew no bounds.

Over the years, she had seen AFMC through many lenses—first as a raw and eager student, then as junior faculty, later as head of department and professor of paediatrics, and subsequently while overseeing training at the national level as DDG (P&T). Now, she had the opportunity to return to the place she loved most as its academic head. In her own words, this was the best thing that could have happened to her.

She was determined to push the boundaries of academic excellence at AFMC, while also promoting the holistic development of the young cadets who joined the college with such enthusiasm and hope. It was her deep conviction that a well-rounded personality was essential for those destined to become officers in the Indian Armed Forces.

As dean, her primary responsibility was to oversee all academic matters. As deputy commandant, she was also expected to assist the commandant in reviewing and refining administrative processes to foster an environment that would nurture academic excellence. Typically, the dean steers clear of administrative matters—which are often considered cumbersome—preferring instead to focus fully on academic affairs. Similarly, the commandant usually handles administration independently. It is a division of responsibilities that generally works well, allowing each to concentrate on their respective domains.

However, Madhuri had observed during her earlier faculty years that a disconnect often existed between the academic staff and the administrative team. These misunderstandings frequently became obstacles in delivering the best possible outcomes for students. Her experience at Army HQ had also equipped her with a broader understanding of how administrative systems function at higher levels. She was keen to bring those insights to AFMC, aiming to bridge the gap between the two spheres and streamline functioning. She knew this would only be possible with the commandant's support. So, before taking any steps in that direction, she decided to have a candid discussion with him.

Soon after taking charge, she had an in-depth conversation with the commandant on these matters. By then, Madhuri had already developed a reputation, not just as an academician, but also as someone who could resolve complex administrative issues. Her personality was defined by unflagging enthusiasm, immense self-confidence, a positive outlook, and a determination to tackle even the most tangled problems. She had a rare gift for simplifying complexity and finding out-of-the-box solutions. And, just as importantly, she had the persistence to follow every issue through to its conclusion.

She was also known for being forthright in her dealings—a quality that occasionally unsettled people, particularly her seniors. At times, this directness sparked apprehension, and at other times, even mild resistance as a defensive reaction. Nonetheless, she shared her vision as dean with the commandant right at the start and sought his approval to be actively involved on both sides of the aisle (academic and administrative). The commandant was a thorough gentleman, soft-spoken, and highly accomplished in his administrative duties, particularly in the areas of accounts and procurement—fields in which Madhuri admittedly lacked familiarity. She acknowledged this openly, and it was soon agreed between them that she would learn the nuances of accounting from him, while contributing her own strengths in other aspects of administration. In return, he would entrust all academic responsibilities to her and support her efforts to improve coordination between faculty and administration.

With this spirit of mutual respect and collaboration, Madhuri began her new chapter as the first lady dean in the history of AFMC.

The Dean's Residence

The dean's residence at AFMC is an earmarked house, strategically located to allow direct entry into the institutional premises while also offering access to the main road outside. This thoughtful layout proved to be a practical advantage, enabling Madhuri unrestricted mobility through various modes of transport. She made immediate use of this convenience by adopting a bicycle for all internal movements from her residence to different parts of the AFMC campus.

Her intent was to promote this environment-friendly practice among her staff, in addition to the undergraduate students who were already required to use bicycles within the college premises. This simple, yet symbolic act was noticed by the media, and soon, Madhuri's initiative went viral, drawing attention to the cause and giving it the publicity it needed.

The residence itself was a well-designed, compact house. Having retired by then, I had joined Madhuri in Pune without the distractions of professional commitments and was thus able to help her settle into our new home quickly. With some support from the establishment, we spruced up the surroundings and transformed the house into a space we grew to love dearly. In time, we even built a wood-fired oven adjacent to the house, which proved particularly useful during informal gatherings with students at our residence.

Madhuri's Personage

Over the years, Madhuri had added many dimensions to her personality, evolving into a figure of distinct character and charm. It feels fitting to capture those traits at this point, as they played a significant role in shaping how she approached her new responsibilities.

To ensure no facet is overlooked, I have chosen to present this reflection under the title: 'The ABCs of M's Mystique and Magic.'

The ABCs of M's Mystique and Magic

M is **A**ssured, **A**uthoritative, and **A**dmirable,
She is **B**old, **B**rave, and has **B**rains formidable.
Competent, **C**apable, and **C**onfident is she,
Dynamic, **D**etermined, and **D**ignified is thee.
Energetic and **E**xtrovert, **E**xcellence is her thirst,
Fit and **F**eisty, **F**amily is always **F**irst.
Guts and **G**umption, she has **G**lamour in tow,
With a **H**eart of gold, **H**umour and **H**appiness are always in full flow.
She is **I**ntelligent and **I**ntense, her **I**magination is fine,
But also is she **J**oyful, **J**olly, and a Master-**J**uggler of time.
Knowledge is her passion, **K**indness her motto,
Live wire she is, **L**eads from the front with **L**ogic as her veto.
Mindful and **M**eticulous, she is **M**entor and **M**otivation,
A **N**o-**N**onsense girl; **N**o is **N**ot an option.

Open and forthright, she is **O**riginal all the way,
Practical and **P**assionate, **P**oise and **P**erfection make her day.
A die-hard **Q**-batcher with a **Q**uicksilver mind,
Rapid in thought, a **R**esponsible **R**ajmata is her kind.
Sharp and **S**ure is **S**peedy the **S**printer,
Sincere and **S**table, she is the real **S**how-**S**topper.
A **T**eam person that she is, **T**rusted and **T**ransparent,
She is indeed **U**nique and the **U**ltimate diva apparent.
Warm, **W**ise, **W**onderful, and **W**insome,
Worries for her are never troublesome.
She is the **X**-factor in all relations,
Personal, social, and professional.
Yes for work and **Y**es for fun,
Blessed with eternal **Y**outh, age is always on the run.
Zero error for her is the only option,
Zing with **Z**oom and **Z**est is her obsession.

The ABCs above attempt to summarise the qualities that Madhuri consistently brought to her role and employed fully in service of the students at AFMC. Her academic achievements as an undergraduate were already legendary, and she naturally became a role model within the institution. She had a particularly special connection with the undergraduates, whom she viewed as her own children.

Madhuri's 'M' now also stood for mother, adding a new dimension to her cherished personal motto of being a soldier, doctor, and teacher. As dean, she became a mother figure to more than 500 young students. With a combination of firmness and affection, she embarked on her mission with deep resolve and moral clarity.

She also carried the additional responsibility of ensuring a supportive environment for postgraduate trainees, including young officers, many of whom had families. She understood that a well-managed administrative setup was key to allowing them to focus on their demanding study schedules. As dean, she was also tasked with the training of future nursing officers and those enrolled in specialist nursing programmes.

Altogether, she had to cater to a diverse student population, each group with its own unique needs. She saw her role not as a set of separate responsibilities, but as one continuous, integrated mission, and she was very clear on how she intended to deliver the best for all.

Madhuri's Perspective Plan

Against this backdrop, Madhuri formulated her perspective plan for the institution. At its heart was the idea of integrated training, which meant merging theory and practical experience in a symbiotic manner to ensure better retention and deeper understanding in the art and science of medicine. She believed that while rigorous mental discipline was crucial to mastering the fundamentals of medicine, it also needed to be complemented by the constant presence of empathy while dealing with patients. This formed the foundation of what she called the 'Head and Heart Principle'—a vital requirement for all doctors, and even more so for those who serve in the armed forces. She also strongly believed that the spirit of research must be actively nurtured within the medical fraternity, and there was no better place to begin than at AFMC. Academic rigour needed to be balanced with well-being; hard work was essential, but so was the capacity to enjoy life in the right measure.

Administrative support was a key enabler in her plan, whether it was round-the-clock access to viable dining facilities (especially important for PG trainees with erratic schedules), or fitness facilities to ensure the well-being of both body and mind. She also recognised the need for support systems such as childcare arrangements so that young mother-trainees could focus on their demanding academic work with peace of mind.

The vision plan Madhuri laid out was not just an aspirational document; it was a detailed blueprint. It included both the theoretical framework and a phased implementation strategy, with timelines and clearly defined deliverables. Once the plan was drafted, she first discussed it with the commandant and then presented it to the broader AFMC community—students, faculty, and administrative staff—urging everyone to move forward together towards the shared goal of holistic training at AFMC.

This wasn't her first such endeavour. Back in 2010, when she had taken over as head of the paediatrics department, she had outlined what she called *Vision Plan 2020* for paediatrics. By 2017, that plan had progressed significantly and was well on its way to completion. Implementation had begun soon after she first conceived it and continued even during her tenure as DDG at Army HQ. Now, as dean, she had the opportunity to carry it forward to its conclusion—something that gave her great satisfaction.

The second major vision she had shaped was also during her time as DDG: a comprehensive, long-term plan for the development and optimal deployment of the armed forces' specialist medical pool. It was intended to enhance inter-service efficiency and was largely successful. The plan remains in use, with necessary updates to keep pace with advancements in medicine.

These two experiences, combined with the administrative insights she had gained during her posting in Delhi, prepared her well for the vision she now set out for AFMC, a vision she was determined to bring to life during her tenure as dean.

Let's take a look at some of the key improvements, enhancements, and innovations introduced by Madhuri.

1. Positive Work Culture

Madhuri began implementing her ideas by redesigning her daily routine to balance the dual responsibilities of being dean and deputy commandant. With her primary focus on academics, she dedicated her mornings to matters related to students, faculty, teaching, and overseeing the execution of academic improvement plans. Administrative matters were taken up in the afternoon, and she made it a point to regularly brief the commandant on significant academic developments.

Her aim was to foster an atmosphere of trust and mutual respect at the senior level, which is essential for effective leadership. She also wanted to send a clear message to both faculty and administrative staff that the two wings were not separate or competing entities but complementary parts of the same institution. In any organisation, a degree of friction between the technical and administrative arms is common, and AFMC was no exception. But when the two senior-most functionaries are aligned, the tone shifts and real progress becomes possible. This larger vision—of a united and collaborative institution—was central to the success of the vision plan she had shared with the commandant.

In typical Madhuri fashion, she wasted no time in reimagining her physical workspace as well. She cleared out excess furniture to make her office more spacious, replaced dark upholstery with light pastel shades to brighten the environment, and added neatly arranged vases, real plants, and fresh flowers to bring warmth to the space. A clean and uncluttered desk completed the transformation into an efficient, welcoming workspace.

She also noticed that her clerical staff lacked comfortable working conditions and promptly made the necessary improvements. For Madhuri, ensuring that her team felt cared for and comfortable wasn't just an afterthought; it was essential. And she had a natural instinct for making people feel seen, valued, and empowered.

Everyone was aware of Madhuri's quick decision-making ability. She made it clear from the outset that if an issue could be resolved over the phone, there was no need for a face-to-face meeting. She cut down long waiting times in lounges, and all meetings—whether with staff or faculty—were direct and to the point. Everyone was expected to state the issue at hand, share any problems, and offer possible solutions.

Madhuri had a remarkable ability to distil complex matters down to their essence and approach them methodically. Giving practical guidance and direction was her forte, and she did it with characteristic aplomb. She placed high value on everyone's time, especially the faculty, who had to juggle teaching, patient care, and administrative tasks daily. Having been part of the faculty herself, she knew first-hand that administrative staff often lacked a full understanding of these time constraints. Resolving this disconnect was one of the key issues she was determined to address during her tenure.

2. The Undergraduate Sphere

Among her many responsibilities, it was the undergraduate domain where Madhuri most wanted to make a lasting impact. Students arrived at AFMC directly from civilian life, raw, unshaped, and full of potential. The goal was to mould them into strong, independent, self-confident individuals, equipped with both intellectual rigour and emotional depth, with the head and the heart in the right place.

She envisioned that those who entered the portals of AFMC should not only be academically accomplished but also possess talents and interests in other spheres, such as sports, music, dramatics, and co-curricular pursuits that build character and broaden perspectives. A blend of such talents enriched the community and helped shape well-rounded personalities. The ultimate aim: to produce doctors who were not just skilled, but sensitive and sensible, making them ideal custodians of healthcare in the armed forces.

3. The UG Selection Process

When it came to the UG selection process, Madhuri made a concerted effort to ensure that the right aspirants were selected. As chairman of the selection board, she led the final interview process, ensuring that pointed, thoughtful questions were asked to assess each candidate's suitability for the armed forces. This special interview process is a unique privilege granted only to AFMC, owing to the specific requirements of service life.

Her efforts to attract top-calibre students to AFMC had already begun during her tenure as DDG. Now, as dean, she was in a position to further that impact. The very fact that a woman had risen to become dean of AFMC and done so with dignity, distinction, and strength was a powerful signal. AFMC, she believed, was one of the finest institutions for women to serve the country, offering an adventurous life, strong camaraderie, and a deep sense of purpose rooted in national service.

She also made it a point to interact with the parents of incoming students, reassuring them about the quality of life and support awaiting their children. She often said, 'You are handing us a raw product. It is now our responsibility to shape them into fine lady or gentleman doctors, who will serve with compassion and commitment.'

Thanks to these efforts, AFMC began to attract some of the finest young minds to fulfil the armed forces' medical needs.

4. UG Training

The foundation of any undergraduate medical institution lies in the quality of its faculty and in that respect, AFMC had few equals. The college was staffed with some of the best doctors in the armed forces—professionals with strong reputations and clinical prowess—committed to teaching the next generation.

To build on this base, Madhuri introduced an integrated model of teaching, merging theoretical instruction with practical exposure from the early stages. Traditionally, subjects were taught in silos. This meant that students would learn one speciality at a time and were expected to integrate the knowledge on their own as they progressed. But in reality, medicine isn't practiced in silos.

Take, for instance, gynaecology and paediatrics which are intimately connected disciplines where the health of the newborn is a direct extension of maternal health. Yet, the two departments often worked independently, with little coordination. Such compartmentalisation was common across many specialities. Recognising this, Madhuri formed interdisciplinary teams from within her talented faculty to design integrated training modules that better reflected real-world scenarios.

She also introduced competency-based training capsules—well ahead of their time—which later became the cornerstone of modern medical teaching methodologies.

Another notable innovation Madhuri introduced in the training curriculum was the use of role-play-based learning sessions designed to highlight the human aspects of medical care. These sessions focused on bedside manners, the importance of politeness, and the often-unnoticed impact of rudeness, arrogance, or impatience shown by doctors or nursing staff. These seemingly minor behaviours can significantly affect a patient's sense of well-being.

The sessions were recorded on video and subsequently institutionalised as part of sensitisation training for all healthcare personnel. In fact, Madhuri herself participated in one of the dramatised sessions, taking on the role of an ayah who, as is sometimes the case, behaved rudely towards patients. The exercise powerfully demonstrated how even non-medical staff play a vital role in the patient care experience. Madhuri hoped that this inclusive and experiential form of training would instil greater awareness and empathy across the entire chain of care delivery, ultimately leading to better patient welfare.

To further enhance hands-on training, she also increased the frequency of clinical sessions for students. While this did place additional demands on the faculty, she managed to balance the load by adjusting work schedules and encouraging flexible hours. The highly motivated faculty responded with commitment, putting in long hours without hesitation.

Madhuri herself had always loved teaching and was known for her knack of reviving interest in even the most neglected subjects. On more than one occasion, during her morning rounds, if she found that a faculty member had been delayed, she would step in without hesitation and conduct the class herself. Her grasp of the core subjects was such that she needed no preparation. And yet, through her unique takeaways method, she was able to imprint key learning points in the students' minds with clarity, structure, and precision.

5. The Attendance Factor

Having experienced the difference that consistent attendance made in her own academic journey, Madhuri placed great emphasis on it during her tenure as dean. During her early days as a student at AFMC, the initial euphoria of newfound freedom had caused her to miss a few classes, and the result showed in her early assessments. Learning from that setback, she corrected course and went on to excel. That personal lesson became a guiding principle she wanted her students to benefit from.

She firmly believed that AFMC students had access to some of the finest faculty in the country and that skipping this opportunity was a serious loss. Consequently, she enforced a strict rule of 80 per cent minimum attendance. To ensure compliance, she introduced a graduated system of consequences, ranging from extra classes beyond regular hours, to staying back during term breaks (thus missing the chance to go home), and finally, rustication for chronic non-compliance.

Exceptions were made only for those participating in college-approved activities—sports, academic contests, or co-curricular commitments—and even then, only up to a 5 per cent waiver. She was also cautious about students over-committing to extracurriculars at the cost of academics and actively curtailed such tendencies.

While her tough stance on attendance wasn't always popular among the students, Madhuri held firm. For her, there could be no compromise when it came to academic discipline.

6. The Postgraduate Domain

Madhuri had completed her own postgraduate training in Mumbai after missing the opportunity to pursue it at AFMC.

Rather than carry any resentment, she had turned that challenge into an opportunity, using her time in Mumbai to build herself into a well-rounded and resourceful clinician. The experience of having to travel across the city to gain clinical exposure from a wide range of hospitals and senior mentors was something she greatly valued in hindsight.

It was this enriching aspect that she now sought to bring to the PG training experience at AFMC. She felt that while the AFMC PG students were fortunate to have a strong in-house faculty and excellent clinical material available through the command hospital, this also placed them in something of a comfort zone. Their exposure was high in quality but narrow in scope.

To address this, she introduced a twinning arrangement with BJ Medical College in Pune. This allowed the PG trainees to rotate outside of AFMC, giving them broader exposure to both patients and a diverse teaching faculty. It broke the confines of a single-institution mindset and encouraged them to learn from varied environments and clinical settings.

Understanding that PG students often worked around the clock and frequently missed regular mealtimes, Madhuri also introduced a 24/7 food counter within the Officers' Mess premises. This not only provided much-needed access to nutritious food at odd hours but also ensured their safety by minimising the need to venture out at night in search of meals. The initiative was deeply appreciated and addressed a long-standing practical need.

7. Research-Driven Learning

One of Madhuri's primary areas of focus in strengthening the PG curriculum was research. Although postgraduate students are required to submit a thesis as part of their training, this was often approached as a formality rather than an opportunity for genuine inquiry. The research tended to be superficial—more of a checklist item than a meaningful academic pursuit. Madhuri made a concerted effort to change this mindset and methodology.

She strongly believed that postgraduate education must cultivate a deeper spirit of inquiry and a drive for original learning, which are essential for advancing the practice of medicine. She was a firm advocate of translational research, which bridges the gap between theoretical knowledge and practical application. In her view, an early exposure to this approach was critical, and the foundation for it had to be laid during undergraduate training itself. She believed that the basics of research methodology must be instilled at the UG level, so students would be better equipped to undertake meaningful research during their postgraduate years.

To advance this goal, she also proposed changes to the annual research project approval process in the armed forces under the aegis of DGAFMS. Madhuri suggested the establishment of a dedicated research cadre within the armed forces and emphasised the need for stability and support for those pursuing careers in this domain. Her vision included setting up a central research hub at AFMC with a network of regional nodes in command hospitals and other major institutions, each node focusing on research aligned with regional medical priorities. This Hub and Spoke model, she argued, would help channel limited resources towards projects with tangible utility for the armed forces, rather than spreading them thinly across superficial studies.

Her proposals were practical and forward-looking. However, they also required a shift from long-standing systems, and naturally, met with some resistance from the establishment. Despite the lukewarm response, Madhuri pursued her vision with characteristic persistence. She took it upon herself to initiate the creation of the central research hub at AFMC. By the time she moved on to her next assignment in 2019, she had successfully established a fully functional multidisciplinary research unit (MRU).

She received vital support from her senior and friend, Dr Soumya Swaminathan, who later rose to become DG of ICMR and chief scientist at WHO. With her help, Madhuri secured funding and backing from the Department of Health Research to build the MRU at AFMC in a mission-mode project. Dr Balram Bhargava, who succeeded as DG ICMR, continued to extend full support.

In its first phase, the MRU included a sleep lab, a molecular and epigenetic lab, and a 3D printing lab—pioneering facilities that Madhuri envisioned as the launchpad for a strong research culture. She was ably assisted by Col Karuna Datta, who had completed her PhD in Yog Nidra and brought infectious energy to the effort.

Today, the initiatives that took root in 2019 have gained recognition and momentum. Madhuri also opened AFMC's doors to collaborative research with premier institutions based in Pune such as the National Centre for Cell Science, National Institute of Virology, and National AIDS Research Institute, laying the groundwork for high-quality research partnerships.

8. The Field of Nursing

In the armed forces, nursing is a distinct and respected service, with qualified nurses commissioned as officers in their own cadre. Their role is crucial in delivering quality care across all levels of the forces. The main training hub for nursing officers' functions under AFMC in Pune, with additional training centres in designated command hospitals. Specialist training is also conducted at the College of Nursing in Pune. All of these fell under Madhuri's area of responsibility.

Having worked closely with nursing officers during her clinical years, Madhuri had developed immense respect for their skill, commitment, and quiet competence. She often acknowledged that their practical experience had, on many occasions, been life-saving. In fact, she would say that nurses often outperformed doctors when it came to bedside efficiency.

One of her key concerns was improving administrative facilities for the nursing establishment at Pune. Some infrastructure upgrades had been initiated earlier but had since stalled due to contractual complications. Through deft handling and strong relationship-building, Madhuri was able to break the deadlock and revive the work. The new residential block for nursing officers was soon completed. She was delighted to inaugurate the facility and celebrate the moment with the nursing community, who responded with joy and appreciation.

Beyond infrastructure, she also took a close look at their academic curriculum, streamlining it to strengthen training standards and better align it with the practical demands of their roles.

Another important area she addressed was staffing and availability. While posted as DDG at Delhi, Madhuri had closely studied the system governing the deputation of nurses for refresher and specialist training. She found that too many nurses were being sent for training simultaneously, creating shortages in hospital staffing. To remedy this, she introduced two key reforms. First, she proposed the creation of a reserve pool of nursing staff within the armed forces to compensate for those temporarily away on training. Second, she introduced a staggered training calendar to avoid bulk deputations.

As dean at AFMC, she was now in a position to implement these changes on the ground. Initially, the nursing staff viewed the new policy as a restriction on their opportunity for career growth. However, Madhuri made it a point to explain that striking a balance between individual aspirations and service requirements was essential. Over time, the community understood the rationale, and the policy was accepted in the right spirit—as a step towards better functioning and care delivery across the board.

9. Infrastructural Enhancements at AFMC

Madhuri always believed that a strong academic environment could thrive only when supported by sound administrative infrastructure. Residential blocks for students needed to be well maintained. Informal refreshment facilities near their hostels and clean, orderly dining arrangements for daily meals were essential for their comfort. Sports and other recreational provisions were seen as vital extensions of student life. Co-curricular activities such as debating clubs, adventure outings, and music festivals also needed to be encouraged in the right measure. Intercollegiate competitions in these areas were critical in order to cultivate a sporting and resilient spirit but also to nurture leadership qualities in students who were soon to become officers in the Indian Armed Forces.

It was with this holistic outlook that she chose to take an active role in administration as the deputy commandant. Initially, the administrative staff was not very comfortable with Madhuri's insistence on being kept informed of daily activities. They had been accustomed to reporting directly to the commandant and following his directives.

However, through persistence and persuasion, Madhuri gradually won them over and soon streamlined several processes for the larger good. Her efforts resulted in substantial improvements in infrastructure. One of the most notable achievements was the inauguration of a new academic-cum-cultural block, aptly named the Aprameya Complex. Aprameya is another name for Lord Krishna, representing the transcendental—what lies beyond measure. Medicine, with its boundless pursuit of knowledge, could be viewed in a similar light. Likewise, the development of the human mind holds limitless potential. Hence, it was a fitting name for a complex where students could explore not only medicine but also other human pursuits that would enhance their capabilities as doctors. The complex included spacious halls for lectures and examinations, as well as spaces for the music club, dramatics and debating societies, and several indoor sports activities.

Madhuri also engaged directly with the students, seeking suggestions on ways to improve their daily routines. In response, canteen facilities near the boys' hostel were upgraded significantly. Television and internet access were added to support both entertainment and self-study. At the students' request, washing machines and a café were made available for both boys and girls. She encouraged the girls to develop terrace gardens and create mural-style paintings on the interior hostel walls. Small coffee and ice-cream kiosks were established near the mess to further enhance campus life. The overarching aim was to foster a positive and vibrant environment through administrative measures—an environment that would, in turn, support strong academic performance.

In a small way, I too was able to contribute to the rejuvenation of AFMC's infrastructure. During my tenure as the quartermaster general prior to retirement, I discovered that AFMC—despite being a tri-service institution—had inadvertently been excluded from the infrastructure fund distribution due to a procedural oversight. After investigating the matter, I was able to restore the flow of resources to the institution. As a result, during Madhuri's tenure as dean, many projects that had long been stuck in bureaucratic limbo finally saw the light of day.

10. The Cadets' Mess

The Cadets' Mess at AFMC is a large facility capable of seating all 500-plus cadets under training at once. Madhuri saw in it a valuable opportunity to instil proper mess etiquette in her students. In the armed forces, many traditions govern attire, table layout, and the formal serving of meals. She felt that select days of the week could be used to gradually introduce students to these customs.

While it was relatively easy to guide the boys in wearing their uniforms correctly, she was surprised to learn that many of the girls were unfamiliar with how to drape a sari. Madhuri introduced these protocols gently and over time. Eventually, a marked improvement was seen in the students' conduct. They came to understand the distinctions between formality and informality and recognised the importance of maintaining decorum in the mess premises.

Her aim was to transform the mess from a mere building into an institution the students would take pride in and that mission was largely accomplished.

11. A Crèche for the Toddlers

An important initiative taken by Madhuri to support young mothers at the institution was her effort to establish a crèche for toddlers. To provide a secure and safe space for young children within the AFMC campus, she sought and obtained permission to repurpose a disused residential house for this facility. While it took time to complete the necessary administrative formalities, six months later a bright, cheerful crèche-school was up and running within the AFMC premises. It was formally inaugurated by the spouse of the chief of army staff. Run under the management of a professional agency, the crèche functioned efficiently throughout Madhuri's tenure as dean.

12. Introducing a New Tradition

Shortly after we had settled in, the lively atmosphere of AFMC reminded me of my days at the NDA. One of my fondest memories was the commandant's tea—a monthly gathering at the commandant's residence atop Peacock Bay for cadets who had excelled in any area, be it academics, sports, or other fields. The function served as an informal meet-and-greet between the commandant and the achievers. His spouse was always present and would ensure that there were ample treats for the young guests—a highlight for us cadets and a strong incentive to perform well and earn repeated invitations! As both a good student and a keen sportsperson, I had the good fortune of attending many such gatherings.

Recalling that experience, I suggested to Madhuri that she consider introducing a similar tradition in the form of a monthly dean's tea, where she could engage with her students informally. She loved the idea—being naturally drawn to young people and their energy—and saw it as a chance to gather feedback on their daily lives while also giving them a chance to enjoy some hearty treats at the dean's residence.

The idea took off, and soon a stream of students began visiting our home each month. Madhuri would prepare one dish for the gathering herself, and in a fun twist, the students were also expected to cook one dish using ingredients provided at home. The wood-fired pizza oven at the dean's house proved to be quite the hit as everyone thoroughly enjoyed making their own pizzas. Initially, the students were a bit apprehensive about the setup, but Madhuri's cheerful, engaging nature quickly put them at ease. Over time, these evenings became lively, joyful affairs that we both looked forward to.

13. The AFMC Marathon

The AFMC Marathon was institutionalised during Madhuri's tenure as dean. The opportunity arose when a prominent banking institution proposed organising a Plankathon to promote healthy lifestyle practices. Madhuri agreed to host it at AFMC but laid down clear guidelines to ensure the event aligned with the institution's values and standards. A well-known film personality was slated to be the chief guest, generating considerable excitement across the campus.

Madhuri firmly instructed the organisers that AFMC cadets—who were, after all, the primary hosts—must not be relegated to the background but be given front-row access to the proceedings. When, at the last minute, the organisers attempted to sideline this commitment, Madhuri made it clear that if they did not follow the agreed guidelines, they were welcome to pack up and leave. Her firm stance ensured the event went ahead exactly as planned, and the cadets thoroughly enjoyed the experience.

Since that memorable beginning, the AFMC Marathon has become a staple event on the Pune Marathon Calendar, attracting larger crowds with each passing year.

14. Festivals on Campus

Madhuri understood that many young cadets at AFMC were unable to visit their families during festivals like

Diwali, Holi, and others. With her characteristic enthusiasm, she resolved to recreate a sense of home for her 500 children on campus. As a result, each festival became a celebration filled with unrestrained joy. Sweets were prepared in the Cadets' Mess, and food-making competitions were organised among the students, complete with generous prizes. A formal committee would be constituted to evaluate the dishes—judging originality, taste, and innovation—turning the entire event into a cherished memory.

During Holi, Madhuri would join the festivities with the same gusto, often diving into the colour-filled ponds alongside the cadets. Her fun-loving spirit made her immensely popular, and the students would momentarily forget the firm hand with which she managed academics and discipline. Over time, the bond she shared with the student body grew so strong that she was affectionately given the title 'The Rajmata.'

15. Religious Events

In Indian homes, a deep emphasis is often placed on cultivating spiritual values in children. Without bringing in any overt religious bias, Madhuri ensured that functions at the mandir, gurdwara, masjid, and church were conducted with dignity and grace. She attended all such gatherings in her personal capacity, focusing on the universal values and goodness that flowed from them. Her approach highlighted the importance of being good human beings above all else. She moved with warmth and ease among the students and staff and often expressed how blessed she felt to be a part of such inclusive moments.

16. The Annual Intercollegiate Sports and Music Festival

These festivals were a long-standing tradition at AFMC, and Madhuri strongly supported them. They challenged the students' organisational abilities and brought out their best. However, she also understood the need to ensure that youthful exuberance didn't spill over into indiscipline.

To that end, she came up with a clever solution: she formed quick reaction teams (QRTs) made up of the 'big boys' of the college, i.e., students she knew well, not just in terms of academics but also in terms of discipline, attendance, and temperament. Interestingly, she would often assign leadership of these QRTs to students known to be a little mischievous. She believed that by giving them responsibility for maintaining decorum, they would rise to the occasion. The QRTs were tasked with staying vigilant and curbing any disruptive behaviour at its onset.

This system worked remarkably well. The cadets on duty felt honoured to be entrusted by the Rajmata and lived up to her expectations. Under her leadership, all such events were conducted smoothly. In these moments, Madhuri's presence transcended her formal role as dean. She became a trusted leader, respected and beloved by the student body.

17. Inclusion on the TED Talk Map

In yet another imaginative initiative, Madhuri helped place AFMC on the TED Talk map. The suggestion came from the faculty and students themselves. Since TED chooses its venues based on academic rigour and organisational capacity, she saw this as a unique opportunity to promote holistic personality development among the cadets.

With her backing, the proposal received a positive response, and the first TED Talk was held on campus thanks to her efforts. The high calibre of speakers ensured enthusiastic participation, and the sessions were deeply appreciated by the audience. It became a meaningful platform for stimulating the minds of both students and faculty.

18. Student Counselling

Madhuri was acutely aware of the psychological pressures faced by the student community. While some students turned to substance abuse to cope, others slipped into depression, sometimes exhibiting violent or suicidal tendencies. She kept a close watch on vulnerable students and actively counselled those in distress. In serious cases, she also reached out to their parents.

Recognising the need for professional intervention in certain situations, she established a dedicated counselling centre, where trained psychologists and counsellors could provide guidance. Sessions could be held privately if the student wished. These efforts proved effective and well-received.

Her experience also led her to envision a more contemporary solution: an online, anonymous, and menu-driven counselling service. Realising its growing relevance, she has continued to work in this field to this day.

19. Other Projects

Madhuri also spearheaded several other valuable projects. She felt that the Officers' Mess needed a well-appointed lounge. Taking a hands-on approach, she personally sketched out the proposed structural modifications, selected the colour scheme, and chose the furniture and furnishings, transforming the lounge into a space truly worthy of hosting important guests at AFMC. A new gymnasium and salon complex were additional enhancements to the mess facilities. The highlight, however, was the creation of a state-of-the-art pub within the same complex. Affectionately referred to as The PubMed—a witty nod to both its AFMC location and the well-known medical database—it quickly became a popular and vibrant gathering spot. The addition of a wood-fired pizza outlet called Pizza Kilnic made it the most happening place in that part of the cantonment.

Events of Significance

It would be appropriate to bring this part of Madhuri's career to a close by recounting some key events that had a lasting impact on her professional journey.

As mentioned earlier, soon after assuming her role as dean at AFMC, Madhuri presented her vision plan to the entire institution. She laid out clear deliverables against defined timelines and pursued them with unwavering commitment. In recognition of her exceptional service, she was awarded the Ati Vishisht Seva medal by the honourable president of India in 2018—a richly deserved feather in her cap.

Parliamentary Delegation Visits AFMC

In early 2018, a parliamentary delegation was scheduled to visit AFMC to review its functioning and consider ways to support its further development. The commandant discussed the matter with Madhuri and requested her to present AFMC's achievements on his behalf. The aim was to offer the delegation a comprehensive view of the institution's progress and potential.

Madhuri took up the task with characteristic diligence. Having already formulated a vision plan at the start of her tenure, she was able to anchor her presentation with clarity and purpose. She highlighted the remarkable transformation that AFMC brought about—how it shaped civilian youth into military doctors who were not only skilled in medicine but also instilled with the compassion and empathy needed to serve as soldier-doctors in the Indian Armed Forces.

She showcased the infrastructure enhancements that had been implemented to foster a positive learning and training environment. Looking ahead, she proposed elevating AFMC to the status of an institute of excellence—a move that would ensure greater autonomy and sustained funding for future growth. She also underscored the need for a dedicated research wing at AFMC, one that could engage in translational research and contribute to national health priorities as well as the unique medical needs of the armed forces.

At the end of her presentation, Madhuri fielded several pointed questions with poise and confidence. She then took the delegation on a well-planned tour of the campus. By the end of the visit, the members of the parliamentary delegation were deeply impressed and conveyed their satisfaction with AFMC's functioning. They assured her that all necessary support would be extended at the earliest.

Appointed to PM's STIAC

In the latter half of 2018, Madhuri received an unexpected call from the principal scientific advisor (PSA) to the prime minister of India. He congratulated her and informed her that she had been nominated to serve on the PM's Science, Technology and Innovations Advisory Committee (STIAC). He expressed hope that they would meet soon.

For a moment, Madhuri was stunned. She politely told the caller that he might have dialled the wrong number; perhaps he intended to reach someone else. She also explained that, as a serving military officer, she was not aware of any such deputation and believed no external appointment could be made without the approval of her military superiors. The PSA reassured her that she was indeed the intended nominee. He explained that her name had emerged after a thorough selection process, and that the appointment came from the highest authority. He congratulated her once again and told her to await further details regarding the inaugural meeting in Delhi.

Madhuri was speechless. The news had come out of the blue, and she had no idea how to process it. Within hours, it began circulating on social media, and congratulatory messages started pouring in from friends and well-wishers.

Unfortunately, as Madhuri had feared, her superiors were not entirely pleased. They questioned why she had not informed them earlier. When she explained that she herself had no prior knowledge, her explanation was met with scepticism. However, once formal communication regarding her appointment was received, the matter was no longer pursued.

Madhuri navigated this sweet-bitter development with measured grace in the days that followed. I, however, was immensely proud of her achievement. To the best of my knowledge, she was the first serving officer to be appointed to the PM's STIAC—a distinction that, in my view, deserved far greater recognition. The fact that it wasn't may be interpreted in various ways.

Since her appointment, Madhuri has had opportunities to present her views on medical education, healthcare, and research at the national level. Over time, she has been inducted into numerous other scientific committees across the country, a fitting reflection of her wide-ranging capabilities.

The Annual Review Bug

This episode traces back to the concluding phase of Madhuri's tenure as the DDG at Army HQ. Though the working environment did not quite match Madhuri's naturally exuberant temperament, she continued to give her all, operating with full vigour and commitment. She has always had a natural disposition for putting in her best, without allowing negative thoughts to weigh her down.

At the end of any tenure, it is customary for an officer to be reported upon by the immediate superior. Accordingly, Madhuri submitted the requisite document a week before her departure for Pune, anticipating that the process would be completed before she left the station. However, this did not happen. She proceeded to Pune, trusting that the formalities would be concluded in due course.

Once in Pune, Madhuri immersed herself wholeheartedly in her new assignment. Several months passed with no update on her annual appraisal. The delay raised concerns as something seemed amiss, and there was a sense that she might have been adversely affected. Well-wishers advised her to take preventive steps, and she accordingly applied for redress on the basis of her apprehensions.

Her concerns were formally examined and as feared, inconsistencies were found in the report submitted about her. These were set aside, thus safeguarding her prospects for promotion. This much-needed reprieve came just in time—in the latter half of 2018—allowing her to be considered for the next rank. Both of us breathed a sigh of relief. This was the first time Madhuri had faced such a situation in her otherwise steady career, and it came at a particularly sensitive juncture.

We reflected on the strange parallel in our professional journeys, noting how both of us, at different times, had faced critical moments that tested our resolve. In both instances, we were fortunate to have support that helped us overcome those hurdles. It reaffirmed our shared belief that sincere and honest work is ultimately rewarded in the armed forces, in one form or another.

Subsequently, Madhuri's promotion to the rank of lieutenant general was approved. As expected, she was placed last in seniority among her batchmates, since the earlier issue regarding loss of seniority had not been ruled in her favour. We knew this would inevitably delay the promotion, and we briefly considered whether we should file for reconsideration.

But Madhuri felt her focus needed to remain firmly on her mission at AFMC. Any seniority case, she felt, could be taken up at a later time, if at all. And so, we dropped anchor, allowing her to concentrate fully on her role at her beloved alma mater.

Social Snippets of Interest

Since Pune was our hometown, our time there was peppered with warm family gatherings. The lush green surroundings of the Cantonment and the charming premises of AFMC made for a perfect setting. For us, it was an opportunity to host our loved ones with warmth and care, especially since, during our earlier brief visits to Pune, we were usually the guests.

One particularly memorable occasion was the celebration Madhuri organised for Teju's birthday in February 2018. Teju had been told to come directly to our place after work for a casual, fun evening themed around *Punjabiyat* (the unique cultural identity and spirit of the Punjabi people). She was also asked to bring a suitable change of clothes for the occasion.

Madhuri, with her characteristic flair, transformed our residence into a vibrant mini-Punjabi dhaba. She set up makeshift *chullas* (stove or cooker) and a *tandoor* (clay oven), added wooden tables and chairs, and even placed a few colourful *charpais* (cot) to complete the ambience. The decorations were bright and bustling, just like those that attract customers to roadside dhabas. The menu was equally authentic, and it included tandoori roti, dal makhani, sarson da saag, lassi, and, of course, gulab jamun for those with a sweet tooth. The air was filled with lively Punjabi music and dance numbers that were guaranteed to get everyone on their feet.

When Teju arrived, she didn't even recognise the house and drove past the gate! It never crossed her mind that her otherwise elegantly understated mother-in-law would transform the home into a full-blown dhaba. Once she stepped inside, we all had a fabulous time. Madhuri has always lived by the motto 'Work hard and party harder,' and that evening was no exception.

Madhuri was a well-known figure in civilian circles as well, and she maintained a wide network of friends and acquaintances. There were frequent official visits from her superiors at AFMC, many of whom knew us personally. Hosting them at home for a meal became routine. Since I had retired as a senior military officer, I too had friends in the higher echelons of the military community in Pune, which kept our social calendar busy during our AFMC days.

Madhuri, with her impeccable hosting instincts, ensured that each gathering felt personal and memorable. Her eye for décor, her thoughtful selection of menus, and her attention to the dining layout were all part of the experience. These occasions were more than mere social engagements for her; they were a creative outlet, a hobby that brought her joy and provided her with the kind of mental relaxation that helped her perform even better at work.

A Moment of Grief

Not all memories from our AFMC days were joyful. One deeply saddening event unfolded during one of our social gatherings. We had invited my mother over to celebrate Madhuri's birthday on 15 October 2018 for a special afternoon meal. My elder brother and his family were present, as were Nikhil and Teju. My mother, who had turned eighty-seven a couple of months earlier, had not been keeping too well, and we hoped that a change of setting might lift her spirits.

After lunch, she felt tired and decided to rest for a while. A little later, she experienced some giddiness, and we admitted her to the command hospital for a check-up and further observation. Over the next couple of days, she began to feel better and was even expected to be discharged the following day. But that afternoon, while asleep, she likely lost her balance while trying to turn on her side and fell off the bed.

She was gently helped back into bed by the medical staff and appeared unhurt. However, later that evening, she slipped into a coma. Further investigations revealed that she had sustained a cranial haematoma during the fall.

The next morning, she was taken in for an emergency procedure to remove the blood clots beneath her skull. The doctors performed the intricate surgery with great care, and after a few days, she regained consciousness. However, the temporary stoppage of blood supply to the brain had caused paralysis in her limbs and facial muscles.

The hospital staff cared for her with exceptional devotion over the next month. Once her condition stabilised, we brought her home. From then on, my elder brother Sanjeev and his wife Padmaja cared for her with immense patience and love until she passed away on 29 April 2020.

This remains one of the more painful memories from our time at AFMC. It is a lingering thought in our minds, whether we could have done something more for her. That question still returns to us from time to time, and we can only hope that, with time, healing will come.

The Children and I

It feels appropriate to close this section with a small update on the children and myself. Of course, they were no longer the children we always remembered. Nikhil was now in his early thirties, with Teju not far behind. His business had picked up momentum and was now expanding into other continents. He and his partners continued to work with determination and drive. Teju, who had initially worked with Voltas in Mumbai, had moved to Mercedes in Pune. They had not yet decided to grow their family, though we hoped they might change their minds in the near future.

Vibhuti remained in Michigan and had settled well into her master's programme. She had been bravely wrestling with mathematics, while simultaneously upgrading her skills in subjects of her choice. She had made a brief trip to Pune after my retirement. Seeing me unemployed, she gifted me a small Beagle pup in June 2017. Ever since then, he has kept us on our toes at home.

In his early days, he gnawed through much of the wooden furniture. Now, grown into a handsome boy—still thoroughly undisciplined—in his pristine coat of whites, browns, and fawns, he brings us endless love and joy. He is a near-replica of our beloved old Coco, and so we gave him the same name.

In late 2017, after six months of retirement, I attempted to re-enter the civilian workforce. But within a year, I realised that I was no longer inclined to function under someone else's authority. The desire to retain my independence led me back into my own domain and that space continues to be one I cherish deeply.

In May 2018, Vibhuti completed her master's degree in information science. We were as thrilled as she was and travelled to Michigan for the graduation ceremony. It was a proud moment watching her walk up to receive her certificate from the dean. Her academic focus had been on a rather unique combination: human psychology, computers, and visual graphics, specialising in human-computer interface (HCI), which qualified her professionally as a UX/UI designer.

Earlier, she had completed a summer internship at Microsoft, and after graduation, she was offered a role in their design team in Seattle. She made the cross-country shift from Michigan to Seattle on her own, found herself an apartment, and settled into her new life.

Vibhuti had truly grown into a self-made individual. She tackled life on her own terms and remained confident in her ability to meet challenges head-on. We could see that she was developing strong wings, and we encouraged her to keep flying high.

Adieu and a Fond Farewell

In February 2019, during a visit to AFMC for the Annual Research Conference, the head of AFMS indicated to Madhuri that she was likely to be posted out of AFMC. Given the earlier setback with her seniority, it was unlikely that she would be considered for one of the top medical service appointments upon promotion. In that light, it would have been fitting for her to stay on as the commandant of AFMC and retire from there. It would have brought her great satisfaction to continue guiding AFMC on its path to excellence in the final leg of her career.

However, other factors were in play. There appeared to be someone else in the running for the coveted appointment of dean, and the hierarchy seemed inclined to make a change. Madhuri's request to stay on at AFMC was turned down. She was initially offered a posting in Delhi, but she was not keen on yet another desk job. Instead, she volunteered for an operational assignment that would allow her to serve closer to the troops.

At that time, the position of major general medical in Northern Command, responsible for medical support in the operational zones of Jammu, Kashmir, and Ladakh, was falling vacant. Madhuri expressed her interest in this post, preferring a challenge in the field over a bureaucratic role. Her proposal was initially met with scepticism, but she persisted and eventually, her request was approved. Within weeks, she received her posting orders. She was to report to HQ Northern Command in May 2019.

Madhuri embraced this new assignment with her usual zeal. I too was glad for her as it would open up new vistas of service, expose her to conditions previously unfamiliar, and bring her in close contact with the troops in forward areas. She would be able to see for herself the challenges they faced and take meaningful steps to improve medical support on the ground. It was, in every sense, a new and exciting chapter.

As soon as the posting orders arrived, the student fraternity at AFMC began preparing for a farewell befitting their beloved Rajmata. A special event was held at the Cadets' Mess. The highlight was a poem composed and recited by one of the students—an emotional tribute placed in Addendum section. It made it clear just how deeply they would miss her.

For someone who was always in control of her emotions, Madhuri found herself overwhelmed. Her eyes welled up as she tried to hold back her tears. In return, Madhuri had also written a poem to express her own feelings—a farewell song which a faculty member sang on her behalf. It was set to the tune of Terry Jacks' *Seasons in the Sun* and titled *Dean's Farewell Song*. The emotional connection between her and the students was unmistakable, and those bonds remain strong even today.

As we look back, we realise what an incredible time it was. Many of those students are now accomplished doctors and continue to stay in touch. Every Teacher's Day, Madhuri's WhatsApp overflows with messages and good wishes, each one a testament to the affection and respect she still commands. But the time had come to move on and take on the next mission.

Postscript by Madhuri

The best memories I carry from AFMC are the times spent with the cadets. They would often poke fun at my strictness through skits and plays during their social events, bringing tears of laughter and joy. They even made a short film in the dean's residence and graciously offered me a role! I took my role of being a strict mother with a heart full of love very seriously.

The song I wrote to express my feelings was sung by my colleague, Deepti, as a parody of the line 'Goodbye to You, My Trusted Friends . . .' It was my personal way of bidding farewell to my alma mater.

While I became the Rajmata, Rajeev gracefully stepped into a quiet but strong supporting role. Most senior officers apply for post-retirement appointments or nominations but Rajeev had no such desire. He was very clear: 'No job for me. That will only separate us again. I now want to stay with my wife with no requests or applications to higher HQ. I will support her.' I was sceptical at first. We had barely lived together over the years, so I wondered what he would do all day while I remained occupied with work. I am not a poet like him, but needless to say, I could never have continued without this wind beneath my wings.

Yes, he does get bored at times, home alone while I remain busy. And yes, we do have our differences now that we are full-time husband and wife! But our relationship has aged like fine wine. We are learning to embrace even those differences, with grace.

Chapter 17
Operational Medicare

The First Vibes

In her characteristic style, once she had bid farewell to AFMC, Madhuri didn't look back. She had given AFMC her head and heart while she was there. She did have dreams of taking the institution to the next level had she been allowed to continue as commandant. But since that was not to be, she accepted it with grace and turned to embrace the next set of challenges with her usual zest. For her, new challenges simply meant new opportunities. This was the simplicity of her outlook, and she took things in her stride with positivity and energy.

Madhuri and I decided that she would initially travel alone to Udhampur to assume charge, get acquainted with the operational scenario, and understand the people she would be working with. She could then return to Pune to complete the winding up. After that, I would accompany her to the new station. The plan worked out smoothly. Madhuri landed in Udhampur in May 2019 and immediately immersed herself in her new responsibilities. She found the working environment at HQ Northern Command to be extremely positive and felt at ease meeting her new professional colleagues. As always, her cheerful disposition and energetic drive made a strong impression. Many officers in Udhampur were known to me from my earlier years in the army, and I too looked forward to reconnecting with them. Overall, the new environment felt promising.

She returned to Pune after a month to wind up fully. For the journey back, we made arrangements for Coco to travel with us. We first flew to Delhi and then took the overnight train to Udhampur, which was quite convenient. Soon, we were settled in our new home in a beautiful setting. Udhampur, nestled within the Shivalik range of the Himalayas, is wonderfully located. The mountain ranges in the distance painted a picturesque view that we would enjoy every day in the months to come.

Operational Scenario

The Northern Command theatre is vast and complex. It spans across Jammu, Kashmir, and Ladakh, with terrain ranging from hills and riverine belts to dense forests and multiple mountain ranges. There are also the glaciated regions of Siachen, located over 20,000 feet in altitude. Communications—by road, rail, or air—are frequently disrupted by weather, especially during the harsh winters. Avalanches are common, and the effects of high altitude can cause serious health complications. To top it all, active military operations in the area of responsibility (AOR) result in daily casualties from gunfire, artillery shrapnel, mines, and accidents.

Madhuri's first task was to familiarise herself with these intricacies. She would then analyse the medical support system and explore ways to improve its quality and reach. She believed that good medical care was among the strongest morale boosters in operational areas, and she was committed to ensuring that troops received the best possible care, at the right place and at the right time.

I suggested that once she had gone through the briefings and map studies, she should undertake visits to the field to see things firsthand. Many of these journeys would require travelling by road or air, and in some locations, even walking through rugged terrain. Only by physically visiting these sites could she develop a full understanding of her responsibilities. Such firsthand exposure would be key to bridging the gap between policy and practice, enabling her to lead with both clarity and conviction.

Getting into Her Stride

The senior officers at HQ Northern Command were thorough professionals, and they worked well with Madhuri. They encouraged her to go ahead with her field visits and provided all necessary resources and logistical support. Summer was just setting in over the higher reaches of Ladakh and the Kashmir Valley, and it was a good time for such tours.

Her areas of focus included regions both north and south of the Pir Panjal range—Kashmir Valley to the north and the Jammu region to the south—as well as sectors across the Zanskar range in Ladakh. Each of these areas presented a different combination of terrain and military activity, requiring tailored medical planning. The complexity of the terrain, weather, and operations made her assignment both challenging and full of potential for meaningful improvements.

She began her familiarisation tour in the southern sector, as it was still accessible by road. I accompanied her during these journeys. Having served in that region earlier, I was familiar with its operational and administrative nuances, and I tried to brief Madhuri on relevant details ahead of our visits. This helped her engage more confidently and effectively during her interactions. Her visits focused on Jammu, Rajouri, and Poonch, where she concentrated on optimising the use of medical resources. Interactions with senior commanders and feedback from troops on the ground helped shape her understanding.

Travelling by road allowed her to truly absorb the realities of the terrain. Meeting troops where they lived and worked gave her valuable insight into their living conditions and medical needs. This knowledge enabled her to approach medical planning with greater empathy and precision.

North Kashmir, being larger and more varied, was tackled in stages. Madhuri first flew into Srinagar and then travelled further west and north into the higher reaches. Due to poor weather, helicopters were not operational, so she travelled by road for most of the tour. This gave her an intimate view of the difficult conditions under which soldiers served. She made it a point to meet the young medical officers embedded with frontline troops. Her presence reassured both soldiers and commanders that quality medical support was a high priority.

Ladakh was another critical region, and Madhuri visited it in phases as well. She flew to Leh by fixed-wing aircraft and travelled to Kargil and the interiors of Eastern Ladakh by road and helicopter. She was also able to reach the Siachen Glacier and witness the extreme conditions there. The area's altitude causes unique physiological and psychological stress, which must be accounted for in medical planning.

Having covered every corner of her area of responsibility and having met commanders, soldiers, and medical personnel across the board, Madhuri now had a clear, ground-level understanding of her domain. This allowed her to recommend improvements and refine systems with confidence. In military operations, the golden rule is: know your ground. By abiding by this rule, Madhuri had begun to settle comfortably and effectively into her new role.

Strategic Blueprint for Medical Care

The success of medical treatment, especially in operational settings, hinges on the ability to deliver care within a critical time window, first for immediate sustenance and later for complete recovery. In difficult and rugged terrain, where evacuating a casualty can be time-consuming and challenging, it becomes vital to position medical resources as close as possible to the operational zones. This ensures that life-saving interventions can be delivered during the golden hour.

However, complex injuries often require facilities and expertise that are only available at larger, rear-area hospitals. This dilemma—between proximity for immediate care and the need for specialised treatment further back—is a constant reference point in military medical planning.

Even the method of evacuation plays a crucial role. In some cases, the casualty must be moved on foot or astride a mule. To enable quicker movement rearward, road and air connectivity must be swiftly activated. This intricate chain—from initial treatment to evacuation and full-scale medical care—requires constant review and innovation to ensure that effective medical care is available anywhere and everywhere, anytime and all the time. Madhuri was deeply focused on all these aspects.

Having familiarised herself with the different operational sectors, the intensity and nature of operations in each, the common types of casualties, and the available modes of transport (on foot, by road, helicopter, or aircraft), Madhuri began shaping her vision for medical care in the Northern Command. Her core concept, especially for serious injuries, was built around the idea of immediate, in-situ treatment to stabilise life or limbs, followed by rapid evacuation to the nearest node with the appropriate facilities for that specific condition. She envisioned a grid of main and satellite medical centres, linked together to create a time-bound and systematic pattern of treatment.

Given the rigid hierarchy typical in army command structures, Madhuri felt that some flexibility needed to be introduced into the medical evacuation system. For instance, in the case of high-altitude sickness, the most effective treatment often lies in immediate descent to lower altitudes. Yet in some cases, patients were being evacuated to Leh, which, although equipped with excellent facilities, is itself a high-altitude zone. What was medically required was movement to a hospital situated at a lower elevation, often under a different administrative command. Such cases led to unnecessary delays due to jurisdictional formalities. Madhuri stepped in to address this issue with a practical solution—streamlined liaison between commands—to ensure timely and appropriate medical response.

Another key focus area for her was upskilling and reskilling the medical personnel. She introduced sector-specific protocols—for instance, simple adaptations in treatment techniques for gunshot or shrapnel injuries—that significantly improved survival rates. She also pushed for the effective use of telemedicine, which proved particularly valuable in remote, inaccessible regions. Her coordination with ISRO and other relevant agencies led to the establishment of an improved and reliable telemedicine network in the Northern Command.

Broadly, Madhuri believed that with improved communications, greater availability of helicopters, and the presence of forward airstrips in nearly every sector, it was now possible to evacuate casualties more quickly to the most appropriate medical facility. This, she felt, was the best way to ensure high-quality care. She also saw the region as an excellent training ground for medical personnel from the navy and air force, and in her vision plan, she advocated for a pan-service approach to make medical resource utilisation more cost-effective and collaborative across the armed forces.

Some Indelible Memories

Despite the ever-present security considerations and general state of alert, our stay in the peaceful environs of Udhampur was deeply fulfilling. Our residence was perched on a small hillock, and the daily view of the distant mountain ranges—bathed in golden light during sunrise and sunset—was nothing short of ethereal. It remains one of our most cherished and indelible memories from our time in Udhampur.

The Call of Vaishno Mata

Nestled amidst those majestic mountains is the revered Vaishno Mata Mandir. We had visited the shrine many years earlier when Madhuri was posted in Pathankot. Now, it felt as though Mataji had summoned us once again to her divine presence, and we were eager to offer our obeisance at the earliest. Fortunately, soon after settling into our new home, we were able to receive her blessings.

A well-laid walking path had come up since our previous visit, and since both of us strive to stay fit, we chose to make the trek on foot. Though a helicopter facility was available, we felt that walking up to the shrine was a more meaningful way to experience the journey. Reaching the mountaintop within a few hours, we bowed in reverence before the mata. It was a fitting and spiritually uplifting start to our time in Udhampur.

We had the privilege of visiting the mandir again when Madhuri's sisters came to see us, and once more when Nikhil and Teju visited. Our final visit took place just before we left Udhampur. Owing to time constraints, we opted for the helicopter ride that time. On each visit, we felt a deep sense of peace and rejuvenation—an experience that renewed our strength for the journey ahead.

The Amarnath Experience

Our pilgrimage to the Amarnath shrine was nothing short of extraordinary. It was the first week of August, and the yatra was in full swing. However, due to unpredictable weather, the pilgrimage had been suspended several times. One morning, both of us felt an intense inner calling to proceed to Amarnath. A well-wisher had once told us that such an impulse should be honoured without delay. So, without further deliberation, we decided to leave the very next day.

Being posted at HQ Northern Command made it relatively easier to arrange the logistics. Our plan was to travel by road to Srinagar (a six-hour journey), continue to the Baltal base camp (another two hours), and begin the fourteen-kilometre uphill trek early the following morning. We expected to reach the shrine in about six hours, spend a quiet hour in prayer, have a light meal, and then begin our descent, returning to Baltal by evening and back home the next day.

However, early the next morning, we received word that weather conditions had worsened dramatically. The road to Srinagar had been closed to civilian traffic due to safety concerns. We considered our options but felt strongly that we must continue. So, we decided to proceed up to a point just short of the Banihal Pass and take a final call from there.

We halted briefly at an army transit camp. Soon after, we were warned about the threat of shooting stones due to relentless rainfall. We were told to either turn back or move swiftly before the situation deteriorated. Our conviction remained unchanged. We believed the shrine had truly called us and we decided to press on.

What followed was an unforgettable four-hour stretch. Every few kilometres, we encountered falling rocks, and security personnel along the way would stop us momentarily to ensure it was safe before allowing us to continue. With caution and determination, we finally reached Banihal Pass. It was a eureka moment as we entered the safety of the tunnel and crossed into the Kashmir Valley. On the other side, we were greeted by a striking transformation in weather and scenery. Descending into the valley, we were surrounded by breathtaking natural beauty.

By now, it was late afternoon—the time when all movement on the road is usually curtailed. We had to move quickly if we were to reach Baltal. As we hurried along, we suddenly found ourselves in the midst of a large military convoy. I even remarked to Madhuri how unusual it was to see so many vehicles from one of my former formations, moving with such urgency. Only later did we realise that additional troops were being inducted into the valley in anticipation of the abrogation of Article 370.

It was early August 2019. Unknowingly, we had entered the valley just before it was about to go under lockdown. At the time, no one spoke openly of the impending move, and normalcy prevailed on the surface. Along the way, we had to explain our presence to several security personnel. Madhuri used her military network to inform security posts ahead and ensure we were allowed to proceed. After a day full of uncertainty and tension, we finally reached Srinagar, and later that evening, arrived at Baltal. It had been a long, adventurous day, and we were grateful to finally rest before beginning our trek to the shrine the following morning.

The next morning, we woke up at 4 a.m. to make an early start. The first piece of news we received was not encouraging; bad weather had now moved across the Pir Panjals and was affecting the Kashmir region, including the pilgrimage route. It had rained through the night, and slush covered the ground. As a result, the trek to Amarnath had been suspended, and all *yatris* (travellers) were advised to remain in their respective camps. That certainly dampened our spirits.

However, recalling how similar the situation had been when we started from Udhampur the day before, we decided not to give up so easily. We made our way to the starting point of the yatra and met the officer in charge of operations. A couple of young medical officers posted in the area had volunteered to join us on the trek. We assured the officer that we would turn back if at any point the route appeared unsafe, and we wouldn't take unnecessary risks. We were offered mules for the journey, but Madhuri, true to form, chose to walk.

So our little team—Madhuri and I, the two young doctors, the mules, and their handlers—set off for the shrine. The climb was steep and physically demanding. The rain had left the trail muddy, making parts of the trek quite tricky. We even encountered a few short stretches with falling stones along the path. But around mid-morning, the weather shifted dramatically. The sun broke through the clouds, casting a golden light over the mountains, as if smiling at us and congratulating us, perhaps, for passing a test we hadn't even fully understood until then.

A quick breakfast along the way recharged us for the final stretch. Two hours later, we reached a viewpoint where we caught our first glimpse of the holy cave, nearly a kilometre away across a blanket of snow. That first sight of the shrine filled us with renewed energy, and we pressed on eagerly.

Standing in front of the cave, in the sacred presence of the deity, was an indescribable experience. After offering our prayers, we sat quietly, soaking in the atmosphere and listening to stories of the shrine's rich history. The pandit there told us that we had arrived on a Tuesday morning which is considered especially auspicious. That only deepened the sense of grace and good fortune we felt.

The return journey, while shorter, was harder. Descending the slope exerted more pressure on our knees, and by the end, the pain was quite intense. But our determination carried us through. The moment we returned to the base camp, the physical discomfort faded into the background, replaced by a deep sense of fulfilment.

Just then, Madhuri received a message summoning her to HQ for a briefing the next morning at 10 a.m. It sounded impossible but not to her. Without hesitation, she arranged to take the early morning helicopter back to Udhampur. If that didn't work, she would fly from Srinagar to Jammu and complete the rest by road. So, instead of resting at Baltal after the demanding trek, we drove back to Srinagar that very evening and stayed the night.

The next morning, weather conditions grounded the helicopter, so Madhuri flew to Jammu by commercial aircraft and then drove to Udhampur. During the journey, she mentally prepared her briefing. At exactly 10 a.m., she walked into the conference hall and delivered her presentation—calm, confident, and thoroughly prepared, as though she had never left her desk. This moment captured the essence of her professionalism. Her dedication has always been unwavering, regardless of the odds or obstacles. Looking back, the visit to the Amarnath shrine truly felt preordained. Despite the challenges, we made it and felt blessed all over again.

Nomination to the Board of Governors (BoG)

Soon after our visit to Amarnath, Madhuri received unexpected news that she had been nominated to yet another prestigious national committee: the Board of Governors in supersession of the Medical Council of India (MCI). This interim body, set up by the government, was entrusted with overseeing all matters related to medical education across the country until the formation of a new National Medical Commission (NMC). The BoG was also tasked with suggesting structural reforms to the erstwhile MCI. For Madhuri, still a serving officer of the armed forces, it was a matter of honour to be selected for such a critical national responsibility.

However, as with her earlier appointment to the PM's STIAC, this nomination too came with its share of discomfort. Questions were raised about her joining the BoG without prior permission from her HQ. But Madhuri had neither applied for nor solicited this role, so the question of prior approval did not arise. It was the chairman of the BoG who had to step in and clarify that Madhuri had been selected in her personal capacity by the appointments committee.

Once again, Madhuri found herself navigating an uncomfortable moment within the rigid hierarchies of military protocol. Fortunately, her performance at HQ Northern Command remained impeccable and widely appreciated. Everyone was proud of the petite, dynamic officer in their midst, who balanced her operational responsibilities with utmost diligence.

Though her role on the BoG required her to travel to Delhi on weekends, she would be back at her desk in Udhampur every Monday morning, often travelling overnight by train. She handled both commitments with unwavering energy, ensuring no responsibility was left unattended.

A Helicopter Crash

During Madhuri's tenure in Udhampur, another significant event occurred; a helicopter carrying senior officers crash-landed while returning from an official visit within the AOR. Midway through the journey, the aircraft developed a serious mechanical problem. Thanks to the skill and composure of the pilot, the helicopter was brought down with a controlled impact, greatly reducing the potential damage.

News of the crash came as a shock to all. The immediate priority was the swift evacuation of the injured to the military hospital in Udhampur. As soon as Madhuri received word of the incident, she swung into action. The army follows well-rehearsed contingency protocols for such emergencies, and these were executed with speed and precision under Madhuri's supervision.

She ensured the hospital was alerted and prepped to receive casualties, while evacuation from the crash site was coordinated using smaller helicopters capable of landing in restricted zones. These helicopters airlifted the injured directly to the hospital helipad. Thanks to this rapid response, all serious cases were attended to within the golden hour.

The preparatory drills and medical SOPs, practised regularly as part of military readiness, proved invaluable in this moment. The coordinated effort by the staff of HQ Northern Command and the medical teams ensured that all those involved in the crash were rescued, treated, and given high-quality post-operative care. As the senior-most medical officer, Madhuri felt deeply gratified by her team's composure and capability during the crisis.

The Promotion Pantomime

Madhuri had been expecting her promotion anytime from June 2019, after receiving formal approval in December 2018. Her denied request to remain at AFMC was a clear signal that larger forces were at play. Accepting the situation with grace, she moved to Udhampur as directed.

Four officers had been approved for promotion along with her, and Madhuri was the last on that list due to the ongoing seniority issue. To complicate matters further, two additional officers were granted promotion after successful redressal of their cases. These two were allotted the available vacancies for the second half of 2019. This meant that Madhuri's promotion would be delayed further, and the next available vacancy would arise only at the end of February 2020. After waiting nearly a year, this additional delay felt like a double blow. Even someone as resilient as Madhuri felt disappointed and let down by the helplessness of the situation.

Sensing her frustration, I reminded her that she had weathered many storms over the years. This was not the moment to retreat into negativity. That would only give her detractors satisfaction, and she mustn't grant them that so easily. In a matter of days, Madhuri tucked that chapter away and returned to her duties with renewed energy. Her colleagues understood the situation and stood by her, empathising, encouraging, and urging her to stay the course.

By mid-January, her promotion and posting orders should have arrived. Around this time, the new head of medical services visited Madhuri at her HQ and mentioned that he expected her promotion to be cleared soon. However, when Madhuri followed up at the end of January, she was told that the sanction for her promotion had not yet been received. It became clear that another obstacle had emerged, one that lay beyond the jurisdiction of the Medical HQ.

Seeing no other option, Madhuri and I decided to travel to Delhi and seek clarity from those better placed to help. It was evident that the matter had acquired dimensions beyond pure service procedure, and once again, Madhuri would have to rely on her own initiative.

In Delhi, we met a few individuals who were familiar with the system. The general advice we received was to be patient and wait a little longer. But we could sense that the issue had taken on extraneous overtones and was likely beyond the influence of even senior military officials. At one point, we considered whether one should seek an appointment with a higher authority to apprise him of the unjust delay in Madhuri's promotion. After some reflection, however, we decided to hold back.

As the last week of February 2019 arrived, there was still no indication of movement. Queries to the Medical HQ met with polite evasions. The grapevine was buzzing with speculation that the promotion vacancy arising at the end of February might be given to an officer junior to Madhuri. This officer had also been approved for promotion along with her, but as per the norms, Madhuri, being the senior, was next in line to be promoted on 28 February. That would mean the junior officer—despite his approval—would retire without being promoted, simply due to the lack of an available vacancy.

Feeling wronged, the junior officer is believed to have projected his case to the concerned authorities. For reasons that remain unclear, his plea seemed to have found favour, and it appeared that a way was being sought to accommodate him. The simplest solution? Delay Madhuri's promotion. If that happened, she would be leapfrogged by her junior and be forced to wait for the next vacancy once again. Within a system where promotions are strictly seniority-based, this was a serious breach of the norm. Madhuri sensed that no one within the system was able—or willing—to stand up for her at this critical juncture.

Determined not to let it slide, Madhuri resolved to take the matter into her own hands. In the last week of February 2019, she went to Delhi to request a meeting with the concerned officials. Her plan was simple: she would first approach the civilian officer handling the file. If that failed, she would seek an appointment with the next authority in the chain. I stayed back in Udhampur, as she felt she needed to fight this battle alone. I respected that.

She informed her Service HQ that since no one had been able to push her case forward, she was taking the initiative herself. In Delhi, she officially sought an appointment, having informed her medical services chief. By now, time was running out; 28 February was the very next day, and the meeting was still pending.

What struck her most was the serene demeanour of the junior officer who was due to retire at noon the next day. Madhuri couldn't help but wonder whether something had already been set in motion behind the scenes, while she was still scrambling for answers. Eventually, she was told that the official she was to meet was returning from an important engagement and would see her shortly. When he did return, he summoned her in without delay. As soon as she entered, before she could even speak, he offered her a seat and said warmly, 'Congratulations.' He informed her that the sanction for her promotion had finally been received and that there would be no further delay. He wished her all the best.

It was a battle Madhuri should never have had to fight. But she did what needed to be done with quiet resolve and the strength of her convictions. For that, she deserves every bit of admiration.

An ebullient Madhuri called me from the DGAFMS's office to say she was returning to Udhampur with her promotion orders finally in hand. When she mentioned that the other officer had also been promoted through the creation of a special vacancy, I immediately sensed the potential implications of such a decision. Anyone who felt aggrieved by the outcome now had the right to appeal. Hence, it was important that she wear her lieutenant general's rank without delay, by the next morning.

All her accoutrements for the new uniform were still in Udhampur. As luck would have it, I was able to pack everything and catch a train to Delhi within the hour. It was in a buoyant mood that I boarded the train.

The next morning, we assembled at the DGAFMS's office at the appointed time. Now that her promotion had been cleared, even the DGAFMS looked visibly relieved and agreed to formally pip Madhuri in his office. And so, on 1 March 2020, after a fourteen-month wait, Madhuri donned her new rank. It was a historic moment—the first time a husband and wife had both risen to the highest rank in the Indian Armed Forces.

I was deeply proud of her. She had achieved this milestone through sheer grit and perseverance. Meanwhile, she had already been appointed as the deputy chief of army staff (medical) at HQ IDS. The DGAFMS, with a twinkle in his eye, commented that someone of her calibre might find little work to do there. Madhuri, quick as ever, replied with a grin that work had a way of following her and she was certain she would soon find herself working even harder. Little did she know that the COVID-19 pandemic was just around the corner and about to test every assumption.

Both of us returned to Udhampur soon after the pipping ceremony in Delhi. The very next day, Madhuri was officially dined and wined out of the station. Much was said about her professional contributions and her social impact. Always the life of any gathering, she had made many friends in Udhampur and was especially loved by the ladies. Even today, many of those bonds remain strong. Friendships forged in isolated or challenging service conditions tend to last a lifetime and this was no exception.

Postscript by Madhuri

I had relished every moment of my tenure as dean at AFMC. When the time came to relinquish the chair, I felt no appointment could match the stature and meaning of being dean at my alma mater. So, instead of returning to Delhi, I chose to move to the Northern Command. I took great pride in calling myself a doctor-teacher-soldier. As a doctor, I had the distinction of being the first paediatric nephrologist in the armed forces. As a teacher, I had risen to professor, head of department, and then dean, so what more could one ask for?

But as a soldier, I felt something was missing. After my early days in a field hospital, I hadn't had my boots on the ground again. That is why I sought this new challenge. I was mildly taken aback when my superior quipped—perhaps half in jest—'Do you think you are going to Northern Command as a tourist or a senior officer's wife?' He simply couldn't fathom that a woman would willingly volunteer for a posting that many male officers tried to avoid.

Some true stories really are stranger than fiction. Who would have imagined that after being empanelled to the highest rank,

I would wait fourteen long months and still have to fight for what was rightfully mine? But that is exactly what happened. And yet, all the pain and helplessness vanished the moment Rajeev reached Delhi overnight, bringing along my brand-new uniform. The stars and cap I wore were his, carefully preserved for just this occasion.

It was no small feat. We had realised a shared dream. We had grown together—each reaching our respective heights in our professions—without growing apart. When he pinned those stars on my shoulders, I gave him a smart salute, a heartfelt thank you, and said simply: 'We did it.'

Together, we had created history, becoming the first three-star general couple of the Indian Army, and possibly, of the entire Commonwealth.

Chapter 18

The Last Lap

DCIDS in Delhi

After a warm send-off from Udhampur, Madhuri reached Delhi ahead of me to take charge of her new appointment. She was designated as the next deputy chief of integrated defence staff (medical)—DCIDS (med)—in the office of the chief of defence staff (CDS). She had the rare distinction of being the first lady officer to be appointed as DCIDS (med), and that too under the very first CDS of the Indian Armed Forces. Madhuri was also only the third woman to attain the three-star rank in the armed forces, the earlier two being Lt Gen Punita Arora and Air Marshal Padma Bandopadhyay nearly fifteen years before her.

The media spotlight that had once followed her appointment as the first lady dean of AFMC reignited with renewed intensity. In those early days of March 2020, the flurry of social media activity was overwhelming. What she didn't yet know was that an even greater test of her mettle was just around the corner—the impending COVID war would soon command every ounce of her energy and attention.

I followed a few days later with Coco, after dispatching our household belongings from Udhampur to Delhi. The train journey gave me time to absorb the full weight of everything that had transpired. After all the twists and turns of our service life, Madhuri had finally donned the lieutenant general's rank she had so richly earned. February 2020 had been particularly draining for her, and I felt a deep sense of relief that the artificial drama surrounding her promotion was now behind us.

In Delhi, Madhuri had arranged temporary accommodation within the AHRR premises. Within a few days of our arrival, we were fortunate to be allotted a comfortable residence right in the heart of the capital.

DCIDS (Med): The Appointment

The DCIDS (medical) serves as the principal adviser to the chief of Defence Staff on all medical matters concerning the armed forces. Prior to the creation of the CDS post, the DCIDS (medical) reported to the chief of Integrated Defence Staff (CISC), who was responsible for overseeing inter-services coordination. However, with the appointment of the CDS in December 2019, the significance of the Integrated Defence Staff increased considerably, along with its scope of responsibilities.

The structure of command had now shifted: all three services came under the overarching guidance of the CDS, unlike earlier when the respective service chiefs exercised greater autonomy over their domains. Integration became the new mantra, and the CDS was determined to fast-track this process to enhance operational efficiency with broader strategic implications.

By the time Madhuri joined HQ IDS, the CDS had been in office for just over two months. He was familiar with Madhuri both professionally and personally and was glad to have her on his team. Known for being a go-getter, Madhuri had always been mission-focused and result-oriented. The CDS had a clear and expansive vision for the armed forces, and he viewed integration as essential to future readiness. Yet, as in most militaries across the world, there was resistance—territorial instincts and a desire to guard one's turf still lingered. The Indian Armed Forces were no exception.

He believed that Madhuri, with her clarity, drive, and credibility, could help overcome these challenges. Moreover, since the Medical Corps was already a tri-service entity under the DGAFMS, it was seen as the ideal domain to begin demonstrating the benefits of true integration—a low-hanging fruit, so to speak.

When Madhuri was first posted to HQ IDS, the appointment wasn't seen as particularly dynamic. Integration efforts were still nascent. In fact, her superior at Medical HQ even sounded apologetic when he told her that, in the absence of a more prominent posting, he had no choice but to assign her to this role. Madhuri responded in her characteristic way: with composure and clarity. She simply said that she understood how these matters worked, and that no matter where she was posted, or whom she worked with, she would find a way to contribute meaningfully and make herself invaluable to the organisation. That, indeed, was Madhuri's way.

Office Staff

Madhuri had a rather unique experience when she joined her new HQ. On her first day in office, she called in her subordinate officers to get to know them first-hand. One of them mentioned that he was in the last few months of his service and was mainly engaged in winding up formalities after many years in uniform, so she may not find him very useful. The second officer revealed that he had been recently superseded and, as a result, was not inclined to perform with much enthusiasm. The third officer had already completed his tenure and was simply awaiting his next posting. The fourth had medical issues and said he would not be able to contribute significantly. Her immediate deputy too was due to retire in a few months and was mentally preparing for life in the civvy street. That left just one officer willing to work with full energy and commitment!

Madhuri was momentarily taken aback. This was a textbook case of humour in uniform, albeit of a macabre sort. She couldn't help but wonder if this was what her service head had been alluding to when he remarked that she might find it difficult to pursue her professional goals with the usual vigour. However, Madhuri follows the army dictum with conviction: 'When the going gets tough, the tough get going.' She heard everyone out patiently and then told them that within the constraints they had each projected, she would like to know what they would be comfortable doing as part of their daily work. Through her interactions, she identified each officer's aptitude and preferences. Then, she reverse-fitted their individual requirements into the available tasks, allocating duties that aligned with their comfort zones.

She also assured them that she would be available as a mentor and guide for each of the responsibilities entrusted to them, and that she would personally help resolve any obstacles they might face.

Once this rapport was established, the very same officers who had initially expressed reluctance began to engage more seriously. Madhuri remained consistent in her patience and persistence. They were genuinely surprised. Her reputation for being a tough taskmaster with an intense work ethic was well known, and this collaborative, accommodating approach didn't quite fit the picture they had in mind.

Over time, these officers not only became efficient in their individual domains but also went above and beyond to support and execute the broader vision plan Madhuri had laid out. By the end of her tenure as DCIDS (med), that very same team had played a meaningful role in bringing her vision to life.

An Obstacle-Studded Break

Having navigated and resolved the tricky challenge of aligning her office team within the first week of taking charge in Delhi, Madhuri requested a short break to catch her breath. Around the same time, our daughter Vibhuti was due to arrive from the US for a brief trip to complete her visa formalities. We thought it would be a good opportunity to head to our hometown, Pune, for a long-overdue family gathering.

In the second week of March, we went down to Mumbai, where Vibhuti was scheduled to visit the US Consulate to begin her visa process. In the meantime, sporadic reports of the COVID-19 pandemic had started to accelerate. While the initial spread in India had been slow, cases were now rising rapidly across the country, and rumours of a nationwide lockdown were gaining traction.

On 14 March, Vibhuti went to the US Consulate for her fingerprinting appointment. The process was completed smoothly, and she was asked to return the next day with her passport for final stamping. She came back home relieved and optimistic. But later that same afternoon, she received an unexpected message from the consulate that embassies across the world had been instructed to halt all visa processing with immediate effect. This was being done to prevent the entry of potentially infected travellers into the US. The news came as a major setback, especially for Vibhuti. She had planned only a short visit to India and her apartment in the US was closed up, her pet dog had been left with a temporary caretaker, and most critically, she had only taken a brief leave from work. A prolonged stay in India could jeopardise her employment.

The situation was filled with uncertainties. We tried to approach the consular office the next day but met with no success. Understandably, we all felt a bit shaken. However, rather than staying on in Mumbai and risking being locked out of our own hometown, we decided to proceed to Pune before restrictions were formally imposed. It was an unexpected challenge, one that called for patience, calm, resilience, and a supportive environment in which to think clearly.

After reaching Pune, we decided to check whether the US Embassy was accepting requests under exceptional circumstances. Vibhuti's case qualified as such, since the consulate had already initiated the final steps of her visa process and it seemed only fair to complete them. After an intensive online search, we discovered that the American Embassy in Delhi was accepting urgent applications through their online portal. On 16 March 2020, we submitted Vibhuti's request under the category of compassionate consideration.

To our great surprise, the embassy responded positively and granted her an appointment for 18 March in Delhi. This meant a quick, unplanned dash from Pune to the capital. It was decided that Madhuri would accompany Vibhuti, not only for support but also to offer guidance in case any major decisions had to be taken on the spot. Meanwhile, the Indian government was also preparing to implement a nationwide lockdown in response to the worsening global pandemic, following the US travel restrictions on international movement.

On 17 March, Madhuri and Vibhuti flew to Delhi with all the required documents. The following morning, they visited the American Embassy. Vibhuti explained her unique situation, and the staff responded with empathy. They accepted her passport and informed her that it would be couriered back within ten days. With that, Vibhuti would be free to take the first available flight back to the US. She was immensely relieved, and both she and Madhuri returned to Pune the same evening, hopeful that the hardest part was behind them. That relief, however, was short-lived.

Barely had we begun to catch our breath in Pune when the next shock arrived. Given the ongoing spread of the COVID-19 virus, the prime minister announced sweeping restrictions on movement across the country. Starting 20 March 2020, all public transport—air, road, and rail—was suspended, and international travel came to a standstill. Once again, Vibhuti found herself trapped in uncertainty. Her anxiety grew as she had worked tirelessly to establish herself in a field she loved, and now it all seemed to hang by a thread.

She reached out to her employers in the US. They were sympathetic and allowed her to work remotely for the time being, though they couldn't guarantee how long this arrangement would last. US government policy would ultimately determine her employment status. Meanwhile, Madhuri also realised that with travel halted, she could not return to her duty station in Delhi. She promptly informed her office of the situation and assured them of her availability over the phone at all times.

The armed forces too were grappling with this unprecedented disruption. Isolation protocols had to be swiftly put in place to prevent outbreaks. Many soldiers who were on leave now needed to report back to their units, but precautions were essential to ensure no one inadvertently carried the virus back. Discussions were underway for organising special transport and health screening procedures to manage these returns safely.

While we waited for clarity on these broader concerns, we hoped Vibhuti's passport would be returned by the end of March, as promised. But another disappointment awaited us. Around 30 March, the embassy informed us that all its staff had been placed on leave and the premises were closing until further notice. This meant Vibhuti's passport was effectively stuck inside a shut embassy, with no functioning courier service to retrieve it.

It was a double blow as not only was there no confirmation that the passport was ready, but even if it was, there was no way to access it. Vibhuti was understandably distressed. We did our best to lighten the mood, but she wasn't easily comforted. To keep ourselves sane and distracted, we set a daily rhythm of indoor activities which included some light entertainment, an exercise routine between meals, and structured work-from-home schedules. The presence of Nikhil and Teju with us added warmth and reassurance during this period of forced stillness.

Soon after, we heard that the US Embassy had resumed partial operations to assist with critical cases, particularly those involving American citizens stuck in India. Encouraged, I began exploring possible solutions to Vibhuti's dilemma. We were told that with patience, things might start moving. After all, flights were still grounded, so even if the passport was retrieved, there was no immediate urgency. This logic helped calm Vibhuti, and by the second week of April, we received the long-awaited good news: her passport had been collected by an authorised contact in Delhi. Since courier services were still suspended, it would stay in safe hands for the time being. Vibhuti was overjoyed, and Madhuri and I felt a huge burden lift. A major hurdle had been cleared, and we were thankful.

Now all that remained was for international flights to resume—a prospect that still seemed distant. For now, though, we were in a better emotional space. There were even whispers that Air India might soon operate special flights to bring back Indian citizens stranded in the US. However, these flights would only be inbound; outbound travel to the US remained restricted by American authorities.

During the same week that Vibhuti's visa issue was resolved, the chief of Defence Staff (CDS) called Madhuri and asked her to report to duty in Delhi at the earliest. He informed her that a special air force aircraft would be arranged to fly her from Pune so she could rejoin and contribute to the war effort against COVID-19 in earnest. Once back in her office, Madhuri was ready to take on the new and invisible enemy, one that had gripped the nation in a crisis unlike any before.

Meanwhile, Vibhuti and I remained in Pune, trying to determine our next steps. During one of our discussions, Madhuri and I agreed that it would be best for Vibhuti and me to travel to Delhi. With her passport already in Delhi and the possibility of international flights resuming soon, it seemed prudent for her to be there, ready to leave as soon as a window opened.

As domestic air travel had not yet resumed, our only option was to travel by road. To do so, I needed special permission from the Maharashtra State Police. Further, we would have to coordinate interstate travel clearances through Madhya Pradesh, Rajasthan, Punjab, and finally Delhi. It was a daunting task, but I reached out through the army network for assistance. Fortunately, I was well acquainted with senior officers in these regions, and soon the necessary permissions were arranged. Police stations along the route were informed of our travel schedule.

We planned to leave by road on the morning of 29 April 2020, with our first halt scheduled at Mhow, Madhya Pradesh. However, that morning, my ailing mother passed away. Though she had been unwell for some time, her passing still came as a deep shock. My elder brother Sanjeev led the cremation rites, which were completed that same morning. Despite the emotional weight, I decided to proceed with the journey that day itself as it felt better to stay occupied and keep moving, both literally and mentally.

We slightly modified our route and made our first halt at Deolali. From there, we travelled to Mhow, and then to Kota in Rajasthan. At each stop, we stayed within military cantonments to minimise contact with others. The roads were eerily deserted, with no support facilities en route. We had to carry our own food and water each day and prayed our vehicle wouldn't break down mid-journey.

What we did see on the roads, however, was both heart-wrenching and unforgettable. Groups of people—migrant workers—were walking back to their villages, carrying their belongings on their heads or in plastic bags. With economic activity shut down across cities, they had lost their livelihoods and had no option but to return home on foot. Watching them along our journey was a sobering reminder of the human cost of the pandemic.

After three nights and four days on the road, Vibhuti and I reached Delhi on 2 May 2020. Many people had helped make the journey possible, and I remain deeply grateful to them. The main goal was to get to Delhi and that, thankfully, had been achieved.

Madhuri was greatly relieved to have us back. I had driven the entire first half of the journey myself, reluctant to let Vibhuti take the wheel since she wasn't used to driving in Indian conditions. But seeing my exhaustion, she stepped up and drove a fair distance, making the latter half much easier for me. Being reunited in Delhi after all the strain was an immense relief.

The next few days were spent arranging Vibhuti's onward travel to the US. Through the Ministry of External Affairs, we learned that the Indian government would allow passengers with valid visas to board the Air India repatriation flights being sent to bring home Indians stranded in the US. That was encouraging news.

When the first such flight was scheduled, we received timely confirmation and managed to secure a seat for Vibhuti. In the early hours of 7 May, Madhuri and Vibhuti left for Delhi airport. There was a degree of confusion, understandable given that it was the first international flight out after a long hiatus. But once her documents were verified, Vibhuti was permitted to enter. She cleared immigration quickly and was processed under strict COVID protocols. The cabin crew handed out sealed packets containing food and water for the entire journey, and passengers were instructed to strictly follow the safety guidelines throughout the flight.

Approximately twenty-four hours later, we received the call we had been waiting for—a cheerful voice on the other end of the line. Vibhuti had landed safely. That single call wiped away weeks of stress and anxiety. It truly was a happy ending to what could have easily turned into a nightmare. We were thankful that this turbulent chapter had closed with grace, courage, and a touch of luck.

The War on COVID

The medical services, under the leadership of the DGAFMS, were the principal agency tasked with formulating protocols to protect the armed forces from the devastating impact of the COVID-19 virus. While it was inevitable that infections would occur, the priority was to control the spread and ensure the best possible medical care for those affected. This required a dual approach: first, establishing preventive measures on one hand, and second, creating therapeutic facilities for those infected on the other. Protocols devised centrally by the medical authorities had to be implemented across all three services, under the oversight of the respective service heads and their medical organisations.

As the head of the three services, the CDS appointed Madhuri as the primary coordinator of the tri-service medical response. She was entrusted with conceptualising, planning, and overseeing the implementation of protocols across the army, navy, and air force in equal measure. Additionally, she was made the point of contact for coordination with external agencies dealing with the broader fallout of the national health emergency. This involved working closely with both the Ministry of Health and the Ministry of Home Affairs.

Among all the actions taken, the most crucial was preventing the spread of infection. Globally, efforts to develop a vaccine were in full swing, including in India. It appeared that countries such as the USA, UK, and China were making rapid advances. Several Indian companies were also engaged in vaccine research. However, even with eventual breakthroughs, there would still be a time lag for production and distribution. Interim preventive measures, therefore, remained critical.

Based on the evolving understanding of transmission patterns, a series of preventive strategies were drawn up: isolation, restricted movement, social distancing, and avoidance of contact with infected individuals. As part of the prime minister's STIAC, Madhuri was deeply involved in discussions on implementing simple and affordable methods to limit the virus's spread. In one such early conference, she suggested that in the absence of adequate N95 masks, using cloth masks could serve as an effective barrier to reduce the inhalation and exhalation of the virus. Initially, the idea didn't receive much attention as it was simply listed among various optional precautions. But soon, the humble cloth mask emerged as a key preventive tool worldwide. Complex masks with regulated inflow and outflow systems were later developed for aviation and hospital use, but in India, the affordable cloth mask became the lifeline for millions. It was a classic example of how a simple solution could effectively counter a complex problem. Madhuri's early suggestion, taken forward by senior scientists in the PSA's office, eventually became a cornerstone of India's COVID prevention strategy.

In her capacity as a member of the BoG that had replaced the MCI, Madhuri also worked closely with Member (Health) Dr Vinod Paul to draft India's telemedicine guidelines. These guidelines proved immensely beneficial during the pandemic. As a result, telemedicine in India expanded rapidly, with the Ministry of Health and Family Welfare launching the e-Sanjeevani platform. Madhuri, from HQ IDS, was able to operationalise SeHAT, the dedicated telemedicine platform for the armed forces, within just three weeks.

Another key strategy for mass prevention was isolation. This served multiple purposes. First, it helped monitor those arriving from high-risk areas for early signs of infection. Second, it curtailed further spread. Third, it supported the therapeutic management of confirmed cases. The armed forces developed one of the country's most robust multi-layered isolation systems. With soldiers returning to their units from across the nation, it was vital to ensure they were virus-free before resuming duty. These stringent measures became the foundation for maintaining operational readiness in the services.

The armed forces also rolled out an exemplary vaccination campaign, covering their 1.4 million personnel. As part of the coordination committee, Madhuri helped design a comprehensive strategy to prioritise vaccination, with special attention given to veterans. In this war, where the enemy was invisible and lived inside the human body, medical personnel were truly the front-line warriors. The structured and disciplined manner in which the forces conducted their vaccination drive became a benchmark for the rest of the country. Given their capability, discipline, and reach, the armed forces emerged as a vital pillar in India's war against COVID.

Operation CO-JEET

Seeing the scale of devastation the unseen virus was wreaking across India, the prime minister declared a war against it and co-opted the armed forces into the national effort to defeat this invisible enemy. Accordingly, the CDS implemented a tri-service strategy to combat the new menace. The armed forces were tasked with establishing nodal jumbo hospitals in various parts of the country, in collaboration with the Defence Research and Development Organisation (DRDO). The scale of the infection had grown so massive that even railway trains and stations had to be repurposed as temporary hospitals. The army's road and air transport resources were also pressed into service for transporting medicines, medical equipment, and, where required, people.

The overall responsibility of coordinating these diverse medical operations, under the directions of the CISC at HQ IDS, was entrusted to Madhuri by the CDS. She was authorised to liaise with the DGAFMS (head of medical services) for support. Additionally, she was designated as the nodal officer for interaction with DRDO to set up hospitals across the country, particularly for treating civilians. Her responsibilities also included coordination with the Ministry of Health and the Ministry of Home Affairs. This delegation of authority allowed her to integrate the deployment and utilisation of inter-service medical resources for the fight ahead. Thus was born Operation CO-JEET, driven by cooperation and coordination, with an unwavering resolve to achieve *jeet* (victory). Madhuri now channelled all her energy into this warfront, one led by the medical community—doctors, nurses, and paramedical staff.

The first jumbo hospital, with a capacity of a thousand beds, was set up in a greenfield area in Delhi in a record

twenty-one days. DRDO worked with remarkable efficiency to erect the physical infrastructure. Dedicated zones were created for critically ill patients; high standards of hygiene and sanitation were maintained; the interiors were fully air-conditioned to provide relief during Delhi's peak summer; and pressurised oxygen was made available to counter the virus's debilitating effect on the lungs. Advanced diagnostic equipment and information technology tools were introduced to minimise human contact. IT kiosks enabled patients to stay in touch with their families, offering emotional support alongside medical care.

Madhuri's main responsibility was to formulate the administrative protocols and coordinate the deployment of essential manpower to ensure seamless patient care. It was a herculean task. She had to ensure that diverting military medical resources for civilian care did not compromise the operational readiness of the armed forces. A detailed analysis was undertaken to address this concern. During the initial phase, there was justifiable hesitation from the services. The service chiefs were rightly cautious about the implications of reallocating manpower to civilian efforts.

Understanding their concerns, Madhuri proposed a modified doctor-patient ratio to ensure minimum effective care, thus conserving manpower. However, this sparked opposition from the medical teams, who were worried that it would compromise the quality of care. Madhuri remained calm and persuasive, explaining that extraordinary situations demanded unconventional solutions. Manpower economy, she emphasised, was critical to sustaining long-term effort.

This tension created a degree of dissonance in the collective effort. Madhuri briefed the CDS, who recognised the need for clear directives to reinvigorate the integrated approach. An online coordination meeting was convened at the highest level. Many concerns were discussed during the session.

Madhuri voiced a simple yet powerful perspective: in a conventional war, the soldier fights on the frontlines while the doctor supports from the rear. But in this battle, the enemy was a microscopic virus, and the doctors were the frontline warriors. The soldiers, she said, needed to lend their shoulders in support. Her appeal was well received, and firm instructions were issued to all three services to share resources with maturity and mutual respect.

This war demanded a true whole-of-nation approach to deliver a decisive blow to a formidable enemy. The conference proved highly productive. Following this, Madhuri was able to successfully establish jumbo hospitals in Delhi, Ahmedabad, and Lucknow, each of which brought vital relief to the civilian population.

Other Points of Interest

It is often in testing times that innovation finds its true footing. As DCIDS (med), Madhuri launched the SeHAT medical platform—providing inter-service e-health assistance and teleconsultation—in a record time of just three weeks. Her close association with NITI Aayog helped her adapt the national telemedicine guidelines for use across the three services. Today, SeHAT has become an integral part of healthcare delivery for armed forces personnel, particularly benefiting their families.

Madhuri was a firm believer in the potential of digital health as the future of efficient medical care. With the National Health Authority recently established, she advocated for tri-service interoperability in sharing electronic health records seamlessly. She recommended that a formal policy be framed to make this a reality.

Another important responsibility of the DCIDS (med) was the training of health workers for CBRN (chemical, biological, radiological, and nuclear) casualty management, which was normally conducted through annual workshops. During the COVID era, the relevance of biological warfare preparedness was sharply underscored. However, conventional training programmes were no longer feasible. In response, the first digital online course on CBRN aspects was developed. The DCIDS (med) team worked diligently to convert it into a competency-based digital module that could accommodate over a hundred trainees simultaneously. Its successful institutionalisation has since enabled the conduct of multiple courses throughout the year, for both officers and troops.

During this same period, Madhuri also worked closely with scientists engaged in COVID-related research. She contributed to the design of several studies and collaborated with senior mathematicians and researchers to develop the mathematical model SUTRA, which predicted the intensity and duration of COVID waves. A scientific paper based on this model was published and shared with empowered groups under Member Health, NITI Aayog, and the Ministry of Health and Family Welfare.

The Social Quotient

While the war against COVID continued in earnest, encouraging developments were quietly unfolding on the home front. Vibhuti, who had returned to the USA in May 2020, had settled back into her work routine and was visibly relieved to be reunited with her beloved pet, Churro.

In mid-August 2020, she happened to meet a warm and wonderful person, Shreyas. Their friendship grew steadily over the following months amidst the scenic backdrop of Seattle. Towards the end of the year, we had our first virtual interaction with Shreyas and sensed an affectionate bond forming between the two. With this happy note, the new year arrived.

As our daily battles with the formidable Mr COVID intensified, it was heartening to see Vibhuti and Shreyas grow closer. We encouraged them to visit us in the new year whenever possible. On Vibhuti's birthday, 7 March 2021, Shreyas surprised her with a proposal at his home—an event that was both touching and beautifully orchestrated. He had enlisted the help of a close friend to decorate the house with flowers and hundreds of candles—a combination Vibhuti loved. When she walked in, she assumed the preparations were simply for her birthday and didn't notice the prominent board beside the birthday card that read: 'Will You Marry Me?'

Shreyas waited for her reaction, but seeing none, gently dropped to one knee to draw her attention to the real occasion. Overwhelmed by joy and caught completely by surprise, Vibhuti collapsed into his arms with a heartfelt 'yes.' It was the most unexpected and precious gift she could have received.

We were overjoyed and invited them to visit India at the earliest opportunity. After speaking with Shreyas's parents and receiving their warm consent, we decided to hold an engagement ceremony during their trip. Meeting Shreyas in person for the first time was an absolute delight. Tall, strong, and charming, he won us over instantly.

After a brief stay in Delhi, we travelled to Pune and hosted a graceful engagement ceremony at our family home. This was the house where Vibhuti had spent much of her childhood, and it had always been her wish to get engaged in that very space.

The first step had been taken when Shreyas proposed on her birthday. The second step—the engagement—was marked by the blessings of both families. Now, only the wedding remained. However, with pandemic-related restrictions still in place, planning a formal ceremony was proving difficult. That is when Vibhuti played her masterstroke. With her usual decisiveness and flair for organisation, she declared that Mr COVID was not going to delay the next big milestone. She decided to get married on Shreyas's birthday, which was on 12 May 2021.

Vibhuti had planned that on Shreyas's birthday, all the preparations would appear to be for his special day. In reality, the main event was their registered marriage, quietly arranged to take place in her own home in the charming suburb of Bellevue, Seattle. With the help of a close friend, she arranged for a court official to conduct the ceremony at her residence. Under the pretext of birthday celebrations, she even bought formal attire for both herself and Shreyas. Her friend assisted in decorating the house with care and love.

Just twenty-four hours before the scheduled ceremony, she broke the news to both sets of parents and invited us to attend the event online. So well-kept was this secret that Shreyas only realised something was amiss when Vibhuti insisted he get dressed in a formal suit and wear a bow tie. Still fumbling with it, he stepped out onto the rear patio, only to be greeted by a fully arranged courtroom setting, ready for their solemn wedding ceremony.

In that moment, Shreyas understood that Vibhuti had outdone him. While he had taken her by surprise with a birthday proposal, she had gone a step further and planned their wedding on his birthday. His parents joined the ceremony online from Michigan, and we did the same from Pune. It was a beautiful and unique way to circumvent the restrictions that COVID had imposed on us all. And as if that weren't enough, the 12th of May brought with it another incredible joy; Nikhil and Tejas were blessed with a baby boy on the very same day. The day that marked Shreyas and Vibhuti's wedding also marked our becoming grandparents. It was a confluence of blessings so rare, so joyous, that words could scarcely contain the happiness we felt.

After Madhuri's retirement at the end of October 2021, Vibhuti and Shreyas, accompanied by his parents, came down to Pune in January 2022 for a formal wedding ceremony. COVID continued its mischief even then, affecting several of us. But since we were all vaccinated, everyone recovered in due course. For us personally, despite the occasional hiccup that COVID caused, it was a joyful culmination to not just Vibhuti's journey, but to our service lives as well.

Bidding Farewell

The saga was drawing to a close. The first wave and the Delta wave had been weathered. India had shown the world that a nation could triumph over adversity when united in purpose. Despite inadequate public health infrastructure—shortages of PPE, testing kits, laboratories, ventilators, and hospital beds—we had pulled through. We brought back citizens from overseas, vaccinated a vast population with indigenous vaccines, and were beginning to bounce back economically. It was time to bid farewell on a high note.

At Madhuri's formal dining out, the chief of Defence Staff spoke warmly about her contributions. His wife, Mrs Madhu Rawat, graciously hosted a special ladies' lunch in Madhuri's honour to mark her appointment as an advisor to the Defence Wives Welfare Association. (Little did we know then that we would tragically lose both of them in a helicopter crash just two months later.)

The army chief also hosted a dinner at the prestigious Battle Honours Mess, where Madhuri was invited as the guest of honour. It was a rare distinction being dined out separately by two chiefs at the Officers' Mess.

Even before she had hung up her boots, the governor of Maharashtra appointed Madhuri as the vice-chancellor of the Maharashtra University of Health Sciences, one of the largest state health universities in India, with over 500 affiliated colleges. She moved into this new role with grace and enthusiasm, transitioning from uniformed service to civilian leadership with confidence. After all, she now carried the armour of thirty-nine years of unblemished service and the depth of experience that came with it.

Postscript by Madhuri

The last day in uniform is always emotional, always nostalgic. I was no different. The weight of never wearing that uniform again, the heavy DMS boots, the army fatigues—it all began to sink in.

I had to return my identity card for destruction. That card had stayed with me for all thirty-nine years of my service. Officers are required to apply for a new ID whenever two identifying features change. But somehow, I was sentimentally attached to my original card, and I had held onto it from the very beginning. It still described me as 'Capt Madhuri Kanitkar, Short Service Commission Officer, HQ 12 Infantry Division.'

During the farewell, the small but spirited DCIDS (med) team delivered a speech that I will cherish forever. With great warmth and affection, they said that the small DSC Platoon—

usually a unit of re-employed soldiers on security duty—had been transformed into a Ghatak (Commando) Platoon under Madhuri's energetic leadership. They shared how she led from the front, worked shoulder-to-shoulder with each team member, and relentlessly pushed towards the mission goals they had set together during the COVID crisis. It was the best compliment I could have received.

The very next day, on 1 November 2021, I joined the Maharashtra University of Health Sciences as its vice-chancellor. Then came another moment that will forever remain etched in memory. On 26 January 2022, I was honoured with the Param Vishisht Seva Medal, the highest peacetime military award for distinguished and meritorious service. I had the opportunity to don the uniform once again to receive the medal from the honourable president of India.

Both Rajeev and I had the rare honour of being recipients of the VSM, AVSM, and PVSM. Rajeev had also been awarded the Sena Medal. It felt like the perfect, fairy-tale ending to a great journey.

We had grown together but never grown apart.

And with that, we bid our goodbye . . . until we meet again, in another story, another time.

Epilogue

When I began writing this story, my initial intent was to focus solely on Madhuri. To jog my memory, I started by making brief notes for each decade of her service. A broad nine-to-ten-year timeline seemed appropriate to chart the key developments and shape the narrative. However, I soon realised that to truly do justice to her story, I needed to begin with her childhood and the influence of key members of her immediate family—insights that were crucial in understanding the person she became. And so, those formative aspects found their place at the very start.

As I moved past her early years, I couldn't help but note that I too had entered the picture quite early, becoming part of her life and, perhaps unknowingly, influencing some of her life choices when she was still in her teens. She often teases me about being a 'cradle-snatcher,' given the firmness of the decisions she took at such a young age.

What started as Madhuri's story soon evolved into our story. Over the years, in our recurring game of hi and bye, we strengthened our bond with a simple but powerful commitment: to grow together without growing apart. Eventually, our journey expanded to include our children and close family and friends, each of whom played a significant role in our military life. Their presence and support became integral to this story, giving deeper meaning to what was originally meant to be only about Madhuri. In essence, this has become a family story set against the backdrop of a military life.

I have attempted to present the various dimensions of this narrative through my personal lens. At times, to ensure accuracy in the sequence of events and timelines, I consulted with Madhuri. Her insights helped enrich the story with her own perspective on the events she experienced. There are places where I have been sharp, especially when I felt that she hadn't been given her due. That sentiment is mine alone, and I take full responsibility for those moments. To her credit, Madhuri never tried to influence me, even once, as I went about recording this account.

For me, this has been a rollercoaster ride, reliving the turbulent, eventful years we spent together in military service. As we look back, we both recognise that the organisation we served is unparalleled. It gave us the privilege of living a clean, dignified life . . . a life filled with hard work and rewards, with setbacks and moments of fulfilment, all taken in stride with grace and composure.

From a family perspective, I must acknowledge that Madhuri shouldered an exceptional share of the responsibility when it came to raising the children. She was truly a one-(wo) man army, managing Nikhil and Vibhuti with remarkable strength and discipline. During our most challenging times, the unwavering support of the organisation proved invaluable. Equally important was the steady encouragement and reliable presence of our family and friends. It made all the difference and allowed her to become what many know her as today: a soldier, a doctor, and a teacher—all rolled into one. At the same time, she never faltered in her roles as the eldest daughter in her family, the mother of our children, and, often, their stand-in father too. As for me, I could not have navigated life without her constant physical or virtual presence beside me.

In the larger context, this effort to sketch her journey has been my way of honouring Madhuri, both the person and the personality. When I reflect on how seamlessly she managed to merge her professional and personal worlds into one cohesive whole, it feels almost unreal. But that is her hallmark—unique, as only she can be. The numero uno in every field she has walked, worked, and conquered.

I hope to always be by her side now that she has traded in her olive greens for a civilian role. She has plunged into the field of medical education, research, and healthcare with renewed purpose. Her dream is to integrate these three pillars and harness digital technology to ensure holistic wellness for the citizens of this great nation. She truly believes that a fit body in a fit mind is the way forward to make Bharat (India) a truly developed nation. That, in essence, is her dream now.

—Lt General Rajeev Kanitkar

Addendum: A Cadet's Tribute

मधुर माधुरी की छाया मे

इस कॉलेज के दिन जाते हैं मस्ती में
राजमाता की बस्ती मे, ढलती शामों की हस्ती में।
हाथ उठा के, मध्धम मुस्काके,
नटखट अंदाज मे ठेंगा दिखा के, बातें जो बतलाती हैं,
वो याद सदा रह जाती हैं, हम जितनी बातें आज करें,
वो सारी कम रह जाऐंगी,
और इस कॉलेज की मान प्रतिष्ठा
ऊंची और हो जाएगी।

खेल कूद मे आगे हैं, त्योहार संग मनाती हैं,
जब मैम चले हैं वर्दी में, तो थोडा सा इठलाती हैं
मंच पे आके, हमको बहला के,
एक छुट्टी काट चली जाती हैं।
पर इनको अपना डीन बताके
बात गजब हो जाती है।

सफर चुना है ऐसा की, आज यहा कल वहां गए,
तो दुख कैसा कि दूर हो गए,
जब बाते है और यादे हैं।
और मिलना चाहेंगे फिर से,
थोडा बढकर, थोडा सजकर
कुछ करना चाहेंगे हम भी
बिलकुल आप जैसा बनकर।

—Cadet Hrithik Rai

Acknowledgements

We would like to begin by expressing our deepest gratitude to our parents, who gave us both the opportunity and the freedom to pursue our military careers, which were firsts in our families. This book would not have taken shape without their blessings.

Next, we extend heartfelt thanks to our family and friends, whose care, concern, and unwavering support helped us navigate the many ups and downs of professional life. Their steadfast presence made this journey possible.

We are especially grateful for the patience and understanding shown by our two children, Nikhil and Vibhuti. They endured the rigours of a disciplined upbringing and, in doing so, helped us manage our professional responsibilities with greater ease. A special word of thanks to their respective life partners, Teju and Shreyas, for reviewing the initial draft and sharing their valuable feedback.

We are indebted to Mrs Kiran Bedi, who encouraged us to share our story, believing that it might offer useful pointers to others in similar situations.

We are also extremely thankful to the wonderful organisation, the Indian Armed Forces, in which we had the opportunity and privilege to serve. It provided us the fabric upon which we could weave our respective journeys in service, with pride, honour, and dignity.

A special note of gratitude is due to Hay House Publishers India, who stood by us as a strong pillar of support in this unique endeavour. In particular, we deeply appreciate Associate

Editor Aditya Jarial's clear, consistent guidance and editorial support, which were instrumental in bringing this story to its successful completion. We are also thankful to Raghav Khattar for his insight, encouragement, and belief in this book from the very beginning.

And finally, it would perhaps be most fitting to acknowledge each other for being able to live the mantra of 'adjust, adapt, and adopt,' and in doing so, grow together, even as our paths kept us physically apart for long stretches of time.